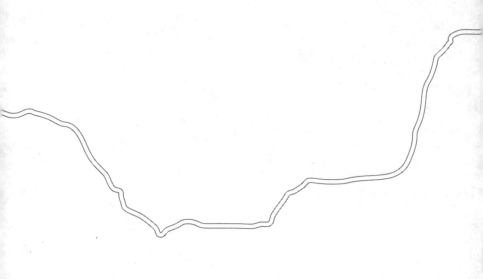

Touring the Sierra Nevada

CHERYL ANGELINA KOEHLER

UNIVERSITY OF NEVADA PRESS ▲▲ RENO & LAS VEGAS

University of Nevada Press, Reno, Nevada 89557 USA
Copyright © 2007 by University of Nevada Press
Unless otherwise noted in the caption, all photographs
copyright © 2007 by Cheryl Angelina Koehler
All rights reserved
Manufactured in the United States of America
Design by Carrie House / HOUSEdesign llc
Library of Congress Cataloging-in-Publication Data
Koehler, Cheryl.
Touring the Sierra Nevada / Cheryl Angelina Koehler.
p. cm.
Includes index.
ISBN 978-0-87417-700-8 (pbk. : alk. paper)
1. Sierra Nevada (Calif. and Nev.)—Description
and travel. I. Title.
F868.S5K64   2007
917.94—dc22   2006037619
The paper used in this book meets the requirements
of American National Standard for Information
Sciences—Permanence of Paper for Printed Library
Materials, ANSI z.48–1984. Binding materials were
selected for strength and durability.
FIRST PRINTING
16 15 14 13 12 11 10 09 08 07
5 4 3 2 1

To Puck, the courageous mountain dog

Contents

Preface

Wander here a whole summer, if you can. Thousands
of God's wild blessings will search you and soak you
as if you were a sponge, and the big days will go by
uncounted.

       —from *Our National Parks* by John Muir

For you, my dear friends, I have gathered into these pages many seasons of wild blessings soaked up on countless big days spent wandering through the Sierra Nevada, California's great central mountain range.

The wildest of these blessings tumble down from among the Sierra's loftiest peaks: craggy, ice-bitten stone spires that rise to more than 14,000 feet. Others come from high, rock-strewn passes and glacier-scraped basins, where granite and water commune with the sun, moon, and stars. The blessings flow in multitudes along the Sierra's snow-fed creeks and roaring rivers, gathering by the thousands in meadows full of wildflowers, in dense forests of pine and fir, and in endless groves of shimmering aspen. They pile up on the shores of icy lakes and hide within deep, stony canyons.

The blessings stand quietly in the grassy oak forests of the western foothills. They fill the ancient bedrock mortar holes made by generation upon generation of Native Americans grinding acorns and seeds into meal for their daily sustenance, and they rustle among the reeds that some tribespeople still gather and weave into handsome baskets. Blessings lie in heaps in the dusty corners of Gold Rush–ghost towns alongside piles of unrealized dreams.

They roam with the wild creatures through the forests, out into the rangelands, and across endless miles of sagebrush. Wherever they are found in this wild western land, the blessings soak us to the bone. They stay with us as memories, inciting a yearning to return again and again.

Guide to the Guide

This book is designed to introduce this splendid corner of the world to all types of travelers. The 10 extensive driving tours cover the full 400-mile length and 50-to-80-mile width of these mountains, the longest continuous range in the United States. Much of the Sierra Nevada is public land: national forests, national parks, and wilderness areas, as well as many state and county parks. These are places where we can go to learn about our history and about the spirit of nature that resides within us all. It is not necessary to be a hiker or avid recreation seeker to discover this grand and welcoming region, but you should have some reliable means of transportation, basic good sense, and a healthy respect for the challenges of travel through a high mountain wilderness.

REVELATIONS ON INTERSTATE 80

Interstate 80, from San Francisco, California, to Reno, Nevada, provides one of the easiest trans-Sierra crossings. This route intertwines threads of California history, running from near the Golden Gate to Sacramento on the American River and along the famous immigrant route through Donner Pass. The California gold rush, the transcontinental railroad, Sierra winter recreation, and the geography of the range all get an introduction in the course of this journey. The chapter ends in Reno, a highrolling town with a surprising depth of character, and a good place from which to launch many other Sierra adventures.

TAHOE

Lake Tahoe is renowned for its deep, clear waters and its spectacular setting in a high rocky basin. It is also notorious for its casinos, crowds, posh resorts, and crowded beaches. On a spin around the lake, the traveler will find advice on how to find places of solitude and grandeur away from the madding crowds.

CENTRAL SIERRA CROSSINGS

U.S. 50, Highway 88, Highway 4, and Highway 108 carry travelers over the Sierra in the middle part of the range. Each presents spectacular scenery and uncounted opportunities to wander off into blissful solitude or radiant adventure. The chapter includes more history of trans-Sierra travel and some introductions to Sierra flora and fauna.

U.S. 395: MONO COUNTY

This itinerary covers the Mono County portion of u.s. 395, a highway that runs along the base of the Sierra's steep eastern escarpment. This is the western edge of the Great Basin, a vast, arid region that encompasses the state of Nevada and portions of several nearby states. The tour begins in Antelope Valley, south of the Carson Range and Lake Tahoe, and leads through Bridgeport Valley, to Bodie ghost town, to Mono Lake, and on into the volcanically active Long Valley Caldera region at Mammoth Lakes.

U.S. 395: OWENS VALLEY

The tour of u.s. 395 continues southeast into the broad, deep, and dry Owens Valley, flanked by 14,000-foot peaks that rise up on either side. This land has a long and varied history of human habitation, with recent controversy over the exploitation of its natural resources. From this sublime place, adventures take on a most extraordinary character. You will visit such wonders as a forest of 4,000-year-old bristlecone pines, the Sierra's largest glacier, and Mount Whitney, the highest point in the nation's contiguous 48 states.

THE SOUTHERNMOST SIERRA

The Sierra's seldom-visited southernmost region is a land of solitude and subtle beauty, where weathered mountain granite rolls softly away into the Mojave Desert. Surprising discoveries here are the mighty Kern River, forests of Joshua trees, and many sublime views.

THE HIGH SIERRA

No roads traverse the highest Sierra, and so this rugged region must be explored on foot or astride a horse or mule. However, visitors can easily ramble into some stunning country in Sequoia and Kings Canyon national parks, strolling among magnificent groves of giant sequoias, standing within one of the country's deepest gorges, and pondering the highest peaks of this magnificent mountain range.

YOSEMITE NATIONAL PARK

This chapter looks in on magnificent Yosemite National Park in each of its varied seasons. There are visits to the famous falls and monoliths of the valley, rambles to many splendid spots in the Yosemite backcountry, and surprising discoveries of overlooked sights near the park's entryways.

GOLD COUNTRY

In its 326 miles from the foothills near Yosemite to the Sierra Valley in the north, Highway 49 threads through the famous Sierra Nevada Gold Country. Highlights along this tour include the Gold Discovery Site at Sutter's Mill, countless mining towns, both highly restored and tumbled down, winery visits, and gorgeous river chasms.

THE LOST SIERRA

In the far northern part of the range, the diminishing Sierra peaks hide their stony heads under a thick cloak of conifers and then disappear altogether beneath the newly formed lava rock of the Cascade Range. Known as the Lost Sierra, this region sees far fewer visitors than nearby Tahoe, but those who come find great recreational opportunities and a treasure trove of natural and human-made wonders, including world-renowned railroad sights.

PLANNING YOUR TRIP

Each geographical chapter of this guide ends with a section called Practical Matters. These include: when to visit; driving routes and alternate means of transportation; lists of where to find the greatest concentrations of lodging, dining, and camping options; and lists of resources and publications where you can get more detailed information on each region.

Acknowledgments

In 2000, when I was just beginning work on this book, a potential collaborator inquired as to which Sierra Nevada peaks I had climbed. My answer was that I did not *do* peaks but that I simply liked to *be* above 10,000 feet. Six years later, after traveling far and wide through the Sierra Nevada, I have come to believe that the appeal of this great mountain range can be found at every elevation. My greatest delight has been to see that my elderly parents derive as much joy from a simple Sierra driving tour as I gain on a long backpacking expedition. So first and foremost, I want to thank Paul and Angelina Koehler for that insight and for their unending support of this project.

Another senior citizen who has helped me see the Sierra in a new light is photographer Erlda Parker, whose generous contributions to these pages required a keen eye, a steady hand, and an adventurous spirit.

Quite a few of my research assistants were perfectly pleased to accompany me on the more vigorous adventures, and so I am truly grateful to my sister, Charmaine Koehler Lodge; my husband, Mark Middlebrook; and long-time friends Kit Robberson and Beth Burleson for their many contributions of time, insight, and photographs. Others to whom I offer my thanks for companionship and encouragement are: Mondara and Jera Lodge; John and Renee Kramer; Sarah Michael; Niko Bakulich; Adrienne Baker; Steve, Sam, and Annie Tillis; Ben Greensfelder and Sandra Bao; Kit Duane; Diane and Larry Rich; Andy Kinkaid; Steve Knox; Frankie

Wyka; Ron and Dodi Middlebrook; Robin Hathaway; Sue Kauer; Ed and Tricia Kloth; Lark Godwin Leet; and the entire Tribe of Burning Lamb.

There are many people I want to thank for helping me with logistics, teaching me fascinating things, and steering me toward the best sights in their particular locale. Among them are Julia Dillon, Bob Greensfelder, Chris Burt, Bob Peters, Tom Bopp, Jane Russell, Harry Reeves, Bill Bowie, Markus Albertz, Michael Baldrica, Suzi Brakken, Scott Lawson, Rick Stock, Nicole Ryan, and the High Shaman of Burning Lamb, Joxe Mallea-Olaetxe.

Also, I want to thank the Amador County Grapegrowers Association, the Tahoe National Forest Sierraville Ranger District, Feather River College, the United States Geological Survey, Mountain Adventure Seminars, Montecito-Sequoia Lodge, Donner Ski Ranch, Tahoe-Donner, Dodge Ridge, Squaw Valley USA, Dow Villa Motel, River Street Inn, the Feather Bed, Yorkshire House, Crescent Hotel, Haskins Valley Inn, Pullman House Inn, Bridgeport Inn, and the fabulous Plumas County Visitors Bureau for the many services they provided.

Last but not least, I want to offer a mountain of thanks to all those who took up the cause of getting this book into print: Chris Burt and Kit Duane, formerly of Compass American Guides for the first valiant attempt, and for the third and now successful attempt, the staff of the University of Nevada Press. Editor Margaret Dalrymple and Managing Editor Sara Vélez Mallea made many excellent suggestions on my numerous revisions, and it was their belief that this book could shine that gave me hope of getting through the long process. But the person who gave of himself most to make this book shine brightly is copyeditor Ben Greensfelder. His remarkable talent in ferreting out and fixing inconsistencies and errors was surpassed only by his miraculous reengineering of clumsy passages.

Oh, and thank you to the Steller's jays for all the entertainment.

Introduction: Know Before You Go

A little knowledge can go a long way for Sierra newcomers making decisions on where to go, when to go, and what to pack. Even those expecting to spend their nights cocooned within four walls and a roof will find the visit more enjoyable by knowing what to expect of Sierra weather and travel conditions.

Weather and Climate

California is renowned for its mild "Mediterranean" climate. Winters are warmer and summers are cooler here than they are at similar latitudes in other parts of the United States, because of the moderating effects of the Pacific marine air layer brought ashore by the prevailing westerly winds. The marine layer continues to have a moderating effect as it moves up the western slope of the Sierra Nevada, but with each gain of 1,000 feet in elevation, temperatures drop approximately three to five degrees Fahrenheit. This means that on a summer's day when it is a sweltering 100 degrees in the western foothills town of Sonora (at an elevation of 1,826 feet), it could be in the 60s or 70s at an elevation of 9,625 feet in Sonora Pass. High winds in the passes can make it feel much colder.

In summer, persistent high-pressure weather systems create a long period of drought across California. However, this does not mean that the Sierra will see no rain in summer. The prevailing winds carry a certain amount of moisture up the range's western slope, and as this moisture condenses in the higher elevations, it can produce afternoon thunderstorms. This storm water runs off quickly and the lightning produced by the storms is a major source of forest fires. In the eastern Sierra, summer thunderstorms often are created by storm systems moving in from the Gulf of Mexico.

As autumn arrives, California's prevailing high-pressure system gradually shifts and alternating systems of high and low pressure bring a series of moisture-laden storms from the west. These systems bring mostly rain to the coastal and central regions, because of the warm marine layer, but at the Sierra's higher elevations, snow will fall wherever temperatures are below 32 degrees Fahrenheit. The first "winter" storm usually comes in October, with the frequency and severity of storms building to a peak in January or February and tapering off through spring.

The Sierra's western slope can receive prodigious amounts of snow in winter; sometimes three or more feet fall within a couple of days. But by the time the storm systems cross over the Sierra crest, they have lost most of their moisture, and thus on the east side of the range (in the rain shadow), precipitation amounts are characteristic of a desert climate.

The Sierra Nevada is key to California's water supply. Its snowpack acts as a very effective storage system, releasing water gradually throughout the spring as it melts. In some years, the winter storm systems do not develop and the state becomes dangerously depleted of the stored water it relies on to get through the summer drought.

Some Cautionary Advice

The following safety considerations are important information for anyone venturing into this high mountain region, and especially for those going into wilderness areas.

1. At all times, Sierra travelers should be prepared for cold temperatures in the higher elevations. A chill can progress quickly to hypothermia, so always carry **protective clothing** on a high-country hike, even if the day is warm and sunny. Be aware, too, that the thinner atmosphere of the higher elevations holds less oxygen and less moisture, and it gives less protection from ultraviolet rays, so be sure to go out equipped with plenty of **water** and adequate **sun protection.**

2. Do not drive to any remote area described in this book without a vehicle that is properly equipped and maintained for extreme weather and road conditions. Likewise, be aware that basic services are generally nonexistent at wilderness destinations.

3. Above 8,000 feet, it is very common to experience shortness of breath during moderate exertion. Know the signs of **altitude sickness:** headache, dizziness, fatigue, shortness of breath, loss of appetite, nausea, disturbed sleep, and a general feeling of malaise. These should be treated with an immediate return to a lower elevation (below 8,000 feet). Failure to heed these symptoms can allow the condition to progress on to pulmonary edema and even death.

4. **Lightning-strike** deaths in the Sierra Nevada are almost a yearly occurrence. Summer thunderstorms can come up very quickly. Carry rain gear and stay away from high, exposed places when a thunderstorm threatens.

5. Be vigilant about **fire** and remember everything Smokey said. Watch for smoke and check in at information and ranger stations along the route if there is any sign or report of fire. Also, please consider the possibility that a campfire is not an absolute necessity while camping out. Campfires pollute the air, make us stay up too late, and keep us from watching the stars—which is one of the things we're out there to do in the first place, isn't it?

6. **Mosquitoes** can be rampant in early and mid-summer. They breed in moist meadow areas as the snow melts. Their numbers diminish as the ground dries out through the summer.

7. **Poison oak** is very prevalent in the foothills, but disappears above approximately 5,000 feet. Learn to recognize the local variant of "leaves of three" and let it be. Take advantage of protections such as adequate clothing and poison oak cleansers, and make sure to clean the toxic oil off the family dog as well, because petting him is a common means of exposure.

Poison oak *(Toxicodendron diversilobum).*

Climate Statistics from Sierra Nevada Region Weather Stations (listed north to south)

Weather Station (elevation in feet)	Average Temperature (°F) high/low				Average Precipitation (inches)				
	JAN	APR	JUL	OCT	JAN	APR	JUL	OCT	YEAR
Quincy (3,405)	47/22	65/31	91/43	73/31	7.6	3.2	.1	2.8	41.2
Portola (4,849)	42/18	58/27	86/41	67/29	4.2	1.4	.3	1.3	21.7
Oroville (170)	54/36	71/47	96/63	78/50	6.4	2.3	.1	1.6	30.0
Reno, Nev. (4,403)	45/21	64/33	92/51	69/33	1.1	.4	.3	.4	7.5
Truckee (6,017)	40/14	53/25	81/41	64/28	6.0	2.3	.4	1.8	32.1
Nevada City, Calif. (2,779)	50/30	62/37	88/53	69/41	10.4	4.3	.1	3.0	55.7
Tahoe City (6,227)	40/20	50/27	77/45	60/32	6.1	2.0	.3	2.1	32.0
Woodfords (5,649)	44/23	59/31	85/53	66/37	3.6	1.1	.4	1.4	20.9
Sacramento (22)	53/40	71/49	93/60	78/53	4.0	1.3	0	1.0	18.9
Bridgeport (6,470)	42/8	58/22	83/40	67/22	1.4	.4	.5	.3	9.3
Sonora (1,748)	55/32	67/40	95/57	77/43	6.2	2.9	.1	1.8	32.9
Yosemite N.P. HQ (3,963)	49/26	64/35	90/53	74/39	6.2	3.2	.4	1.6	36.4
Mammoth Lakes (7,800)	42/18	55/28	80/48	63/33	3.3	1.1	.6	1.1	19.6
Bishop (4,107)	53/22	71/36	97/56	76/37	1	.3	.2	.2	5.4
Huntington Lake (7,018)	45/24	50/27	74/47	59/36	5.3	2.9	.2	1.8	35.1
Fresno (334)	54/37	75/47	99/65	80/50	2	1	0	.5	10.6
Grant Grove (6,598)	44/26	49/30	75/51	60/40	7.9	4.1	.1	1.6	42.8
Independence (3,950)	55/28	73/42	98/64	78/45	1.1	.3	.1	.2	5.2
Porterville (390)	56/36	76/48	98/65	82/50	2	1.1	0	.6	11.1
Bakersfield (492)	57/38	76/50	98/70	81/55	1	.7	0	.3	6.1

8. **Bears!** There are no longer any man-eating bears in California. Although the grizzly (a.k.a. brown bear) is pictured on the state flag, it was hunted into statewide extinction by 1925. The bear you see roaming the Sierra is a black bear. It is largely herbivorous and disinclined toward interaction with humans. Unfortunately, black bears easily develop a taste for human food left out on picnic tables or dumped in unsecured trash receptacles. They will investigate the smells of snacks emanating from tents, tear open unguarded backpacks, and leap from limbs to take down food hung in trees. Bears that have learned to scavenge in parking lots for their dinner have become adept at breaking into cars to get to the delicacies in coolers and supermarket bags, which they can see through the car window. One forest ranger told me how some bears have learned to recognize certain car models that are easy to break into, and if they have success with a red car last week, that's what they'll try breaking into for weeks to come. The old-style vw Beetles were one of the bears' favorites, since the airtight construction allowed the cars to pop cars open like water balloons under the weight of a flying bear. Please remember that "a fed bear is a dead bear"; "problem" bears often have to be destroyed or relocated for rehabilitation. In places like Yosemite Valley, where proper food storage is strictly enforced, bears have been returning to their more reclusive habits. In recent years, the only places I have seen black bears at all have been at unsecured dumpsters. Please help the bears live out their natural lives. It's fun to see them, but it's better for them if we never do.

9. Finally, please understand that **this is not a guidebook for wilderness sports such as backpacking, rafting, skiing, and rock climbing.** It is important to consult with professional resources for specific advice on safety and planning for those types of adventures. Anyone making a long hike into the wilderness should carry a map and compass and know how to use them. It is also important to consider all clothing, equipment, and food that might be needed in emergency situations, as well as the physical abilities of every member of the party. Backcountry campers must carry a wilderness permit. These are obtained from the ranger station in the district of the hike.

Touring the Sierra Nevada

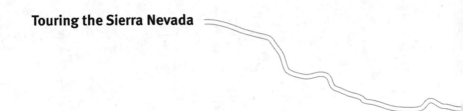

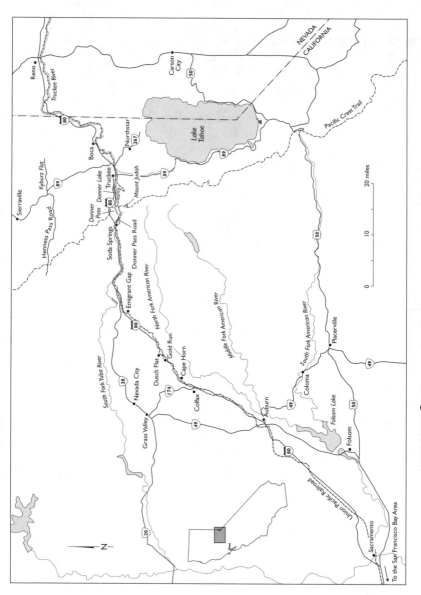

INTERSTATE 80 FROM SACRAMENTO, CALIFORNIA, TO RENO, NEVADA

1

Revelations on Interstate 80

Of all the magnificent Sierra Nevada views that I carry in memory, there is one that is unique because it was so unexpected. It came about on a midwinter's morning as I was walking my dogs on a high ridge in the California Coast Range, at a point just east of San Francisco Bay and 150 miles west of the Sierra Nevada.

The previous day had brought rare weather to coastal California. The marine air layer, which can bring prodigious snows to the Sierra Nevada, generally brings only rain to the San Francisco Bay Area. However, once or twice each winter, the temperature drops low enough that we receive a light dusting of snow at the highest elevations. On this particular February morning, a powerful storm had just departed, leaving our coastal peaks richly dressed in a regal cloak of glistening white.

I took this fine occasion to head for the hills of Berkeley's Tilden Park. As we started up toward a ridge that tops out at 1,800 feet, a full-grown snowman suddenly loomed on the path ahead. The manifestation of this pale phantom stirred the fiercer instincts in my noble hounds, and they bravely attacked and subdued the ephemeral interloper so that we were able to pass by in safety. When we attained the ridge, my companions stopped to cleanse themselves of the sweat of battle in a substantial snowbank while I gazed eastward in the direction of California's Central Valley.

Through the newly storm-washed air, a panorama of startling clarity stretched out on the far horizon, where straggling bands of storm clouds were still making their retreat. For a long moment I stood unable to believe what I was seeing. Seventy miles away to the northeast, the city of Sacramento rose like a cluster of toy blocks in the middle of the expansive green carpet of the Sacramento Valley. Another 80 miles beyond, a magnificent saw-toothed rampart of snow-covered peaks was etched against the sky.

Up until that moment, it had been my belief that this legendary view of the Sierra Nevada from the California coast existed only in the pages of history, in the times, more than four centuries ago, when the Spanish explorers first wrote the words "*las sierras nevadas*" (snowy saw-toothed ranges) on their sketchy maps drawn from shoreline vantage points. I truly believed that this view was now lost in the dust of human activity since the time of the California Gold Rush. But on this brisk winter's morning, it seemed that a window had opened to the past and the distant range was there before me, waiting to be discovered anew.

Through the Golden Gate to Sacramento (el. 25 feet)

The entryway to San Francisco Bay, known as the Golden Gate, is an historical gateway into Northern California. One of the earliest of the European explorers to sail into the Bay and on up the Sacramento River was Captain Pedro Fages. In 1772, Fages and his crew arrived at the confluence of the Sacramento and San Joaquin rivers and made the first written record of viewing the Sierra Nevada.

More than two centuries later, Interstate 80 (I-80), which runs roughly parallel to Fages's route, serves as a busy corridor for travel between the Bay Area and Sacramento, California's capital. For through travelers on I-80, Sacramento usually means nothing but a major snag in the traffic flow, but from the early years of California settlement until the advent of paved highways, a stop here would have been welcome and almost inevitable.

SUTTER'S FORT

Sacramento sits at the confluence of the Sacramento and American rivers, a spot where the seed of modern California history was planted in 1832 when John Augustus Sutter chose it as the site for New Helvetia, the

Interstate 80 and the Union Pacific Railroad through Emigrant Gap.

utopian community he hoped to establish here in the Mexican province of Alta California. He procured this stretch of river bottom in a grant from Juan B. Alvarado, then governor of the province, and built an adobe fort as the home and haven for his self-sustaining community. Within a decade, Sutter's Fort was burgeoning with settlers arriving by ship from the coast or trickling in via newly blazed overland routes. Sutter became known as a magnanimous host, and some historical accounts state that he also got along well with the Indians, providing them with work as servants. Other sources maintain that it was a situation of pure exploitation of the increasingly beleaguered native population.

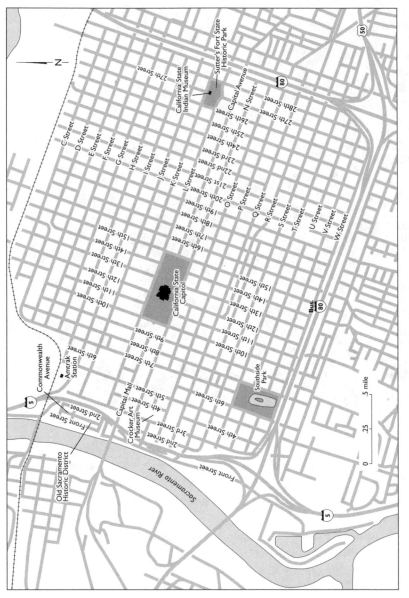

DOWNTOWN SACRAMENTO

Sutter's Fort State Historic Park

California State Indian Museum

Capital Avenue

N Street

27th Street
28th Street

26th Street
25th Street
24th Street
23rd Street
22nd Street
21st Street
20th Street

O Street
P Street
Q Street
R Street
S Street
T Street
U Street
V Street
W Street

C Street
D Street
E Street
F Street
G Street
H Street
I Street
J Street
K Street
L Street
19th Street
18th Street
17th Street
16th Street

15th Street
14th Street
13th Street
12th Street
11th Street
10th Street

California State Capitol

15th Street
14th Street
13th Street
12th Street
11th Street
10th Street

9th Street
8th Street
7th Street
6th Street

6th Street

Commonwealth Avenue

Amtrak Station

Capital Mall

Crocker Art Museum

5th Street
4th Street
3rd Street
2nd Street
Front Street

Front Street

2nd Street

Old Sacramento Historic District

Sacramento River

Southside Park

4th Street

-N-

50

80

80

Bus. 80

5

5

0   .25   .5 mile

Sutter realized that to provide enough bread for his many guests and workers he needed a new flour mill. To build it, he needed lumber, and the forests upriver were the logical source. Sutter sent his best handyman, James W. Marshall, off toward the forests to look for a suitable place for a sawmill. Marshall chose a spot 45 miles upstream from Sacramento on the South Fork American River. The site was in an enchanting valley that the native Nisenan people called Cullumah (or Coloma, as it was transliterated).

The sawmill was in operation on January 24, 1848, when Marshall saw shining particles in the millrace. (The millrace is a narrow diversion channel where the waterwheel harnesses energy from the flow of the stream). When Marshall pulled the golden flecks from the water, he had a good notion of what they were. He also had thoughts on how this discovery might change his world, and so without saying a word, he went back to the fort to show the flakes to Sutter. The two conspired to keep the news out of the public ear for as long as possible, but the secret lasted about two weeks; not long enough for Sutter to finish construction on the flour mill at the fort.

One of the first men to see the breadth of the opportunity was Sam Brannan, an ambitious young entrepreneur who was the publisher of San Francisco's first newspaper, the *California Star*. Brannan quickly opened a store at Sutter's Fort and made plans for another on the embarcadero, the nascent port of Sacramento. Then he went back to San Francisco and with a bottle full of gold flakes went through the streets yelling, "Gold! Gold! Gold from the American River!"

Sutter's loss was unavoidable. There was no stopping the machinery of greed, nor that of Manifest Destiny. It seems an extraordinary coincidence that the Treaty of Guadalupe Hidalgo, in which Mexico officially ceded the Southwestern territory to the United States, had been signed on February 2, 1848, a matter of weeks before the world learned of the discovery at Sutter's Mill. Mexicans had known of the presence of gold in California while it was still their province. A placer (a surface deposit) of some substantial size was worked near Los Angeles from 1842 until 1845. The Indians were aware of it, too, but the soft yellow metal held no value in their hierarchy of natural resources.

In memory of Sutter's
vision of New Helvetia.

Sutter's laborers began to leave in droves for the goldfields, and many more gold-seekers began to stream through Sutter's Fort with no thought of becoming productive members of New Helvetia. Unable to reconfigure his dream, Sutter fell into despair and destitution as New Helvetia was subsumed by the burgeoning city of Sacramento. Today, visitors to the fort see it presented in a state of arrested animation, depicting the days just before the discovery of gold.

Sutter's Fort State Historic Park is located in midtown Sacramento between K and L streets and 26th and 28th streets. Further description of the Gold Discovery Site at Coloma can be found in chapter 9.

CALIFORNIA STATE INDIAN MUSEUM

Walking behind Sutter's Fort to the entrance of the California State Indian Museum (26th and K streets), I find myself pondering the historic role that the fort played in the decline of California's native populations.

On entering this museum (and tribal centers elsewhere), I feel heartened at the growing effort to reconstruct traditional cultural practices. This museum serves as a central resource and learning center for those who want to look into the past, present, and future of California's native peoples.

The museum's estimate of California's native population at the time of the European influx ranges between 300,000 and 1 million people. The first human presence in the Sierra Nevada is estimated at around 11,000 years ago, and the complex mosaic of tribal language groups found in California supports that figure. California's early ethnographers, such as S. Powers, R. B. Dixon and A. L. Kroeber, outlined three main language groups and well over a dozen dialects in the Sierra alone. In the eastern Sierra they found five distinct groups speaking Uto-Aztecan (Shoshonean) languages: the Northern Paiute, Mono Lake Paiute, Monache (Western Mono), Owens Valley Paiute, and Tubatulabal (upper Kern River Valley). Around Lake Tahoe and within the Truckee and Carson river drainages they found the Hokan-speaking Washoe people. On the western slope were Penutian-speaking tribes: Maidu in the north, Miwok in the central Sierra, and Yokuts in the southern Sierra.

Most tribes were migrating hunter-gatherers enjoying an abundance of food resources: fish, shellfish, insects, game, seeds, fruits, roots, and herbs. The Paiute were known to practice agriculture and irrigation, and everywhere, the people engaged in complex forms of resource management. Homes were built of earth, brush, or bark. Intricate baskets of various designs served as gathering, carrying, cooking, and storage containers.

As you travel through the Sierra, there will be several more opportunities to visit museums and tribal centers with programs, exhibits, and activities on the ancient crafts, lore, and cultural practices of the Sierra's native peoples.

AUSPICIOUS MEETINGS IN SACRAMENTO

The **Old Sacramento Historic District** sits at the west end of central Sacramento, beside the Southern Pacific Railroad tracks and on the bank of the Sacramento River. As the River Otter water taxi or a dining cruiser pulls up to the docks, the scene can be reminiscent of the day when William H. Brewer, principal assistant to Josiah D. Whitney's Geological Survey of California, first visited Sacramento. It was September 20, 1861, less than a year after the Survey was commissioned. Brewer describes it in his journal (published under the title *Up and Down California in 1860–1864*):

> We left the city [San Francisco] by steamer for Sacramento, 120 miles, at 4 p.m. and did not get into the river until after dark. The sail up the bay is very fine. The islands and shores of hills are bare and brown now — I mean bare of trees — only dried grass. The effect of the setting sun, illuminating this with its mellow light, was most beautiful indeed. Mount Diablo stood up, a grand object, in the landscape.
>
> The Rev. T. Starr King, the celebrated orator and clergyman, was on board with us. I got an introduction and had a pleasant time with him. He is as agreeable in conversation as he is eloquent in the rostrum. Night closed in on us before we entered the Sacramento River, and when I got up in the morning we were lying quietly at the wharf of that new city, the capital of the state, the "Albany" of California.

Today, visitors can still awake right at the wharf as Brewer did, but they will be aboard the ***Delta King,*** one of the steamships that brought travelers here from San Francisco between 1927 and 1940. It is permanently moored here in Old Town Sacramento and serving as a hotel. (Its better half, the famous *Delta Queen,* is still in service on the Mississippi River.)

Not long after Brewer met Thomas Starr King, the reverend would play a significant role in the establishment of what eventually became Yosemite National Park (see chapter 8). By coincidence, Brewer would meet another (soon to become famous) man named King in almost the same spot, exactly two years later to the day. In his journal entry for September 20, 1863, Brewer wrote, "At Sacramento I took steamer, and meeting an old friend, had a pleasant trip. On the way down two young men came up to me, asked if my name was Brewer, and introduced themselves as two young fellows just graduated last year in the Scientific School at Yale College, who this summer have crossed the plains. Their names are Gardner and King."

That would have been James Terry Gardner and Clarence King, soon to become members of Brewer's sturdy band of surveyors. Gardner's version of this meeting, in a letter written to his mother a few months later (and quoted in the footnotes to *Up and Down California*), is somewhat more colorful than Brewer's:

> [The steamship] was crowded with people from the mines. Many rough, sunburned men in flannel shirts, high boots, belts, and revolvers were around me, but among them one man attracted my attention. There was nothing peculiar about him, yet his face impressed me. Again and again I walked past him, and at last, seating myself in a chair opposite and pretending to read a paper, I deliberately studied this fascinating individual. An old felt hat, a quick eye, a sunburned face with different lines from the other mountaineers, a long weather-beaten neck protruding from a coarse gray flannel shirt and a rough coat, a heavy revolver belt, and long legs, made up the man: and yet he is an intellectual man — I know it . . . I went to Clare [Clarence King], told him the case, and showed him the man. He looked at him, and, without any previous knowledge to guide him in the identification, said, from instinct, 'That man must be Professor Brewer, leader of Professor Whitney's geological field-party.'

Within a week, Gardner and King joined Brewer and cartographer Charles F. Hoffmann on the Geological Survey of California. With their bulky surveying equipment packed onto mules, the team would trek into some of the most remote regions of the Sierra. The story of those adventures continues later in this chapter.

AN ETHEREAL VISION: THE TRANSCONTINENTAL RAILROAD

In the 1850s, the dream of iron rails connecting the two oceans hovered on the brow of America like an ethereal vision. The Sierra, as always, posed a formidable barrier to progress, as did the looming clouds of civil war. Politics played a part as well. The route taken by a trans-Sierra rail line would enhance the fortunes of those near its path and ruin the speculators along the paths not chosen.

While the concept of the transcontinental railroad was well established before the California Gold Rush, it took the exigencies of that massive human endeavor to create enough momentum to move the project forward. It also took the unstoppable intent of someone prepared to meet the challenges. That person was Theodore D. Judah, a civil engineer who in 1856 completed a 22-mile railroad linking the port in Sacramento to the foothill town of Folsom. Judah envisioned his Sacramento Valley Railroad as the terminus of the transcontinental project, and he was prepared to convince Washington of that vision. But first he needed California to sign on with him. He started by enlisting Leland Stanford, Mark Hopkins, Charles Crocker, and Collis P. Huntington, four Sacramento businessmen who at the time were all busy trading in goods required by the miners. When Judah first approached them in 1860, the Big Four, as they would become known, quickly grasped the significance of the moment. Ultimately, they would succeed with Judah's vision, creating the Central Pacific Railroad Company, but Judah would not see that success; he was destined to die of yellow fever, contracted on a lobbying trip to Washington via the Panama Canal.

Stanford made it his project to become elected governor of California. From this high place he worked the political angles, while Huntington went after capital and Crocker hunted down sources of manpower. Crocker's success came via a large force of disenfranchised Chinese miners and their connection to a much larger potential labor force from China's Kwantung Province.

The work of building the railroad began in 1863 and took on momentum in 1864 and 1865 as the Chinese workers carved out the roadbed and laid the track through many perilous sections cresting the Sierra at Donner Pass. They blasted out more than a dozen tunnels through solid rock, working through the winter in these caverns as avalanches thundered past the openings. In summer they worked suspended on ropes on the steep granite cliffs, building ledges like the one around a particularly spectacular prominence called Cape Horn (named after the treacherous promontory that haunted the memories of so many travelers who had arrived in California by ship via the long route around South America.) The success of the Chinese work force is often attributed to a strong work

(opposite) Old Town Sacramento re-creates a bit of the city circa 1860.

OFFICE
Central Pacific Railroad.

54 HARDWARE, IRON, STEEL & COAL

HUNTINGTON, HOPKINS & C°
54

ethic, but in part it came from the fact that they were a unified force, self-contained by virtue of language and cultural habits. While the non-Chinese railroad workers ate meals provided by their bosses and drank from the ever more polluted Sierra creeks, the Chinese fed themselves following their ancient culinary traditions, which included boiling all their water and consuming it as tea, thus avoiding waterborne illnesses. They brought with them an ancient knowledge of medicine and set up their own apothecaries, such as the one you can visit in **Fiddletown** (see chapter 9). Several other intriguing remnants of the Sierra's Chinese culture will be found in this book's tour of the Gold Country, but the real legacy of this era is the vibrant urban Chinatowns in California's cities, where the workers gradually settled.

SACRAMENTO SIGHTS

A fuller story of the building of the railroad can be found at the **California State Railroad Museum,** which is located on the north end of Sacramento's historic district at the corner of 2nd and I streets. This is one of the nation's most respected train museums, offering exhibits, events, and summer rides along the river levees on a train pulled by a steam locomotive. Next to the train museum is the popular **Discovery Museum,** a history, space, science, and technology center with a whole section devoted to the California Gold Rush.

Another museum highlight in Sacramento is the **Crocker Art Museum,** which occupies an ornate Classic Revival mansion on the south side of Old Sacramento on O Street between 2nd and 3rd. The mansion and original collection were a gift to Sacramento from Margaret Crocker, the wife of Edwin Crocker, Charles Crocker's brother. The museum itself is a testimony to the impressive wealth brought to California by the railroad and the Gold Rush, but within the Crocker collections, you also see how that wealth spawned a unique school of California art. Two pieces, Charles Christian Nahl's *Sunday Morning in the Mines,* 1872, and Thomas Hill's *Great Canyon of the Sierra, Yosemite,* 1871, provide examples of how the Sierra landscape and the unique nature of California's gold-era society influenced the new movement. To delve further into this subject, visit the collections at the Nevada Museum of Art in Reno (see the end of this chapter) and the Oakland Museum in Oakland, California.

Another Sacramento attraction within walking distance of the historic center is the **California State Capitol,** located between 8th and 15th and L and N streets. Labels on the vegetation in the attractively landscaped Capitol Park provide a short course in the state's botany.

Also of interest to those who want to linger outdoors in the Sacramento area are the extensive state parks along the American River. The parks continue northeast upstream to **Folsom** (el. 218 feet), where the large Folsom Lake State Recreation Area surrounds a huge reservoir called **Folsom Lake.** At many points along the riverbank in Folsom, there are huge "dunes" of rounded river rocks — a wasteland of stony debris deposited during extensive dredging for gold in the latter years of the gold era. Folsom's charming **historic district** lies just below the Folsom Lake dam. The quaint shops and entertaining eateries along Sutter Street are joined in the historic district by the **Folsom Powerhouse,** which delivered Sacramento its first electric power on July 13, 1895.

To rejoin I-80 from Folsom, take the Auburn-Folsom Road along the west side of Folsom Lake to Auburn.

Gold Run to Dutch Flat

Leaving the Sacramento area, I-80 heads northeast past Auburn and Colfax and into the lush foothill greenery. At Gold Run, an impressive pink cliff looms up beside the highway. This cliff is a human-made scar in the earth that runs 250 feet deep and a half-mile wide for a full two miles. From this chasm miners washed auriferous (gold-bearing) blue gravel in a highly profitable but destructive stint of hydraulic mining in 1859. The best way to investigate the cliff is to make a U-turn at the next interchange and go back to the **Gold Run Rest Area** on the westbound side of the highway. It features several signboards with information on local history (both natural and human) and a short interpretive trail along the pink cliff.

A mile northeast of the Gold Run Rest Area, an exit off I-80 puts travelers on the road to **Dutch Flat** (el. 3,144 feet), a gold-rush town that still has many of its original stone buildings. In 1864, Dutch Flat became the western end of the Dutch Flat and Donner Lake Wagon Road, a route established to supply the railroad construction. The road ran up to Tinker's Station at Donner Pass, Coburn's Station (now Truckee), and on to Lake's Crossing (now Reno).

Emigrant Gap (el. 5,243 feet)

A few miles east of Dutch Flat, the first jaw-dropping views of the Sierra Nevada's bold granitic rooftop come into view. Westbound travelers can stop at the Emigrant Gap Scenic Viewpoint to look down into **Bear Valley,** a sight that apparently struck fear into the emigrants. Here they faced the necessity of lowering their wagons on ropes down the precipitous cliff to reach the valley floor. It would be the last great impediment to their westward journey.

Ten miles east of Emigrant Gap, just past Cisco Grove, is Big Bend, on the Yuba River. It was here that members of the Elisha Stephens Party, first emigrant group to cross the Sierra with wagons, overwintered in 1844–45 when they were caught in deep snow. This was a large group with many women and children. They had intended to follow one of the routes blazed by the renowned explorer, Joseph Reddeford Walker (see the beginning of chapter 3), but a chance meeting with a friendly Paiute at the Humboldt Sink in Nevada caused them to redirect their course. Drawing a map in the sand, the Paiute, who gave his name as something that sounded like Truckee, explained that directly to the west they would find a river flowing down from the mountains. The course of this river would be the best route over the crest.

The party found the river (which was later to be given the transliterated name of this Paiute guide), and by mid-November they had worked their way up to the confluence of Donner Creek and the Truckee River, near the present-day town of Truckee. Here the party was caught in early season snow. They attempted to continue along this creek, but as they reached Donner Lake, they made the decision to split their forces so that a group could go ahead on horseback to get relief supplies. Then the party split again, leaving three young men at the lake with the most cumbersome wagons while the rest pressed on in search of a route that might be passable for the smaller wagons. Remarkably, the main group was able to hoist several wagons and the oxen over a high rocky ridge and continue on to Big Bend at the Yuba River. There the party split yet again, the men going ahead and the women and children making camp in the fast-falling snow. Among those who camped at Big Bend was Mrs. Martin Murphy, who gave birth there to Elizabeth Yuba Murphy, the first Euro-American child to be born in the Sierra. The men arrived at Sutter's Fort and were able to return to Big Bend in February to retrieve the women and children.

Back at Donner Lake, the three young men built a cabin of saplings, rawhides, and pine brush, and they slaughtered the starving cows, hoping to survive off the meat. But as time passed and relief did not arrive, they decided to make snowshoes to help them walk over the pass on the 10 feet of soft snow that had accumulated. The youngest man, 18-year-old Moses Shallenberger, found walking on the crude snowshoes beyond his endurance and he turned back to the cabin. There he waited several months to be rescued. His journal describes how he survived by trapping foxes (which he found very tasty, but in short supply) and coyote (which he found almost inedible).

The following year, several other California-bound emigrant parties followed the Truckee route. Winter snow set in later that year, and all were able to pass through the mountains with little mishap. But the winter of 1846–47 found the Donner Party stranded east of the summit at Donner Lake. That story continues later in this chapter.

Take either the Big Bend or Rainbow Road exit off of I-80 to visit the site of the Stephens Party camp at Big Bend, one of several places to investigate the emigrant stories in depth. Here, at the **Tahoe National Forest Big Bend Visitor Center,** you will find more information and exhibits on the history of travel through this corridor, along with recreation information for the Tahoe National Forest. This is a good place to pick up a map for the Mount Judah hike described a little later in this chapter.

Donner Pass (el. 7,088 feet)

Within a mere two decades of the Stephens Party's passage through Donner Pass, trans-Sierra travel became far less grim, due to the coming of the Central Pacific Railroad in the late 1860s. With such improved access, recreation seekers quickly discovered what winter had to offer just off the station platforms, in the Soda Springs area west of the pass. Soon there

were several hotels to serve them. The original Fenton, Tinkers, and Old Summit hotels are now gone, but the names appear on newer structures. The Summit is where Charlie Chaplin filmed snow scenes for *The Gold Rush* in the 1920s.

Beginning in 1913, motorists could cross over Donner Pass on the Lincoln Highway (Highway 40), which remained the major thoroughfare until 1966 when the interstate was laid through Donner Summit, a few miles to the north. At least one remnant of the older route is still very much in use. Now called Donner Pass Road, it loops off of I-80 at the Soda Springs exit, providing access to most of the Donner Pass ski resorts and Donner Lake.

The first ski resort to appear on the south side of the road bears the distinction of being one of the Sierra's oldest. The Soda Springs Ski Area dates to 1926, when Oscar and Herstel Jones opened their Soda Springs Hotel on the rail line and attracted winter sports enthusiasts by packing ski trails and offering sleigh rides. Today, families enjoy skiing, snowboarding, snowshoeing, and snow tubing here at bargain prices, as they do at nearby **Donner Ski Ranch.**

A refreshing anti-commercial ambience can be found at the Sierra Club's **Clair Tappaan Lodge,** built by club member volunteers in the 1930s. For decades, a stay at the lodge has included a cot in a bunkroom or a tiny private cell, use of communal restrooms, doing daily chores, and listening to presentations at mealtime designed to update members on the latest environmental initiatives.

In winter, club members might use the lodge as a launch pad for a cross-country ski tour on backcountry trails to the club's Peter Grubb, Benson, Bradley, and Ludlow huts. Those who prefer something less ambitious ski close to the lodge on the club's tiny system of trails, which butts right up against **Boreal,** a popular night skiing spot whose entrance is located over the northern ridge on I-80. Boreal is the home of the **Western SkiSport Museum,** which is operated by the Auburn Ski Club, an organization that dates back to 1930.

The big player in Donner Pass skiing is **Sugar Bowl,** where state-of-the-art facilities combine with a fascinating history. It all began in the late

(opposite) Beside a ski trail at Royal Gorge. Photo by Mark Middlebrook

1930s, when Austrian skiers Bill Klein and Hannes Schroll became interested in skiing the area around 8,383-foot Mount Lincoln. With backing from Walt Disney and the Southern Pacific Company, they opened their renowned ski resort in 1939, putting in a beautiful Bavarian-style lodge and California's first chairlift. It was not long before Hollywood and the glitterati arrived to rub elbows with the top international ski racers. The latter came to compete in the breathtaking Silver Belt Race, held yearly until 1975, while the serious partiers came for the kitschy, Polynesian Tiki Cup races of the 1960s.

Cross-country skiers head south from Soda Springs to **Royal Gorge,** a resort boasting the nation's most extensive system of groomed track (330 km, or 205 miles). A popular destination on this system is distant Point Mariah, where views stretch out in the direction of 4,417-foot-deep Royal Gorge. On a cold afternoon there, I found an exposed outcropping of greenish metamorphic rock that served as a dry place to sit while I admired the distant black chasm. Beside the rock was a pine tree that had twisted into a marvelous bonsai-like krummholz against the incessant wind. The whistling winter wind high up in the trees seemed to be singing a Lerner and Loewe song in honor of the location, while at the same time, a mixed-voice choir of peep-meisters chirped excitedly about the feast of insects that was hiding within the pine needles. Some incessant tweeters nearby laid down an ostinato that was punctuated by a two-note whistler. Some far-off honkers marked the cadences and the woodpeckers provided intermittent percussion.

Mount Judah (el. 8,238 feet)

Donner Pass is a place of solitude in summer. At most, you might run a few hikers out on a nature walk or a pair of pensive rock climbers scaling a wall. This quiet season is when I like to hike up Mount Judah to survey the landscape.

To find the Mount Judah trailhead, first locate the signs indicating the summit of Donner Pass on Donner Pass Road. Across from Donner Ski Ranch and beside the Sugar Bowl Academy you will find a short segment of paved road that leads to an informal parking area. The trailhead is indicated by a large signboard for the Pacific Crest Trail off to the left.

The first part of the trail is steep and rocky, but that provides a good excuse to go slowly and admire the tall Jeffrey pines among low-growing gardens of manzanita and huckleberry oak. Manzanita is a genus comprising about 60 species of beautiful crimson-limbed shrubs named for their tiny fruits, which resemble apples. The brushy huckleberry oak advertises its membership in the *Quercus* genus by producing tiny acorns, which are a source of sustenance to many small members of the Sierra's animal kingdom.

Farther on, the Mount Judah Loop turns off to the east as the trail spirals upward in a clockwise route around the north and east sides of the mountain. Along the way, it passes a vista point at Coldstream Pass, a place where many emigrant parties negotiated their ascent to the crest. After a long southward traverse you will be at the top of Mount Judah. From here, the loop continues to the southwest to rejoin the Pacific Crest Trail.

At the top of Mount Judah, a string of tattered Tibetan prayer flags flutters in the wind. Perhaps placed there by an ardent hiker, the dancing flags seem to designate the peak as an international peace zone, broadcasting goodwill to all points within its prospect. To the south are Mount Lincoln (el. 8,383 feet), Anderson Peak (el. 8,683 feet), and Tinker Knob (el. 8,949 feet), along with a lower, but quite striking formation that has the look of a big slanting tabletop or hinged trapdoor tilting westward. Geologists often use the image of a trapdoor to describe the uplifted fault block that forms the Sierra Nevada. In this spot, the steep drop-off to the east (known as the eastern scarp) is a rampart of intricately eroded earthen flutings. The gentle westward slope stretches like a great green tablecloth, folding into deepening ridges where the American River carves out its route toward Sacramento.

A faint brown line threading along the eastern rim of the tabletop is the **Pacific Crest Trail.** Donner Pass is but one of many Sierra access points to this 2,500-mile-long trail that reaches from Canada to Mexico. Heading south from Donner Pass, the trail passes through the heart of the **Granite Chief Wilderness.** It continues on through the 63,960-acre **Desolation Wilderness,** emerging at its next major highway crossing at Echo Summit on U.S. 50 (see chapter 3).

A knobby formation called **Castle Peak** dominates the northern

Looking east-southeast from the summit of Mount Judah; Northstar-at-Tahoe ski runs appear in the distance.

quadrant of the Mount Judah panorama. At 9,103 feet, it stands like a fort keeping watch over the freeway and the once-formidable rocky passes.

To the east, the twin lines of the interstate and the Lower Truckee River slip together around the northern end of the Carson Range at the Nevada border. The Carson Range dominates the entire eastern horizon, rising up to loom over Lake Tahoe and culminating in a cluster of bare peaks at the lake's southern end: Freel Peak (el. 10,881 feet), Monument Peak (el. 10,067 feet), and Jobs Sister (el. 10,823 feet).

On your return down the Mount Judah trails, notice the glacier-polished granitic outcroppings and slopes of broken talus. These formations are a minuscule part of the Sierra's great granitic *batholith,* a vast body of rock that formed underground 200 million to 60 million years ago. This batholith makes up the core of the Sierra Nevada, and defines it as a single range. Here, too, you see the variegated rubble of volcanic surface flows. Volcanic rock breaks down to form a fertile medium for the wind-stunted whitebark pine and lodgepole pine on the ridges, and mystical forests of red fir below. The rich soil also supports a magnificent summer display of wildflowers.

Anyone setting out on even a modest five-mile day hike such as this one should go with the knowledge that this is a high mountain wilderness, where harsh conditions can catch hikers unawares. Carry sufficient water, wear adequate shoes and protective clothing, and bring a good trail map. The Big Bend Visitor Center (see the Emigrant Gap section earlier in this chapter) and the Tahoe National Forest Truckee District station at 9646 Donner Pass Road are nearby places to pick up the free Forest Service brochure with a map and description of the Mount Judah Loop Trail.

Donner Lake (el. 5,933 feet)

From the summit, Donner Pass Road descends by spectacular twists and turns toward Donner Lake, where homes, condo complexes, and a few modest motels dot the shore. In summer, children in a vacation trance mosey across the highway to visit the lake, and motorboats lazily ply the waters, minding the 35-mph speed limit.

Donner Lake was formed in the ice ages when a moraine (a huge pile of glacial rubble) blocked eastward-flowing Donner Creek. The moraine is now the site of **Donner Memorial State Park**. The statue at the entrance to the park marks the site of the cabin where Moses Shallenberger of the Stephens Party spent the winter of 1844–45.

It was here that the California-bound emigrants of the Donner Party were forced to overwinter in 1846–47. Their westward trek from Independence, Missouri, had been fraught with delays caused by overloaded wagons, mechanical breakdowns, poor group dynamics, ill advice, and finally, by early snow that fell hard and heavy at the pass in October 1846. Of the 81 unfortunate souls who waited out the six months of winter at Donner Lake, only 45 reached safety. The others succumbed to cold and

Heading east from Donner Pass on the old Lincoln Highway (U.S. 40) to Donner Lake.

starvation. Nearly half of those who survived are alleged to have resorted to eating the flesh of the departed.

Interpretive signs indicate the location of the Donner Party campsites at the park and at another site to the northeast on Highway 89, but the more informative exhibits are in the park's museum, where there are numerous displays and a short video on the tragedy. Artifacts on display

THE DONNER PARTY

The Donner Party has a mystical meaning in the settlement of the Far West: it is Greek tragedy, moving one to pity and terror, the bloodletting par excellence; the ultimate cup of grief into which all the tears avoided by former parties are shed. All of the bad judgment and bad luck somehow skirted by the others is heaped upon the hapless heads of the one party on which the furies pour their pent-up vengeance at having been cheated of their victims these five long years during which dumb, stumbling men had overcome the unscalable mountains, unendurable salt and sand deserts. It is the ultimate tragedy without which no distant frontier can be conquered; and which gives a structural base of blood and bone and suffering and sacrifice and, in a sense, of redemption, to a new people creating a new life in a new world.

—from *Men to Match My Mountains*, Irving Stone

include many small items recovered from the sites, plus items that the survivors carried to Sutter's Fort. One artifact is a doll that received a full recounting of the Donner Party ordeal from young Patty Reed once she was safely at Sutter's Fort. Here, too, is the fateful letter to the Donner Party from one Lansford Hastings, a businessman with interests in California, whose *Emigrants' Guide to Oregon and California,* published the year before, had made him an ostensible authority on westward travel. Hastings convinced the group to follow an alternate "cut-off" route through the Great Basin. This diversion wound up costing them several extra weeks of travel time, with the result that they arrived at Donner Lake in October, much later in the season than was advised for crossing the Sierra.

The museum's exhibits also cover the Emigrant Trail, local prehistoric culture, and the railroad-building era. The park's campground facilities would have seemed luxurious beyond belief to the Donner Party.

Truckee (el. 5,820 feet)

Donner Pass Road crosses I-80 and skirts north of the busy junction of I-80 and Highway 89, then enters Truckee, a still-bustling old railroad town on the banks of the Truckee River. Train travelers can walk from the station right to the Truckee Hotel, as they did when the establishment first opened as the American House in 1873. The proprietor claimed at that time that his hotel was "pleasantly located, convenient to the railroad, and yet far enough to relieve lodgers of the unpleasantness caused by the noise of passing trains." These days, the clatter of the trains is pleasant compared to the din of weekend partiers and car traffic.

A leisurely Truckee walking tour might take in the numerous historic brick halls and Victorian "painted ladies" now serving as trendy shops, eateries, and elegant B&Bs. The presence of so many old buildings is especially remarkable considering that the town succumbed to fire in 1868, 1869, 1871, 1873, 1875, 1878, and 1891. Current-day restoration is bringing more and more of the remnant early structures into appealing use, a situation in stark contrast to Lake Tahoe towns to the south, where modern development has spared almost nothing of historic value, unless it happened to be nailed down to a state park or national forest.

The Central Pacific Railroad first chugged into Truckee from the west in 1868. When the golden spike was driven in Utah the following year, Truckee became an important stop on the transcontinental railroad. Sierra lumber was soon on its way east and west, and before long, ice, too, was being loaded onto the railcars. The especially cold winter conditions that exist along this stretch of the Lower Truckee River produce a bumper crop of ice, and before the days of mechanical refrigeration, the substance held a premium value at hotels in distant cities. It was also very cheap to harvest, due to the large pool of newly unemployed Chinese railroad laborers.

Around the turn of the century, Truckee entrepreneurs discovered yet another virtue to the town's extreme winter conditions. They began a tradition of winter carnivals, drawing in thousands of visitors by rail with the allure of fabulous ice palaces constructed in the center of town. The carnivals continued until 1919, when an especially elaborate ice palace was destroyed in one of Truckee's notorious serial conflagrations.

The next episode in Truckee's winter ventures began in 1920 when Charlie Chaplin and crew arrived to film the snow scenes for *The Gold Rush*. The film depicts the gold rush in Alaska, but Truckee must have been a far more practical place to work. Chaplin's crew stayed at the Stone Cold Inn, the handsome wooden building on the corner of River and Bridge streets. (There is speculation that the inn got its name when the Chinese ice-cutters were housed there in unheated rooms.) The inn has changed hands, names, and uses over the years. The last time I checked, it was a stylish and comfortable B&B called the River Street Inn.

Cross the river here and you will be on Highway 267, an alternate route to Tahoe that passes through the Martis Valley, a rich natural area threatened by sprawling development. Watch for signs identifying the **Martis Creek Lake National Recreation Area** on either side of the road. The Army Corps of Engineers maintains this preserve of marshy lowland and boggy lake, as well as a very pleasant campground. Brewer's blackbirds, green-tailed towhees, and yellow warblers sing here in the sagebrush, while birds of prey keep their watch from the woodland perimeter. On an early morning visit, I found the lake teeming with waterfowl. White pelicans and ducks floated serenely out into the bogs and channels while herons stalked along the reedy shoreline, and Canada geese flew formations over the shallow lake.

In the evening, several coyotes made an appearance in the dry sage corridors that surround the wetland. The wild canids were taking great interest in the domesticated members of their clan that are brought here daily by locals seeking a place for an off-leash romp.

Martis Creek Lake is also known as an especially favorable habitat for wild trout. It was used in 1971 to initiate a program to reintroduce the threatened Lahontan cutthroat trout. The Lahontans failed, but rainbow trout have flourished, making for great fishing (catch and release only).

A white pelican (*Pelecanus erythrorhynchos*) on Martis Creek Lake.

A RIDE ON AMTRAK'S CALIFORNIA ZEPHYR

In the winter of 1931, Southern Pacific debuted the glorious Snowball Special, an overnight train that took winter sports devotees from Oakland to Truckee for $4.85. In addition to the usual sleeping and snack cars, the Snowball Special featured a car set up as a ski shop and another that served as a dance hall for those who wanted to party all night on the way to the slopes. The Snowball Special ended with World War II, but Amtrak's California Zephyr still runs through Truckee once a day throughout the year with a fare of around $40 for a similar itinerary. In winter, a shuttle bus ferries skiers from the Truckee train station to all the major Tahoe resorts.

Determined to experience the California Zephyr in winter, I boarded the train in Oakland one December morning in 2003 for the eight-hour ride to Reno. The advice of a friend came to mind as rain pelted the train car windows. "Make sure to pack plenty of food for that trip through Donner Pass." The rain would be snow in the Sierra.

The train was nearly empty, and the space around my seat on the second story of the coach car was so ample that it took the first hour to decide exactly how to arrange my belongings. The second hour was spent touring the train's extensive facilities—the airy lounge car with its swiveling seats and huge windows; the dining car that looked like a cozy retro-style diner, although they would be serving steak and lobster on white linen that night. The restrooms? Nobody at all was waiting to get into them.

The train stopped briefly in Martinez near the estate where the famous Sierra mountaineer John Muir spent his retirement and did most of his writing. When we pulled into Sacramento's Amtrak station, an emissary from the California State Railroad Museum boarded to act as tour guide for our ascent into the Sierra on these historic tracks. One worrisome little tidbit in this docent's script was the tale of the great blizzard of January 1952, which trapped a 15-car luxury streamliner in heavy snow near Yuba Gap. The 196 passengers and 30 crew members waited, buried under snow for two days before they heard from anyone. Two more days went by before they were rescued.

As we left the flat Sacramento plain, the familiar dome of the Placer County Courthouse in Auburn came into view for a moment before the dense foothill shrubbery crowded in next to the tracks. We made a brief stop near the old California Fruit Exchange in Colfax, and we then pressed on toward the famous prominence called Cape Horn (see the Trancontinental Railroad section earlier in this chapter). The docent cautioned anyone with acrophobia not to look out to the right unless they were prepared to peer down 1,400 feet into the American River Gorge.

At the Gold Run area ahead, the docent spoke about how the railroad company once had to post guards to make sure gold miners didn't blast away the railroad bed from underneath the tracks. The coveted gold still lies trapped below.

As we neared Donner Summit I nibbled my apple with relief, seeing a mere three, or four, feet of snow on the ground. A cross-country skier outside the window tried racing the train briefly, but gave up the cause as we entered a tunnel at the Sierra crest.

Beginning its descent, the train contoured along the steep slope above Donner Lake, running through a series of snowsheds designed to keep avalanches from swamping the tracks. We came out of a shed to round the famous Stanford Curve, where for several minutes of the ride, anyone looking out the left-side windows could see every other car on the long train, front and back.

Railroad snowsheds above Donner Lake.

As we arrived in Truckee, the docent mentioned that in periods of prodigious snow accumulation, townspeople sometimes have to use their second-story windows to exit their homes. On this particular day, conventional doorways were in use, and the Truckee River was flowing ice-free as we passed the site of the old ice-shipping plants at Boca. By the time the train descended to the 4,400-foot elevation at Reno, the snow had dwindled to a light frosting. Casino lights flashed behind the railroad crossing signals as we pulled into town, blocking an impressive 12 intersections to automobile traffic with our triumphant arrival.

NOTE: In January 2004, a month after I took this trip, Amtrak's westbound California Zephyr derailed in heavy snow, trapping its riders for 14 hours somewhere around Emigrant Gap.

A Side Trip from Truckee on Highway 89

The southbound Highway 89 exit from I-80, located west of Truckee, is quite well known to travelers headed toward Lake Tahoe, but the exit onto northbound Highway 89, located east of Truckee, receives far less traffic. The first time I took Highway 89 north along the Little Truckee River toward Sierraville, it was to investigate Kyburz Flat, where I understood there was an historic outdoor bread oven.

The oven is an exhibit at the Tahoe National Forest's **Kyburz Flat Interpretive Area,** located 12 miles north of Truckee and 1 mile east of Highway 89 on **Henness Pass Road.** In autumn, the marsh at the south end of Kyburz Flat is a mosaic of browns, greens, and golds, with great blue herons stalking through the grasses. In spring, the meadow is a riot of wildflowers, but otherwise, the scenery at this obscure spot is not spectacular.

Kyburz Flat is notable because it is an interpretive site preserving three sets of historic artifacts from three very different eras of human activity. The oldest artifact sits right next to the site's main parking area. It disguises itself as a big, broken rock covered with tiny pockmarks; these are petroglyphs that archeologists believe had ceremonial significance to the ancient ancestors of the Washoe Indians who migrated through here in the warmer seasons.

Beyond the rock in an open area to the east is a high, dry spot covered with sagebrush. Various signboards interpret the ruins, which consist of little more than a low stone fence, a pole stuck in the ground, and a hole lined with rocks. But these traces led archeologists to believe that around 1860 this was once a stage stop on the bustling Henness Pass Road. As I've returned here over the years, I've become fascinated with watching the way nature gradually reclaims such sites. A young Jeffrey pine that sprouted between the wagon ruts of the former roadbed is on its way to becoming a substantial tree.

Look north from the stage stop in the summer months, and you might notice a thin line of lush green meandering through the tawny meadow. It emanates from a spring located at the far northern end of the meadow. This spring once supplied water for the summer residents of the Wheeler Sheep Camp, a complex of cabins, barns, and corrals built

BASQUE SHEEPHERDER'S BREAD

Travelers in the western United States sometimes find an item called Basque sheepherder's bread at regional bakeries. It is unlikely, however, that an old Basque sheepherder would recognize any commercial rendition of the bread he and his dog ate during their long and lonely weeks with the sheep in remote high-country pastures. The real thing was baked in a cast iron pot in the ground, or inside a hand-built, wood-fired stone oven back at the sheep company's base camp.

INGREDIENTS (FOR ONE VERY LARGE LOAF):
    4 cups warm water
    2 tablespoons active dry yeast
    2 tablespoons sugar
    1 tablespoon salt
    10–12 cups all-purpose flour
    Olive oil

EQUIPMENT:
    A six-quart, cast-iron Dutch oven with an
        ovenproof lid
    A large mixing bowl
    Aluminum foil

Eugenio Murillo worked as the camptender at Wheeler Sheep Camp in the 1940s. He has just taken these round loaves of bread from the oven. Photo courtesy of Irene Giossi

Preheat the oven. In the mixing bowl, combine yeast, sugar, and one cup flour with the warm water. Stir to mix and set in a warm place for about 15 to 30 minutes. When the mixture becomes bubbly, gradually add the remaining flour, stirring to form a soft dough. Knead the dough inside of the bowl until smooth, then cover with a damp towel, and allow the dough to rise until doubled in bulk. Cut a circle of aluminum foil to fit in the bottom of the Dutch oven. Oil the inside of the Dutch oven (along with the foil and the lid), and place the dough inside. Preheat the oven to 400 degrees and allow the dough to rise again until it is almost to the rim of the pot. Cover with the lid, and place the pot inside the oven. Bake for an hour. Remove the lid and bake an additional 15–30 minutes until the top is golden brown. Remove from the oven and turn loaf onto rack to cool.

by a Basque immigrant named John Martin Gallues in 1913. The Wheeler camp served until 1953 as a base for Basque sheepherders tending flocks in far-flung Sierra meadows. One of the most important structures here was the stone-and-brick, wood-fired oven, where the camptender baked bread every five days to take to the sheepherders. Along with the bread, the camptender brought jugs of wine and supplies the herders would use to prepare their own meals while alone in their outposts. According to Irene Giossi, who spent summers at Kyburz Flat in the years when her parents were tending the Wheeler Sheep Camp, some of the herders were pretty good cooks. When they knew the camptender was on his way to make deliveries, they would prepare a special lamb stew or rice pudding, cooking it in a Dutch oven in an underground pit lined with hot rocks. If the food appealed and the wine flowed, the camptender might stick around for a few hours keeping the lonely herder company.

The camp's wooden shacks and fences have now returned to the earth, but Forest Service archeologists and enthusiastic volunteers have restored the oven to working order. Contact the Tahoe National Forest Sierraville Ranger District, and you can make arrangements to use the oven to bake bread and cook a pot of stew, as I have done every year since I first discovered the site. My friends all look forward to the annual event (which we call Burning Lamb — not to be confused with Burning Man, an event of quite a different stripe held annually in Nevada's Black Rock Desert).

Note: Kyburz Flat should not be confused with Kyburz, a town on U.S. 50 southwest of Lake Tahoe.

Reno (el. 4,490 feet)

In discussions of the Donner Party tragedy, a question occasionally emerges that makes me smile quietly to myself:

"Why didn't the Donner Party turn back to Reno for the winter?"

In October 1846, when the Donner Party came through the Reno basin, they would have found only Washoe or Paiute winter camps.

"But even so," you might say as you wander between casinos through the very light snow of a typical Reno winter, "this would have been a better place to spend the winter than Donner Lake."

DOWNTOWN RENO

Heart of Reno.

Who's to say why the emigrants didn't turn back to the lower elevations of the Reno basin? One possibility was that each day, as they waited in their cold encampments near the lake, they imagined that they were about to be rescued by the members of their party who had gone ahead to Sutter's Fort. It's quite a different dilemma than trying to decide whether to go back for thirds at one of Reno's 24-hour, all-you-can-eat casino buffets.

Gambling was not fully legalized in Nevada until 1931. The first gold-era settlement in the Truckee Meadows area began to take shape in the 1860s, when a man named Myron Lake constructed a toll bridge over the Truckee River to serve traffic going to and from Virginia City and the Comstock Lode. In time, the toll bridge evolved into a thriving commercial center and railway depot, and today, with two interstate highways whisking cars through Reno, the bridge site at Virginia Street is merely an attractive stop on Reno's **Riverwalk** — one that has special appeal on a hot summer's day. Trails continue along the river through a chain of civic parks.

Following Virginia Street south from the river for about three blocks then heading west for two more will bring you to 160 West Liberty Street, the address of Reno's cultural hot spot, the **Nevada Museum of Art.** The museum is housed in an intriguing four-story structure designed by renowned Southwest architect Will Bruder. The architect describes his design as having been inspired by the forms of Nevada's Black Rock Desert, and indeed, moving through its diverse exhibit spaces, you get a sense of travel into a wholly other environment as unexpected views open and close in every direction. Plunk the kids in the cool Children's Discovery Center and go take a peek at several significant Sierra-themed paintings on long-term loan: Charles Nahl and Frederick A. Wenderoth's *Miners in the Sierras,* 1851–52; Albert Bierstadt's *Among the Sierra Nevada Mountains,* 1868; John Ross Key's *San Joaquin Valley,* 1873; and Edwin Deakin's

Views from the rooftop observation deck at the Nevada Museum of Art take in downtown Reno and Carson Range peaks.

Mount Tallac, 1895. Many of the permanent and traveling exhibitions investigate the unique geography and culture of the Sierra and Great Basin regions. The museum's rooftop observation deck affords great vistas of the casino madness with its contrasting backdrop of mountains in every direction.

North of I-80 on Virginia Street, you might find yourself asking, "Can this be Reno?" as you enter the serene campus of the **University of Nevada,** a land-grant college established in 1887. The publisher of this book operates out of the basement of Morrill Hall, the college's original building, where the first generation of students both lived and studied. A highlight on campus is the mineral collection inside the Mackay School of Mines building. (Heirs of Comstock mine owner John Mackay contributed to the university's expansion in the early 20th century.) Also, visitors might be intrigued by the university's Center for Basque Studies, one of a very few such entities in the world. Here students can study both the ancient culture of the Old World Basques in Spain and France, and also that of the Basque diaspora, which has significant roots in the American West and shows its distinctly colorful character in the greater Sierra Nevada region.

Visitors can mix with Basques in the center of Reno by heading for **Louis' Basque Corner,** which is both a popular restaurant and a boardinghouse for former sheepherders on the corner of North Evans Avenue and East 4th Street. Grab a stool at the bar and strike up a conversation with the friendly fellow in the next seat. He might be a former sheepherder who in his youth was lured from the Basque homeland with the promise of work at a Nevada, California, or Idaho sheep ranch. The job would turn into a long, lonely summer spent herding sheep through high mountain meadows, with no companions but a donkey and a couple of sheepdogs. The young men longed for winter to return so they could take leave of the sheep and spend their earnings on a leisurely life, eating, drinking, and playing *mus* (a card game) at places like Louis' or the Santa Fe Hotel at 235 Lake Street in Reno.

At the hotels they dined daily on barley soup, chorizo-laced beans, salad, plates of steak or chops, and savory stews of chicken, beef, or rabbit, all washed down with carafes of hearty red wine. Here or at the social club, they could gather to play *mus* and *pelota* (handball), enjoy festivals with dancing and singing, and most importantly, they could enjoy the company of women.

Practical Matters

With elevation changes of over 7,000 feet on this tour, there is a great variety in seasonal highlights. Most winter visitors come for the snow, which can remain at the higher elevations into June. Summer can be hot at lower elevations, but ideal in the high mountain regions. Summer-like conditions can extend well into autumn. For more on Sierra weather, including climate statistics on Sacramento, Truckee, and Reno, see the introduction.

ROADS

The routes followed in this chapter, Interstate 80, Donner Pass Road/ old U.S. 40, and the portion of Highway 89 north of Truckee, are well maintained and kept open all winter, except on days when the California Department of Transportation snow-removal operation can't keep up with snowfall. In general, winter travel through regions above snowline (approximately 4,000 feet) requires adequate preparation for snow, ice, and cold temperatures. There may be delays, even on clear winter days, and tire chains are required in snowy conditions.

OTHER MEANS

San Francisco, Sacramento, and Reno have major **airports.** Amtrak's California Zephyr serves this route, and **buses** from major California cities serving the Reno and Tahoe casino districts are frequent and cheap.

WHERE TO STAY AND EAT

Hotel rooms of all descriptions are available in Sacramento and Reno. Smaller hotels and B&Bs are available in Auburn, Colfax, and Truckee. The Soda Springs area offers many vacation condominium options, as well as some inns. The best restaurant selections are in Sacramento, Auburn, Truckee, Reno, and around the ski resorts in Donner Pass.

Truckee in particular has a knack for attracting talented chefs to its year-round restaurants.

CAMPING

There are campgrounds in the Sacramento, Folsom, Auburn, and Donner/Truckee areas, and throughout the Tahoe and Humboldt-Toiyabe national forests.

U.S. FOREST SERVICE

Humboldt-Toiyabe National Forest (www.fs.fed.us/r4/htnf/): **Headquarters,** 1200 Franklin Way, Sparks, 775–331–6444; **Carson Ranger District,** 1536 South Carson Street, Carson City, 775–882–2766.
Tahoe National Forest (www.fs.fed.us/r5/tahoe/): **Big Bend Visitor Center,** 49685 Hampshire Rocks Road (Old U.S. 40), Soda Springs, 530–426–3609; **Sierraville Ranger District,** 317 South Lincoln, Sierraville, 530–994–3401; **Truckee Ranger District,** 9646 Donner Pass Road, Truckee, 530–587–3558.

VISITORS BUREAUS

Nevada Commission on Tourism, www.travelnevada.com/about.asp, 401 North Carson Street, Carson City, 800–638–2328.
Placer County Visitors Council, www.placer.ca.gov/visit/, 13411 Lincoln Way, Auburn, 530–887–2111.
Reno-Sparks Convention & Visitors Authority, www.renolaketahoe. com, 4001 South Virginia Street, Suite G, Reno, 775–827–7366, 1–800–367–7366.
Sacramento Visitor Center, 13th & J streets, Sacramento, 916–264-4740.
Truckee Donner Chamber of Commerce, www.truckee.com, 10065 Donner Pass Road, Truckee, 530–587–2757.

REGIONAL GUIDES

Meals, Hank. *Yuba Trails 2: A Selection of Historic Hiking Trails in the Yuba River and Neighboring Watersheds.* Self-published, 2001.
Schaffer, Jeffrey. *The Tahoe Sierra.* Berkeley, Calif.: Wilderness Press, 1994.

2

Tahoe

On most any Friday night when the weather is right, raging streams of automobiles will be flowing from all directions toward one particular Sierra destination — Tahoe. The appeal is the gorgeous surroundings combined with a wide variety of recreational activities. For those who love skiing, gambling, and partying on the beach, Lake Tahoe is a fabulous mountain playground. For those who want to commune with pristine nature, Lake Tahoe leaves something to be desired.

As a solitude seeker, I dismissed the Tahoe Basin for years, feeling that such a crowded place was unworthy of my attention. When it came time to write this chapter, I became determined to discover the untarnished soul of Tahoe. I outfitted myself with a set of blinders and drew up a schedule for visiting the most popular spots in the off-hours of the off-seasons. What I found was a place of matchless grandeur with an engaging history, but a history that I wish had gone a different way.

Da ow a ga

For 10,000 years before the modern era, the native Washoe people came every spring to fish and hunt in the basin of the big lake they called *Da ow a ga*, returning to the lower elevations east of the Carson Range for the winter. Lake Tahoe was, and is, a sacred place to the Washoe. They say that the Maker had intended to put *Da ow a ga* aside for himself, but as he spread the seeds of humanity to different parts of the world, he ran out of

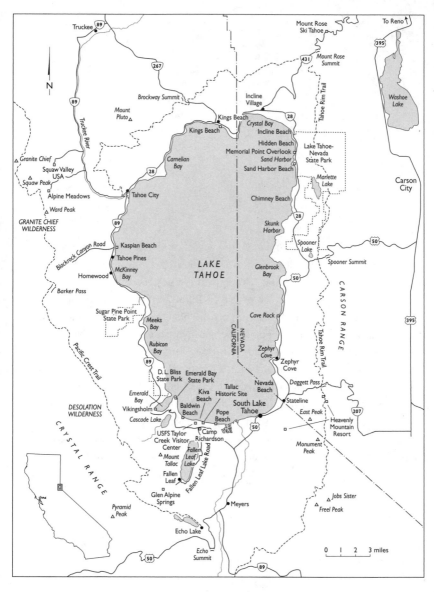

LAKE TAHOE REGION

This southwest-facing view over Lake Tahoe takes in the Crystal Range on the far horizon.

places to put them and decided to give this special place to the Washoe, since he knew they would protect it.

Geologists tell us that the Tahoe Basin is a graben, a block of the earth's crust that has dropped while blocks on either side have risen. The Tahoe graben formed 5 to 10 million years ago when it sank between the rising Sierra Nevada fault block on the west and the Carson Range fault block on the east. At that time, the downshifted block became a deep V-shaped valley (el. 1,645 feet), which provided a path for the ancestral Truckee River to flow in a northward direction. About 2 million years ago, volcanic activity began in the region and lava flowed from Mount Pluto (north of the lake), blocking the river's exit from the basin's north end. The water backed up to fill the basin to a level that reached 600 feet higher than the present surface of the lake, now at 6,229 feet. The Truckee River eventually found an escape route through the northwestern part of the lava dam and resumed its flow toward Nevada.

THE MODERN ERA

The modern history of the Lake Tahoe Basin began abruptly in 1859 with the discovery of the Comstock Lode, a phenomenal deposit of silver and gold located in the nearly treeless Virginia Range 15 miles northeast of the lakeshore. Timber was needed to build and run the mining district, and the magnificent old forests lining the steep slopes of Lake Bigler (named for California's then-governor) were an ideal and ready supply. The trees were felled, flumed down to the lake, rafted to Glenbrook Bay, carted up Spooner Summit, flumed again down to Carson City, and then sent by rail to the mines.

It is interesting to note that five years after the discovery of the Comstock Lode, as the lumber barons were felling Tahoe's trees, the beautiful valley of Yosemite was being set aside as a treasure in the public trust. Tahoe had no such luck — the wealthy built lavish vacation mansions, and hotels sprang up to attract the well-heeled tourists who began arriving via the new transcontinental railroad in 1868. Luxurious steamships became the preferred mode of transportation around the lake, even after the crude West Shore road opened in 1914.

Lake Tahoe culture changed dramatically in 1931 when Nevada legalized gambling, but it took the first televised Olympic Games, held at Squaw Valley in 1960, to make Tahoe into a destination known the world over. The spoiling of the Tahoe Basin went on unmitigated until the implementation of planning and environmental standards in the 1960s.

MARK TWAIN'S TAHOE

At the height of the Comstock mining excitement, a young man named Samuel Clemens (soon to adopt the pen name Mark Twain) came to Virginia City, Nevada, to work as a journalist for the *Territorial Enterprise*. In *Roughing It* (1872), Twain describes how he and his friend Johnny set out on foot over the Carson Range to see Lake Tahoe:

> We plodded on, two or three hours longer, and at last the Lake burst upon us — a noble sheet of blue water lifted six thousand three hundred feet above the level of the sea, and walled in by a rim of mountain peaks that towered aloft three thousand feet higher still. It was a vast oval, and one would have to use up eighty or a hundred good miles of traveling around it. As it lay there with the shadow of the mountains brilliantly photographed upon its still

surface I thought it must surely be the fairest picture the whole earth affords.

Arriving at a stony Tahoe beach, they found a skiff and paddled over the lake until they found a campsite, where they spent an exciting three weeks. Twain writes:

> While Johnny was carrying the main bulk of the provisions up to our "house" (a lean-to) for future use, I took the loaf of bread, some slices of bacon, and a coffee pot, ashore, set them down by a tree, lit a fire, and went back to the boat to get the frying pan. While I was at this, I heard a shout from Johnny, and looking up I saw that my fire was galloping all over the premises!
>
> Johnny was on the other side of it, he had to run through the flames to get to the lake shore, and then we stood helpless and watched the devastation. . . . We were driven to the boat by the intense heat, and there we remained, spellbound.
>
> Within half an hour all before us was a tossing, blinding tempest of flame! It went surging up adjacent ridges — surmounted them and disappeared in the canyons beyond — burst into view upon higher and farther ridges, presently — shed a grander illumination abroad, and dove again — flamed out again, directly, higher and still higher up the mountain side — threw out skirmishing parties of fire here and there, and sent them trailing their crimson spirals away among the remote ramparts and ribs and gorges, till as far as the eye could reach the lofty mountain-fronts were webbed as it were with a tangled network of red lava streams. Away across the water the crags and domes were lit with the ruddy glare, and the firmament above was a reflected hell!

Southwest Shore

This book's tour of Lake Tahoe begins at "the Y," the locals' name for the split between Highway 89 and U.S. 50 on Lake Tahoe's south shore. This junction funnels a disproportionately large amount of Tahoe's traffic, which makes it a very exciting place for those who like being in the center of the action.

From the Y, Highway 89 takes off to the northwest along the lake's western shore. While you're passing through historic **Camp Richardson,** be prepared to stop at the crosswalks. This historic vacation resort remains wildly popular with families, and pedestrian traffic can bring cars to a halt for several minutes while people stroll across the highway with ice-cream cones in hand. Kids on bikes enjoy a great sense of freedom as they tour their vacation paradise.

The private resort of Camp Richardson is unique in this corner of the lake, which is dominated by free-use public facilities. The Forest Service's **Pope Beach, Kiva Beach,** and **Baldwin Beach** are always jammed in good weather, although one might easily find a quiet perch on the little strip of shore at the **Tallac Historic Site,** a luxurious park with three historic estates that date from 1894 to 1927. The estates are now owned by the U.S. Forest Service and open to the public. The centerpiece of the community was the Tallac Resort (now gone, but at one time a sizable complex). Visitors can walk around the remains of the resort's foundations, but most people prefer to marvel at the gorgeous Pope, Baldwin, and Valhalla estates, which have been restored to depict the sumptuous lifestyle once enjoyed by their owners and guests. The Baldwin house is outfitted as a museum, and its grounds are notable for their Washoe native plant garden and cultural exhibits, all maintained by local Washoes. The Pope Mansion offers an art gallery and a set schedule of tours. The Valhalla Grand Hall houses a gift shop, and its summer concerts are but part of the park's impressive schedule of summer cultural arts activities. The beautiful grounds are open year-round. (Pronunciation note: the accent in Tallac is on the second syllable.)

USFS TAYLOR CREEK VISITOR CENTER

Next door to the Tallac site is the U.S. Forest Service Taylor Creek Visitor Center, where you can pick up recreation information for the Tahoe Basin, including trail maps for hikes introduced in this chapter. One of the most interesting exhibits at the center is the **Stream Profile Chamber,** which allows visitors to look into the stream leaving Fallen Leaf Lake as it pours into Lake Tahoe. It's an inside view on the underwater world of the Tahoe Kokanee salmon. In late September and October, you might see the salmon in their red mating colors.

FALLEN LEAF LAKE (el. 6,317 feet)

Many of the Sierra's most exquisite features are the work of the last ice age. This is the case with Fallen Leaf Lake, which sits within a U-shaped, glacier-scraped valley, much like the valleys to the northwest that hold Cascade Lake and Emerald Bay respectively. The Washoe describe the lakes and bay as leaves that fell from a branch as it was being carried by an Indian brave fleeing from the Evil One.

The road to Fallen Leaf Lake starts right across the highway from Tallac. It winds through the forest, through an aspen-rimmed meadow, and on to a lake that is often described as a miniature Lake Tahoe. Indeed, with the traffic and lavish private homes, the scene can be somewhat reminiscent of Tahoe, but the views are rather more intimate.

Touring the little lake by car can be a major headache, since the only way to the far end (and the town of Fallen Leaf) is via the single-lane east shore road, where cars are attempting to go in both directions from hundreds of shoreline vacation homes. However, it is worth the effort in order to make the two-mile hike to the old **Glen Alpine Springs** resort.

Glen Alpine Springs, established in 1884, was one of the Tahoe Basin's first leisure resorts. The soda springs were the main attraction of the location, and they still bubble out of the ground in a rusty froth, which is fascinating, though the marshy ground around the springs provides a fine environment for mosquitoes. The resort's modest structures of native stone and carved wood exude a rustic elegance. Most were added in later decades and are attributed to noted architect Bernard Maybeck. The U.S. Forest Service now maintains the resort as an interpretive site and conference center, staffed primarily by volunteers. Needless to say, amenities are few with this low-budget operation. Bring drinking water, bug repellent, and a picnic, and consider leaving a donation for its upkeep.

To get to the Glen Alpine Springs trailhead, take Fallen Leaf Road through the town of Fallen Leaf past the boat ramp and store. Look for the charming little St. Francis of the Mountains chapel on the left and turn left on Glen Alpine Road. The trailhead is a half-mile up this road. Its parking lot is large but often full, because the trailhead is also a launch point for backpackers headed up to the Crystal Range and the sparkling lakes of the Desolation Wilderness.

Another popular hiking destination from the Fallen Leaf Lake vicinity is **Mount Tallac** (el. 9,735 feet). The trailhead is on the west side of the lake, on Cathedral Road. The five-mile hike up to the dark metamorphic rooftop of Mount Tallac is quite strenuous, but offers the reward of fabulous views of the Tahoe Basin and the High Sierra peaks to the south.

(Note: Anyone setting out on a hike into a high mountain wilderness should go adequately prepared. Hiking guidebooks, such as those listed in the appendix, offer expert assistance for your planning.)

EMERALD BAY

One summer's morning, I found myself out well before the Tahoe crowds were astir, and so I took the opportunity to enjoy my breakfast from a glittering granitic perch in the Vikingsholm parking lot, high above the southwest end of Emerald Bay. The bay was so still that it looked like a great oval mirror, and so deep blue that it rivaled the plumage of the Steller's jay that was trying to steal my breakfast bun. As if in a signal that the day had begun, two jet-skis glided into the bay from the lake, appearing slow and almost silent, due to the effects of the distance. Their wakes made braiding ripples across the placid surface, breaking the azure into a million glistening shards. Then the day's sounds began as two honking Canada geese exited from their nesting spots on Fannette Island and a small motorboat puttered out of the boaters' campground on the north shore of the bay.

The boaters' campground occupies the site of the old Emerald Bay Resort, which opened in 1884. The resort supported a small fleet of fishing boats, many of which now lie sunken offshore in the **Emerald Bay State Underwater Park.** Among the exhibits divers explore at this unique park are a couple of barges, various items from the resort, and a Model A Ford.

Up on dry land, visitors are inevitably drawn to **Vikingsholm,** a beau-

(opposite) The kitchen and dining hall at Glen Alpine Springs.

tiful home of medieval Scandinavian design that Mrs. Lora Josephine Knight had built in 1928–29 to use as her summer residence. It is at the bottom of a steep, mile-long trail from the Vikingsholm parking lot, and you will indeed have to hike this trail, since wheeled transportation is available only for disabled guests. (Arrange this ride at Sugar Pine Point State Park.) Bring a picnic and plan to join a tour of the home's interior. The tiny castle seen atop Fannette Island was Mrs. Knight's teahouse. Tea is no longer served, but the solitude and safety of Fannette Island make it a preferred nesting ground for Canada geese.

Across the highway from the Vikingsholm parking lot sits the rather dreary-looking Bay View Campground. This campground also serves as a trailhead used by backpackers launching trips into the Desolation Wilderness, however most of the foot traffic is aimed at **Cascade Falls,** a

Fannette Island, the only island in Lake Tahoe, sits in the middle of Emerald Bay. Photo by Erlda Parker

An osprey (*Pandion haliaetus*) soars up from its nest beside Emerald Bay.

mere two miles away. At the falls, Cascade Creek fans out over a large area of polished granitic rock before making its final plunge into Cascade Lake. Plan plenty of time to explore.

The longer one stays at Emerald Bay, the easier it is to understand why the campgrounds at **D. L. Bliss and Emerald Bay state parks** are so popular. The two parks comprise extensive lakeside acreage with nice beaches and a great network of shoreline trails, all mapped out on the park brochures. Views along the trails are truly splendid. With more than a century of regrowth since the massive deforestation of the Comstock era and its resulting landslides, the steep slopes are again looking regal with majestic Jeffrey and sugar pines, while views of the old mansions are getting lost in the flourishing greenery. A hiker with sharp ears and eyes might be rewarded with an osprey sighting. These raptors make shrill whistles when someone trespasses beneath their aeries (usually constructed in the tops of dead trees), which look like bundles of sticks.

West Shore

Along the string of small West Shore developments are some of Tahoe's more humble attractions—tiny cafes and motels, four little ski centers, and some modest public beach access. At Meeks Bay, however, the human infestation shows the Tahoe crowd scene nearing its worst. The big campground is jammed with every sort of rig from which all manner of watercraft emerge like flies to buzz the lake. By contrast, **Sugar Pine Point State Park,** just north of Meeks Bay, is an oasis of placidity. Its large campground is open year-round, even in winter, when it serves hearty cross-country skiers. On summer afternoons, those who want to escape to an even-more-civilized past can tour the historic Ehrman Mansion, or just bask in its plush parlor. Black bear, coyote, and mule deer roam up and down the park's mountain-to-lakeshore corridor.

From Sugar Pine Point, the shoreline curves westward to form McKinney Bay, which harbors the small community of **Homewood** and its small ski resort. An old motel here was converted to house the **Tahoe Maritime Museum**. The collections are considered to be some of the best of the genre in the West, and the opportunity to delve into Lake Tahoe's rich nautical heritage has been a welcome addition to lakeside activities.

A mile north of Tahoe Pines (at Eagle Rock and Kaspian Beach) is Blackwood Canyon Road, the only West Shore road that reaches up to the Sierra crest. It's seven miles on pavement and another quarter-mile on dirt to **Barker Pass** (el. 7,600 feet) in the Granite Chief Wilderness. The trailhead here provides access to the Pacific Crest Trail and also to the West Shore portion of the 164-mile-long **Tahoe Rim Trail**. This multiuse trail is open to mountain bikers, but they are barred on alternate days so that hikers and equestrians can have a more peaceful experience.

TAHOE CITY

The little town at the spillway of Lake Tahoe into the Lower Truckee River is an historic gateway to the Tahoe Basin. The arrival of the Central Pacific Railroad in Truckee in 1868 brought the first tourists. At the station, they boarded a stagecoach for a ride along the Lower Truckee River to the fledgling hotels in Tahoe City. By 1900, a narrow-gauge railroad had replaced the stage, and the tracks ran all the way onto the wharf at the fabulous Tahoe Tavern. There, passengers could transfer directly to steamship or beautiful wooden yachts for destinations around the lake.

Today at Tahoe City, one still finds the names of the famous old hospitality houses, but they're on the gated entrances of condominium communities. The automobile has long since replaced the stagecoach, train, and steamships (although a few enterprises do still offer great boat tours). The only place to find much vestige of old Tahoe City is within the hand-hewn lodgepole pine cabins of the **North Lake Tahoe Historical Soci-**

ety, at 130 West Lake Boulevard. The complex of museums is located on a former Washoe campsite on the south shore of the Truckee River, at the river's egress from the lake.

An eclectic array of artifacts introduces many interesting characters, people who lived and worked here in the early 20th century. One was Ethel Joslin Vernon, a longtime Tahoe resident who came to the lake in 1911 to marry Clarence W. Vernon, a member of the Tahoe Tavern orchestra. The couple's honeymoon was a three-week rowboat camping trip in the brisk months of autumn. Ethel loved to hike up in Barker Pass, a place she called "the rim of Heaven." She took long walks with her dog, finding inspiration for her artwork and poetry. Over time, Ethel acquainted herself with local Washoe elders. She wrote down their legends and learned some of their basket craft, which she put to use in making delicate little pine needle baskets. Were Ethel alive today, she would certainly love the Historical Society's Marion Steinbach Indian Basketry Museum, which is housed in the complex's new wing. The exhibits offer a detailed lesson on the forms and materials of Native American basketry, and include displays of dolls, games, hats, jewelry, traps, cages, and cradleboards by craftspeople of many different Indian nations.

Also on the Historical Society's site are the Watson Cabin Living Museum and the Gatekeeper's Cabin Museum. The latter spells out the history of the concrete dam next to the museums. Most any time of the year, there will be several visitors standing on the bridge facing the dam, leaning over the rail to watch the Lower Truckee River swirling turquoise and white and teeming with waterfowl at the lake exit. To drivers crossing the span, it is pretty obvious why this is called Fanny Bridge.

A Side Trip Down the Lower Truckee River

For 14 miles, the lively Lower Truckee River splashes its way from Tahoe City to Truckee alongside Highway 89. In summer, bicyclists whirr along the old railway bed, now a paved bike path, and one flotilla of rafts after another glides along to Alpine Meadows. Beyond this takeout point the glittering waterway is nearly deserted as it passes the entrance to Squaw Valley and a string of equally deserted riverside campgrounds.

ALPINE MEADOWS ROAD

A little under four miles from Tahoe City, Alpine Meadows Road appears on the left. The road follows Bear Creek up to the **Alpine Meadows ski area,** which a young snowboarder I know claims has the best snow in the Sierra. The consensus among skiers is that the resort offers a quieter, friendlier atmosphere than nearby Squaw Valley or the South Lake Tahoe resorts.

If you happen to drive up this road in summer, you might notice a large number of cars parked on the shoulder at the two-mile point. The attraction is the **Five Lakes Trail,** where a mere two miles of hoofing gets you to a beautiful granitic basin with five shallow lakes. From the trail there are glimpses of the ski area.

SQUAW VALLEY USA

Squaw Valley would be just another Tahoe ski resort with great snow and challenging terrain were it not for an extraordinary chain of events that began in 1955. It was in that year that Alexander Cushing, who had fled a drearily successful career as a Wall Street lawyer to open a modest ski resort, applied to the International Olympic Committee (IOC) for hosting rights to the 1960 Winter Olympic Games. In spite of endless assertions by the committee that his efforts were pointless and that the games would be awarded to Innsbruck, Austria, Cushing pressed his idea forward. In a final vote of 32 to 30, the IOC chose Squaw Valley to host the Games, and the entire world looked toward Lake Tahoe.

A frenzy of development ensued as workers scrambled to create the infrastructure necessary to host the games, leaving today's Squaw Valley with an incredible complex of lifts, ski jumps, ice-skating arenas, training facilities, information centers, housing, shops, restaurants, and spas.

Being a novice skier, I was pleased to find that many of the resort's best novice runs are in the good snow on the upper reaches of 8,700-foot Emigrant Peak. However, I found I had pressed my luck when I rode up to 8,900-foot Squaw Peak for the views of Lake Tahoe to the east and of Granite Chief Wilderness to the west. It all seemed worth it until I sprained my thumb on the way down from that high, windswept spot.

To continue the tour of Lake Tahoe, return south on Highway 89 to Tahoe City and turn northeast onto Highway 28.

North Shore

Tahoe's North Shore, from Tahoe City to Kings Beach, is dotted with private communities, an occasional motel and café, and several delightful beach parks with public access. The prettiest is the pebble-lined beach at **Carnelian Bay.** Behind the beach is a restored alluvial wetland surrounded by manzanita and quaking aspen — a showcase for the efforts of the California-Tahoe Conservancy. Here I found a café beside the beach offering both espresso drinks and kayak rentals. East of Carnelian Bay are several white sand beaches maintained by the North Tahoe Beach Center, a project of the North Tahoe Public Utility District.

About 1.5 miles past Kings Beach and the Highway 267 junction, the sudden appearance of the casinos at **Crystal Bay** announces the state of Nevada. The scene is a little more restrained here than it is at the town of Stateline, Nevada, on the lake's southeast corner. Stop in at the Cal Neva Resort and Spa for a taste of Crystal Bay in the 1920s and 30s when celebrities, socialites, and the generally wealthy flocked here to enjoy the rustic locale.

Continuing northeast on Highway 28 to **Incline Village,** you find that you have entered ski country. Diamond Peak Ski Resort is practically in the village, and Mount Rose Ski Tahoe is up (way up!) Highway 431.

SIDE TRIP TO MOUNT ROSE (el. 10,776 feet)
This side trip up to the Nevada Route 431 crossing of the Carson Range at Mount Rose Summit (el. 8,900 feet) offers several different hiking possibilities. A few miles southwest of the summit, the highway passes through an area called Tahoe Meadows where there is ample parking. Hikers, bikers, and equestrians can access the Tahoe Rim Trail here. Hikers with a more casual agenda can enjoy a system of easy trails that fan out through the gentle meadows. A ballet of wildflowers plays in various acts here throughout the spring and summer seasons.

Hikers intent on reaching the top of Mount Rose begin the 12-mile round trip at a trailhead just southwest of the highway's summit crossing. A clear day on the trail might offer a sighting of Lassen Peak (el. 10,457 feet), the southernmost outpost of the volcanically active Cascade Range. Skiers can catch such views while riding the lifts at **Mount Rose**

Ski Tahoe. The resort is based at 8,260 feet, and the lifts ascend to nearly 10,000 feet.

Route 431 continues on to join U.S. 395 south of Reno.

East Shore and the Carson Range

Among the wealthy who flocked to Tahoe in the early- to mid-20th century was a bon vivant named George Whittell Jr. Whittell amassed over 40,000 acres of land beside the lake, including 27 miles of Tahoe shoreline. At Sand Harbor, Whittell built a residence, **Thunderbird Lodge**, which he styled as a French chateau, using the native granite as a primary material. Once Whittell had taken up residence, he put his wealth toward collecting classic cars, yachts, airplanes, and exotic wild animals, all of which he kept at his estate.

The exotic animals are now gone and Whittell's Thunderbird Lodge has become the property of the U.S. National Forest Service. It is open during the summer for public tours. However, visitors will not make it through the gate without an advance reservation with the Nevada Thunderbird Lodge Preservation Society. Tours leave from the Visitors Bureau at Incline Village/Crystal Bay, on Highway 28 near the California state line. Some tours include arrival by boat, the mode in which most visitors reached Thunderbird Lodge during Whittell's day.

In summer, the fine public beaches south of Incline Village attract throngs of vacationers. Between the sandy strips and crescents at **Incline Beach, Hidden Beach, Sand Harbor Beach,** and **Chimney Beach,** huge piles of smoothly sculpted granitic boulders jut out into the cold, clear water. These are ideal spots to sit and peer into the depths or gaze southwest across the lake at the stunning panorama of the Crystal Range. If parking is at a premium, as it is on most any warm summer's day, you can still stop to enjoy this superb scenery at the award-winning **Memorial Point Overlook,** located between Hidden Beach and Sand Harbor. The overlook was one of eight scenic highway projects across the nation to receive honors in 2001 from the American Association of State Highway Transportation Officials. The design disguises the restrooms in a tree house-like structure with lookout platforms and stairways leading down

Vintage shot of the Thunderbird Lodge as seen from an arriving steamer. Photo from University of Nevada, Reno, Special Collections

toward the shore. Interpretive signs provide a concise lesson in natural history.

SKUNK HARBOR

In the rocky cove at Skunk Harbor, a gorgeous little dwelling of native stone sits a few paces up from the sandy beach. The boat docks are nearly washed away at this unstaffed Forest Service holding, but the stone buildings remain in strikingly good condition in spite of the neglect. Entrance into the buildings is prohibited, but you can peek through the windows to imagine what it might have been like in the days when it served as a little getaway spot for a landowner whose main Tahoe residence was on the West Shore. George Newhall built this cozy little retreat in 1923, but a few years after the stock market crashed he sold it to George Whittell (see above). One hopes the Forest Service will one day have the resources to restore Newhall's Skunk Harbor, but meanwhile, a visitor here is ensured near solitude. Unless you arrive by boat, the only way here is to walk or bicycle down the steep 1.5-mile fire road from Highway 28. The gated fire road is found on the west side of the highway, seven miles south of Incline Village on Highway 28. There is no obvious sign to indicate that this is the way to Skunk Harbor, but it's the only noticeable fire road on the west side at those coordinates. There is about enough space to park two cars on the shoulder.

SPOONER LAKE AND THE FLUME TRAIL

Just before Highway 28 makes its T-junction with U.S. 50 two miles south of the fire road to Skunk Harbor, look for an entrance marked Spooner Lake State Park, which is part of the complex of Lake Tahoe–Nevada State Parks. Here, along the crest of the Carson Range, is a mountain biker's mecca. The famous Flume Trail takes its name from a flume built in the 1870s to divert water from newly dammed Marlette Lake to Spooner Lake and down to the Comstock mining district. A little over 100 years later, an avid mountain biker named Max Jones happened along the path of this flume. He found it choked with a retrofit of aluminum pipe and a deep overgrowth of brush, but was so struck with the vision of a recreational path that he single-handedly cleared and rehabilitated the route to accommodate hikers and single-track mountain bikers. He then got permission to set up a mountain bike and cross-country ski center complete with cozy four-season cabins at Spooner Lake.

The extraordinary experience of biking the Flume Trail is not out of range for a novice mountain biker with some prior conditioning, a serviceable mountain bike, a measure of courage, and the good sense to get off and walk the bike through the scary spots. When the flashy riders are whizzing by, just stop while they pass, and gaze out on the stunning views of the sparkling lake framed by massive granitic boulders and tall Jeffrey pines. The Flume Trail connects up to the 164-mile-long Tahoe Rim Trail.

GLENBROOK BAY

Just south of Spooner Lake, Highway 28 comes to an end upon meeting U.S. 50. If you were to turn left and head a mile northeast, 50 would take you across the Carson Range at Spooner Summit (el. 7,146 feet). But our journey is downward and to the southwest, to historic Glenbrook Bay. It was here that Captain Augustus W. Pray arrived in 1860 to plant acres of vegetables, wheat, hay, and oats, and to harvest the lush indigenous grasses. Pray soon realized that there were quicker routes to fortune than farming. He put in a sawmill, which he dubbed the Lake Bigler Lumber Company, and acquired a steamship to bring tourists to his little paradise. A decade later, Pray would sell his empire to Duane L. Bliss, the man credited as the principal architect of Tahoe tourism. In 1896, Bliss launched his own steamship, the S.S. *Tahoe,* and by 1907, he was capturing tourists arriving by train in Tahoe City and transporting them to his new Glenbrook Inn. The inn was a spiffy place, with summer horse racing and one of the first telephone lines on the West Coast. Glenbrook is now a private development.

CAVE ROCK

Until 1931, when the highway around Lake Tahoe was completed, steamship remained the primary means of local transportation, and shoreline features, such as the prominent volcanic formation near Glenbrook known as Cave Rock, were important landmarks. Cave Rock still appears on Tahoe maps as a point of interest, but many motorists driving south on U.S. 50 from Glenbrook pass right through it, wondering later why they didn't see it. The highway tunnels were dynamited through the formation in 1931 and 1958, several decades before competing ideas about the significance of the structure would have made such a reconfiguration taboo.

As scientists examined the shallow cave, located high above the water on the rock's south face, they determined that the contour had been carved by wave action, an indication that the lake surface once lay at a higher elevation. The formation continued to draw scientific interest, but it was the bolts, anchors, and platforms that rock climbers were installing on the rock that brought an outcry from the native Washoe, for whom Cave Rock is an important spiritual site.

Cave Rock is now off limits for rock climbing, but you can still drive through it and not notice that you did.

ZEPHYR COVE

The public can enjoy a county park and public beach at Zephyr Cove. At the Zephyr Cove Resort, there is an opportunity to catch a ride on the paddleboat **M.S. *Dixie II.*** Cruises on the *Dixie* and her sister, the ***Tahoe Queen,*** are an excellent way to see the lake while staying out of the high-season automobile traffic. Tours take in Glenbrook, Cave Rock, and other historic lakeside locations, and many include luxuries, such as meals or nighttime dancing.

South of Zephyr Cove there are two Forest Service beaches, one with a campground. On the occasion of my Flume Trail ride, I made arrangements for a luxurious two-night stay in the campground at Nevada Beach, located within shouting distance of the Stateline casinos. The mattress of sand was a great delight; the full moon created a marvelous ambience as it glinted off the water and illuminated a large and ghostly dead tree, which was fenced off and standing guard over a local patch of endangered Tahoe yellow cress. A little stream meandering through the campground showed signs that a camper must have fallen in on a midnight run to the restroom. As the night stretched toward morning, the shrieks of South Shore revelers blended seamlessly with those of a local band of coyotes.

South Shore

Down at this southeast corner of the lake, U.S. 50 meets Highway 207, which leads up the Kingsbury Grade to **Daggett Pass** (el. 7,334 feet) and on to Minden, Nevada. At the pass, look for the southward turnoff to the Nevada-side lodges of **Heavenly Mountain Resort.** The ski area is spread out all over the combined lofty eminences of 10,067-foot Monument Peak and 9,123-foot East Peak, affording splendid views from its many lifts and mountaintop lodges.

To go for the views on public land, head back to Daggett Pass and turn north on North Benjamin Drive through a steeply situated residential area. The road changes names to Andria Drive and then dead-ends at a large parking lot in the Humbolt-Toiyabe National Forest. Look for the entrance to the Tahoe Rim Trail (TRT) and begin hiking north. Barely a quarter-mile in, the forest cover opens up to provide a great lookout with views of Mount Tallac, Pyramid Peak, South Lake Tahoe, and the Heavenly Mountain Resort complex. With its accommodating bed of decomposed granite and gorgeous gardens of manzanita and Jeffrey pine, the trail provides ample temptation to press on for the 12-mile hike or bike to Spooner Lake (see earlier in this chapter).

Back down on U.S. 50 at Stateline, Nevada, high-rise resort casinos offer glitzy rooms, classy restaurants, pools, clubs, and of course, gambling facilities, but there are plenty of modest joints to choose from as well. Right beside the Marriott hotel is Heavenly's high-speed, year-round gondola. Anyone with a ticket, skier or not, can take a ride up for the views, and any rider who has reached the ripe age of 21 might order a martini at the mountaintop bar. The experience is especially stunning at sunset or on a clear night when the moon is shining.

Along U.S. 50 from Stateline through South Lake Tahoe, Tahoe Valley, and south toward Meyers, the commercial buildup is nearly seamless. In high summer season, the RVs in the campgrounds can be bumper to bumper just like the traffic, and in ski season, the only way to go anywhere quickly is to clamp on the skis. However, nobody seems especially stressed, since just being here is the point.

A vintage casino lodge at Stateline, Nevada.

BUMMING IN SOUTH LAKE TAHOE

Apparently, the scene in South Lake Tahoe is not a modern phenomenon.

AUGUST 21, 1863   The lake is the feature of the place. A large log hotel is here, and many plea-sure seekers are here, both from California and Nevada. I was amused at a remark of a teamster who stopped here for a drink—the conversation was between two teamsters who looked at things in a practical light, one a stranger here, the other acquainted:

No. 1. "A good many people here!"

No. 2. "Yes."

No. 1. "What are they all doing?"

No. 2. "Nothing."

No. 1. "Nothing at all?"

No. 2. "Why, yes—in the city we would call it bumming (Californian word for loafing), but here they call it pleasure."

Both take a drink and depart for their more practical and useful avocations.

—from *Up and Down California,* William H. Brewer

Practical Matters

Elevations here are all above 6,000 feet, making winter reliably cold. Snow often begins in October and ski resorts hope to open in November. The spring ski season can last until June, (although most resorts close in April). Tahoe's summer effectively begins on Memorial Day weekend (at the end of May), but hiking might not be possible in the higher elevations until the snow melts. Wildflower displays often last into August. Autumn is a great time to avoid crowds and enjoy generally pleasant weather. For more on Sierra weather, and climate statistics for various locations in the region, see the introduction.

ROADS

This chapter describes the well-worn 72-mile loop around Lake Tahoe made by highways 89, 28, and U.S. 50. Entrances into the basin are: U.S. 50 (Echo Summit) and CA 89 (Luther Pass) in the south; NV 207 (the Kingsbury Grade) and U.S. 50 (Spooner Summit) to the east; and NV 431 (Mount Rose Summit), CA 267 (Brockway Summit), and CA 89 in the north. While the California and Nevada departments of transportation make every attempt to keep these routes clear of snow and rock debris most days of the year, they have little control over the masses of cars that clog the two-lane roadways during the high summer and winter seasons. High-season traffic backups in the Tahoe City and South Lake Tahoe areas are legendary. Winter conditions can be severe, so be prepared with chains and check for route closures before setting out.

OTHER MEANS

Reno, Nevada, is the closest city with a major airport. **Amtrak** serves Truckee and Reno, although **bus** service is often faster and cheaper. Casino-sponsored bus and lodging packages can be an incredible bargain (just don't blow the savings at the slots). Take advantage of myriad **shuttle and trolley services** between towns and recreation areas to avoid driving headaches.

WHERE TO STAY AND EAT

Tahoe's north, west, and south shore towns still have a few quaint old resort-style motels with mid-20th-century charm. The South Lake Tahoe and Incline Village casino areas have many large hotels. Private resorts, like those at historic Camp Richardson and Zephyr Cove, offer something in between. The majority of the lodging options around the lake are condominium rentals, handled through numerous agencies. For dining options, look in Tahoe City, Kings Beach, Incline Village, or South Lake Tahoe. A few tidy cafés dot the west shore, but one might drive the east shore for miles before finding anything at all.

CAMPING

California-side, there is an assortment of private, state park, and Forest Service campgrounds, many with beaches and boat launches. The Nevada shore offers lakeside camping at Zephyr Cove and Nevada Beach only. Be aware that lakeside campsites are at a premium in summer. For more choice of sites (and more solitude), try one of the Lower Truckee River campgrounds along Highway 89, or head out of the lake basin to a high-country campground.

U.S. FOREST SERVICE

USFS Visitor Center, Highway 89 at Taylor Creek, South Lake Tahoe, 530–543–2600.

Humboldt-Toiyabe National Forest (www.fs.fed.us/r4/htnf/): **Headquarters,** 1200 Franklin Way, Sparks, 775–331–6444; **Carson Ranger District,** 1536 South Carson Street, Carson City, 775–882–2766

VISITORS BUREAUS

Tahoe-Douglas Chamber of Commerce & Visitor Center, www.tahoechamber.org, 195 U.S. 50, Stateline, Nevada 775–588–4591.

Lake Tahoe Visitors Authority, www.bluelaketahoe.com/, 1156 Ski Run Boulevard, South Lake Tahoe, 800–288–2463, 530–544–5050.

Lake Tahoe Incline Village/Crystal Bay Visitors Bureau, www.gotahoe.com, 969 Tahoe Boulevard, Incline Village, 800–468–2463, 775–832–1606.

REGIONAL GUIDES

Carville, Julie Stauffer. *Hiking Tahoe's Wildflower Trails.* Edmondton, Alberta: Lone Pine Publishing, 1997.

Hauserman, Tim. *The Tahoe Rim Trail: A Complete Guide for Hikers, Mountain Bikers, and Equestrians.* Berkeley, Calif.: Wilderness Press, 2001.

Schaffer, Jeffrey P. *The Tahoe Sierra.* Berkeley, Calif.: Wilderness Press, 1998.

Schaffer, Jeffrey P. *Desolation Wilderness and the South Lake Tahoe Basin.* Berkeley, Calif.: Wilderness Press, 2003.

3

Central Sierra Crossings

This chapter makes a big zigzag through the central Sierra, following several routes of great import to the history of trans-Sierra travel. While it's a rare traveler who would follow this whole itinerary on one trip, many will follow a portion of it while seeking out some other Sierra destination, or for a fine loop trip through spectacular scenery. Veteran Sierra hikers and backpackers know these routes as means for reaching the **Desolation, Mokelumne, Carson-Iceberg,** and **Emigrant** wilderness areas.

Early Sierra Crossings

Human travel across the wild, rocky, and often-snowy crest of the Sierra Nevada dates back well before the period of recorded history. From very early times, Native American traders followed trans-Sierra routes to exchange eastern Sierra goods, such as obsidian and pine nuts, for west-side goods, such as acorns and seashells. It took the breaking wave of Euro-American exploration and settlement before winter crossings seemed feasible or warranted.

The first non-Indian to cross through the Sierra was an intrepid Yankee fur trapper named **Jedediah Smith.** In 1827, his party found their way into the Spanish territory of Alta California via the San Gabriel Mountains at Cajon Pass, a route that skirts the Sierra to the south. The Mexican governor, José María Echeandía, heard of their unauthorized entry

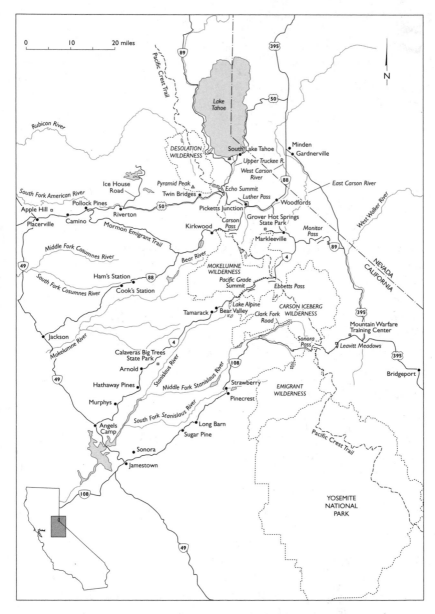

CENTRAL SIERRA

into the territory and ordered them to leave immediately by the same route, but instead, the trappers went in search of a central route and eventually found a way through the snow via the North Fork Stanislaus River, crossing the crest in the vicinity of today's Ebbetts Pass.

The seasoned adventurer **Joseph Reddeford Walker** made the next crossing, beginning his search for a good route in October of 1833. His party followed a river (that would be named the Walker) toward the crest and made an arduous passage over the rocky heights through snow that Walker's clerk, Zenas Leonard, described as "from ten to one hundred feet deep." Leonard's account of the descent has led historians to surmise that the party may have looked down into Yosemite Valley. The huge trees they discovered certainly would have been the giant sequoia. Walker chose a more southerly route for the party's return, making his first of many explorations of the Kern River region, which will be visited in this book's sixth chapter.

In January 1844, **John Charles Frémont** came through in the company of the famed guide and trapper Kit Carson and a large party of men, horses, mules, and a bronze mountain howitzer. They went up the East Carson River to the vicinity of present-day Markleeville, where they met an old Washoe who told them it would be impossible to cross the mountains in the snow. But the party pressed on, finding hot water bubbling out of the ground in the place now called Grover Hot Springs, and beating a path through falling snow to Charity Valley and Faith Valley, where they could see ahead to the western divide. Frémont noted the sublime beauty of the snow-clad forest, the brilliant sky, and the long, mesmerizing views. From the top of Red Lake Peak (el. 10,060 feet), north of today's Carson Pass, he made the first recorded sighting of Lake Tahoe, and from another high lookout, Carson was able to recognize the California Coast Range. After a grueling descent to the South Fork American River, the party eventually arrived at Sutter's Fort.

The public, hungry to know of the land called California, lapped up Frémont's profusely published reports of the trip. They dubbed him "The Pathfinder" and eagerly anticipated the next chapter of his sensational tale. (For more on Frémont's adventures, see chapters 6 and 9.)

Obsolete Sierra transportation.

FIRST IMMIGRANT CROSSING

By the close of the 1830s, overland travel to Oregon was well established, but no emigrant party had yet attempted to cross the Sierra Nevada into California's Central Valley. The first group to do so was the **Bartleson-Bidwell Party.** John Bidwell, who went on to become a California statesman and prominent citizen, noted in his memoirs of the 1841 trip: "Our ignorance of the route was complete. We knew that California lay west, and that was the extent of our knowledge." The party came up the West Walker River in mid-October and crossed the Sierra crest somewhere between Sonora Pass and Ebbetts Pass. As they entered the region now known as the Emigrant Wilderness, Bidwell wrote, "the frightful prospect opened before us: naked mountains whose summits still retained the snows perhaps of a thousand years." They descended west along the Stanislaus River and arrived at the coast in relatively good condition.

U.S. 50: The Johnson Cut-Off

U.S. 50 makes its Sierra crossing along a route closely equivalent to one surveyed and cleared in 1852 by a Placerville rancher named John Calhoun Johnson. Known as the Johnson Cut-off, it ran east up Peavine Ridge above the South Fork American River, negotiating the Sierra crest

SNOWSHOE THOMPSON: THE POSTMAN OF THE SIERRA

One of the more adventurous early travelers through this region was Snowshoe Thompson. Jon Torsteinson-Rue, a Norwegian by birth, took the name John A. Thompson when his family came to America in 1837. As a young man, Thompson was lured to California by visions of gold, but made the wiser decision to take up ranching in the Sacramento Valley instead. However, in 1856, when he saw in the *Sacramento Union* that Uncle Sam was looking for a mail carrier who could brave the Sierra in winter, he could not resist the call. Using his homemade, 10-foot-long Norwegian snowshoes (as skis were then called), Thompson carried the mail over the Sierra several times a month during the snowed-in season, traveling between Placerville and Mormon Station, Nevada (now known as Genoa).

The 90-mile trip took him three days going east, and only two days going west (on account of the more ski-friendly gradient on the western slope, and the higher starting ground on the east). He required little rest, and he was very sparing in his gear, wanting to reserve space for the 60–100 pounds of mail he usually carried. His provisions consisted of crackers, jerked beef, and dried sausage, plus a bible for spiritual sustenance. He carried no blankets, counting on a fire to keep him warm if he needed to stop for the night. (Apparently, he didn't always need to.) If a blizzard struck, he would wait it out on top of a rock, dancing Norwegian folk dances to amuse himself and keep up his body heat. He did not carry a compass, once stating, "There is no danger of getting lost in a narrow range of mountains like the Sierra, if a man has his wits about him." He navigated like a sailor, following the sun and reading the wind, the stars, and the flow of water. There were many occasions on which Thompson rescued prospectors whose skills and judgment were not up to the rigors of the Sierra winter.

Thompson continued to carry the mail every year until he died in 1876 of appendicitis. He is fondly remembered in Genoa with a monument and an annual June festival at Mormon Station State Park.

near Echo Lake at a place that became known as Johnson Pass. The route came into heavy use with the discovery of the Comstock Lode in 1859, losing some of its traffic when the transcontinental railroad was completed in 1868. Pony Express riders used the road during the company's brief period in operation.

ECHO SUMMIT (el. 7,380 feet)

U.S. 50 comes south and west out of the Comstock country through the Carson River Valley, crossing the Carson Range at Spooner Summit and then skirting the crowded southeast shore of Lake Tahoe. Exiting the Tahoe Basin along the Upper Truckee River, the route swings up to Echo Summit, where the views back into the Tahoe Basin are impressive, but marred by the South Lake Tahoe clutter.

Watch for the turnoff to **Echo Lake** at Echo Summit. The lake is a preferred hikers' entry into the glaciated lakes basin of the **Desolation Wilderness.** It is also a popular place to pick up the Pacific Crest Trail. Backpackers appreciate the high elevation of the trailhead and the summer water taxi service that runs the length of the long lake.

While heading west on the descent from Echo Summit, watch to the north between Ralston Peak (el. 9,235 feet) and Pyramid Peak (el. 9,983 feet) for a brief but breathtaking view of **Horsetail Falls.** The falls are on a creek that drops precipitously from the Desolation Basin toward the town of Twin Bridges (el. 6,117 feet). The trail to the falls, which starts from the second of the twin bridges, is notoriously steep and treacherous. To the west, the splendid monumental formation called **Lovers' Leap** rises out of the South Fork American River canyon. This bold protrusion of bare granite is a big draw with rock climbers. Situated practically at its base is a big stone and timber structure called **Strawberry Lodge,** a descendant of the historic Strawberry Station stage stop. Anyone anxious for a bear sighting might want to take a look at the stuffed 1,000-pound Alaskan grizzly inside.

WRIGHTS LAKE (el. 6,941 feet)

Five miles west of Strawberry, a well-paved but long winding road leads north to Wrights Lake. Motorized recreation equipment is prohibited here, and so instead a colorful flotilla of canoes and rowboats bobs near the lake's reedy shores. Waterfowl ply the marshy channels through gardens of wildflowers. Backpacking trails from here lead into the Desolation Wilderness. Back down the road at Lyons Creek is the trailhead to **Lake Sylvia,** a fishermen's favorite and a good place from which to launch a climb up one of the Sierra's most notable landmarks, **Pyramid Peak.** At 9,983 feet, Pyramid Peak is a giant of the Crystal Range, but it is known more for its distinctive pyramidal shape, which is easy to recognize from many distant vantage points. Standing atop Pyramid Peak on August 28, 1863, William H. Brewer wrote:

> The view is the grandest in this part of the Sierra. On the east, four thousand feet beneath, lies Lake Tahoe, intensely blue; nearer are about a dozen alpine lakes, of very blue, clear, snow water. Far

to the east are the desolate mountains of Nevada Territory, fading into indistinctness in the blue distance. South are the rugged mountains along the crest of the Sierra, far south of Sonora Pass — a hundred peaks spotted with snow. All along the west is the western slope of the Sierra, bathed in blue haze and smoke; and beyond lies the great plain, which for 200 miles of its extent looks like an ill-defined sea of smoke, above which rises the dim outlines of the coast ranges for 150 miles along the horizon, some of them over 150 miles distant. It is one of those views to make a vivid and lasting impression on the mind.

The drive on U.S. 50 continues downhill along the steep northern wall of the river canyon. Spectacular pillars of rock poke up austerely from dense mats of manzanita and oak on this exposed northern wall, while the contrasting south wall has a rich green coat of conifers. Gradually, with the drop in elevation, the trees dominate both sides, and then give way to the oak forests of the foothill regions.

ICE HOUSE ROAD
After passing the community of Riverton (el. 3,231 feet) watch the north side of the highway for Ice House Road. This is the main access to Ice House Reservoir, Union Valley Reservoir, Gerle Creek Reservoir, and Loon Lake. Here you will find dozens of Eldorado National Forest campgrounds and three Forest Service rental cabins, one in an old lookout tower. (See the end of this chapter for contact information.)

PLACERVILLE STAGECOACH AND PONY EXPRESS TRAIL
From Pollock Pines to Placerville, a remnant of an old stage road parallels U.S. 50 along its northern flank. Stage stops along the route were identified by their distance out of Placerville, and so the stop near Pollock Pines was known as the **Twelve Mile House.** As of this writing, the Twelve Mile House was sporting the name Sportsman's Hall and serving traditional American fare at 5620 Pony Express Court. Several pages from the 1862 ledger book were posted in the entryway.

(following spread) Pyramid Peak is a distinctive landmark. This view is from Highway 88 west of Carson Pass.

The **Seven Mile House** is in the old sawmill town of Camino. It served for a time as a mill workers' bunkhouse, but as of my last visit was in use as a comfortable B&B and wine tasting room. (For more on the wineries here, see the Gold Country chapter.) Next door, the Camino Community Church was being used as a hat maker's workshop where they were refurbishing Stetsons and Resistols brought in by Central Valley cowboys.

Camino has become the heart (or should I say, core) of **Apple Hill,** a growers' association that literally put itself on the map as a tourist destination. When this marketing cooperative organized in 1964, they had the brilliant notion of inviting the press to a picnic. Media attention hasn't let up since. At apple harvest time, the fruit stands and orchard markets tucked into every curve of Carson Road are jammed with visitors. Many of the stands hawk fresh-baked fruit pies, calculated to give customers an idea of what they might do with all those apples once they get them home. The idea of marketing directly to the public was picked up by local Christmas-tree farmers, flower growers, pumpkin ranchers, winemakers, and even fudge crafters, who set up their stands on Apple Hill. El Dorado County expanded the concept into a network of marked and mapped "farm trails." Many stops are designed especially to entertain children, and so the excitement on the farm trails keeps up from spring until Christmas.

Agriculture and nature are involved in a most interesting collaboration at 2375 Fruitridge Road, which is north of Carson Road about four miles west of Camino. At that address you will find the **U.S. Forest Service Placerville Nursery and National Forest Genetic Electrophoresis Laboratory,** where seeds and cuttings brought from each national forest around the state are nurtured to produce thousands of baby conifers. The tiny trees are tested for resistance to pests and pathogens, and when they are hardy enough for the trip, they are sent back to be planted in their home forests. These plantings can be vital to restoration of burned or damaged groves.

There are other points of interest along Carson Road, covered in the El Dorado Wine tour in chapter 9, that make it worthwhile to continue on this old stage route into Placerville. For a look at the stage line's **Three Mile House,** make a detour south via Jacquier Road to Smith Flat. The first time I went looking for it, I learned that the original wooden frame structure had survived since 1852, and had continued functioning as a hospitality house for many of those years. I found a sign over the entrance to the basement saloon suggesting that a resumption of business might be forthcoming, but the next time through, I found the place completely boarded up again.

U.S. 50 travelers with the time to stop in Placerville can turn to the Gold Country chapter of this book. Those who are continuing on toward Sacramento might want to rest for a moment at Shingle Springs, where 19th-century travelers once stopped for a refreshing drink of spring water. Here, modern-day travelers coasting down into the Great Central Valley can quench their thirst with a last view of the glistening Sierra Nevada peaks.

Highway 88 Through Carson Pass

As I head east out of the Gold Country on Highway 88 from Jackson, I often sense the lush evergreen forest coming on as an avalanche of greenery. Sometimes referred to as the "snow forest," the dense curtain of conifers seems to appear around snow line, which is at around 4,000 feet in this location. Development is minimal along this route, making it easy to imagine the world of the 1860s stagecoach travelers. After 25 miles of jostling since their last stop in Jackson, they would have appreciated getting out for a moment of refreshment at **Cooks Station** or **Hams Station.** At both sites, one still finds businesses offering supplies for travelers.

About 12 miles past Hams Station, watch for Forest Service Route 5, the **Mormon Emigrant Trail,** coming in from the northeast off Iron Mountain Ridge. In the summer of 1848, a group of 46 Mormons laden with wagons, stock, and three cannons started slowly up this gentle divide between the South Fork American River and the Cosumnes River. They were members of the Mormon Battalion, and had come west heeding the Union call for men to help wrest Alta California from the Mexicans. Instead they found themselves in the middle of the uproar over the discovery of gold at Sutter's Mill. They were now forsaking the promise of riches in favor of joining their brethren at the newly established Mormon colony on Utah's Great Salt Lake. Their plan was to follow the route taken by Captain Frémont and Kit Carson in 1844. Barely a mile east of

The Shot Rock.

the junction with the Mormon Emigrant Trail is a rest stop and picnic area called **Shot Rock.** The eponymous rock sits beside the short trail to a vista point, and it is unmistakable. It's a huge granitic boulder that has split right down the middle. From the vista point, the Bear River valley below appears to be paved with massive granitic slabs — smooth ramps that seem to suggest it would be possible to run in leaps and bounds down to the river and up the other side into the 105,165-acre **Mokelumne Wilderness.** On the far ridge stands 9,334-foot Mokelumne Peak, bearing its dark cap of ancient metamorphic rock.

Three miles beyond Shot Rock on Highway 88, you will see a sign for another picnic stop. Called **Tragedy Springs,** the site commemorates three scouts from the Mormon Battalion who died here, apparently at the hands of native warriors. The bodies of the three were found in a shallow grave near a spring. Today's travelers sometimes stop to read the plaque, to picnic, or simply to take a rest while on their own journeys through lives of hope, reward, and sometimes tragedy.

Ahead, Highway 88 skirts the inviting shores of **Silver Lake** (el. 7,250 feet). Those inclined to stay will find several large campgrounds and two historic lodges — Kit Carson Lodge and Plasse's Resort, the latter on a site first settled in 1852 by Raymond Peter Plasse and developed as a resort around 1900.

CARSON PASS SNOW COUNTRY

The Carson Pass route is well known to cross-country skiers, especially those who consider it counterintuitive to buy a pass for use on groomed trails at a resort when there is so much beautiful open country to explore. Volume 2 of Marcus Libkind's *Ski Tours in the Sierra Nevada* details 35 suggested tours in this region, ranging from a simple beginner's jaunt around the meadows at Picketts Junction in Hope Valley (at the Highway 88/89 junction), to a 23-mile expedition from Red Lake (in the pass) over to Highway 4 near Bear Valley.

Downhill skiers and snowboarders head for **Kirkwood** (el. 7,600 feet), where Chairlift No. 4 takes anyone (even a summer hiker) to the summit crossing of the Mormon Emigrant Trail. When Henry William Bigler and the Mormon Battalion came through here on July 22, 1848, deep patches of snow still lingered on the summit. Bigler wrote in his journal: "This day I gathered flowers with one hand and snow with the other."

A little over a decade after the Mormons passed through, Zachary Kirkwood took up residence in the beautiful valley of Kirkwood Creek, and by 1864, his pine-log home was known as the Kirkwood Station. It remains a cozy tavern, now called the **Kirkwood Inn.** Lively groups of bikers and four-wheelers often rendezvous here in the summer, adding their own pages to the colorful history of the place. During Prohibition, a resourceful innkeeper realized that the inn spanned the borders of El Dorado, Amador, and Alpine counties. He mounted the big wooden bar on wheels so that it could be moved easily from county to county, depending on which county's sheriff was visiting the area, and business could go on as usual. (Although "usual" seems to have included a few shootouts, as attested to by the bullet holes in the walls.) The inn was in a quiet mood as we warmed ourselves with a bowl of chili after a day of cross-country skiing on the elegant, groomed trails of the **Kirkwood Cross Country Center,** located just behind the inn.

CARSON PASS (el. 8,560 feet)

The highway negotiates the Sierra crest at Carson Pass via a series of rock shelves that were blasted out of the steep terrain to accommodate cars. If, during a winter drive over the pass, you are gripped by the fear that nature will choose this particular moment to shrug off her snowy mantle, taking you and your vehicle on a fast white ride to a lower elevation, take heart. In anticipation of this very plausible scenario, the Caltrans snow-removal wizards have mounted propane "poppers" in the pass that they use to trigger avalanches at carefully chosen moments (hopefully with adequate time to clean up the fluffy white mess before anyone gets miffed at the delay). The poppers' large metal tubes can easily be seen as you drive through the pass; in operation, they emit thunderous booms to shake the snow loose.

BLUE LAKES ROAD SIDE TRIP

As the Mormon Battalion made their arduous descent eastward from Carson Pass in 1848, they reached an inviting valley at 7,300, feet where quaking aspens lined the sweet-flowing headwaters of the West Carson River. It was the sense of hope that prompted them to give **Hope Valley** its name. While resting here they might have encountered Washoe peo-

Propane "poppers" in Carson Pass are used to trigger avalanches at hours when the road is closed to traffic.

ple from the Carson Valley, who would have been gathering nuts from the pinyon pine or fishing in the river. Summer still attracts anglers to this valley, and many appear to be camping out for the whole season. The only sound that breaks their serenity might be the loud nasal call of the common nighthawk, which often swoops right into the campgrounds around dinnertime.

From Hope Valley, follow Blue Lakes Road south through Faith and Charity valleys to admire the work that nature hath wrought; during the last ice age, an eroding glacier formed a string of paternoster lakes (so called for their resemblance to a string of rosary beads) along its trough. Over time, the stair-step lakes silted in and became the gentle meadows of Hope, Faith, and Charity valleys.

On the north side of Charity Valley, about three miles from the Hope Valley Campground, is the **Charity Valley West End** trailhead start of a splendid downhill hike east along Charity Valley Creek to Grover Hot Springs State Park. The trail follows an old Washoe trade route, also the route used by Captain Frémont and Kit Carson on their expedition of 1844.

The trailhead marker is not easy to spot, but there are usually several parked cars scattered among the trees on the west side of the road right at the trailhead. The trail starts out above the northern rim of gentle Charity Valley, passing through a sea of wildflowers in midsummer with mountain bluebirds darting through the sagebrush and mule ears. The trail winds among ancient, gnarled Sierra junipers and around a surprising array of *erratics* — boulders that ice age glaciers carried along and dropped off in random places. The erratics sit oddly atop beds of granular decomposed granite beside hummocky mounds of andesitic (volcanic) mudflows.

As the trail descends, it enters a long stretch of gigantic stone cliffs, where old-growth Jeffrey pines tower majestically, casting their reflections onto languid pools filled with water lilies. There are many flat stone ledges here that beckon hikers to stop for a picnic. The trail continues through a stunning forest of white fir and a garden of wild roses and thimbleberries before beginning a steep descent through manzanita and huckleberry oak to arrive at Grover Hot Springs State Park. This hike is almost always done as a shuttle trip. The strategy is to leave one car at the

Mule ears (*Wyethia mollis*).

hot springs (see below) and drive the other back to the trailhead. Alternatively, go to the hot springs and hope to make friends with someone who's driving back to Hope Valley.

Blue Lakes Road continues for several miles south from Charity Valley to a junction with the Pacific Crest Trail. At the trail crossing, a spur of the road loops west and then north past the lower, middle, and upper Blue Lakes, while a continuation of the north–south-trending road, passable by 4WD vehicles only, continues on to Highway 4 at Hermit Valley (see later in this chapter). This rough road is a remnant of the old **Border Ruffian Pass Road,** a major route between Carson Valley and Sonora during the silver boom of the 1870s, and still a major route with 4WD clubs.

PICKETTS JUNCTION

Back on Highway 88 and heading northeast from Blue Lakes Road, drivers come to Picketts Junction where many travelers stop at charming Sorensen's Resort, an enclave of wooden cabins set within a grove of aspen. At the junction, Highway 89 comes in from the north out of Luther Pass (el. 7,735 feet) and South Lake Tahoe to join Highway 88 heading east into the narrow **West Carson River Canyon.** A traveler in 1852 described the West Carson's canyon as "the most wild looking chasm eye ever rested upon, and the worst road the human imagination can conceive." The highway is now nicely paved, but the canyon's steep sides still make an awesome impression. Six miles ahead, at the old Pony Express stop of **Woodfords,** Highway 88 continues down into the broad Carson Valley in the state of Nevada, while our tour takes Highway 89 for a southeast turn toward Markleeville.

East Carson River Country

The Sierra Nevada keeps several treasures in this little side pocket on its eastern escarpment, and at any time of year, travelers can slip in and out to grab them via Highway 89 from Woodfords. In the snow-free seasons, two other ways open up into East Carson River Country — Highway 89 through Monitor Pass and Highway 4 through Ebbetts Pass.

The centerpiece of East Carson River Country is the river itself, which draws anglers in search of brown and rainbow trout. The river also hosts the threatened Lahontan cutthroat trout and a rare Paiute/rainbow hybrid. During spring runoff, the trout see a lot of rafters putting in at Hangman Bridge (south of Markleeville) for the run to Gardnerville, Nevada. It's considered a novice run, but with hot springs and good campsites along the way, even expert rafters love to make a go of it.

The only "urban" center in the area is the charming hamlet of **Markleeville** (el. 5,501 feet). With a population that hovers around 200, Markleeville hardly seems important enough to be the Alpine County seat, but when you consider that Alpine is California's least-populated county, it starts to make sense. The county is made up almost entirely of public lands. These protect the headwaters of six Sierra rivers: the Truckee, the south fork of the American, the east and west forks of the Carson, and the north forks of the Tuolumne, Stanislaus, and Mokelumne. Alpine County likes to boast that it has no incorporated town, no doctor, no dentist, no movie theater, no mall, no supermarket, no pharmacy, no hospital, no department store, no fast food, no freeway, and no public transportation, but it is questionable how long these distinctions can be maintained.

At its beginnings in 1861, Markleeville was not much more than a cabin and toll bridge built by settler Jacob J. Marklee. Three years later, Marklee's town had swelled to over 2,500 souls (most came seeking their fortune in the local silver strikes), and Marklee was dead, killed in a quarrel.

Today's population is much more congenial, and even downright accommodating to the thousands of visitors who flock here nearly any time of year with bicycles, fishing poles, rafts, and swimsuits. The bicyclists come to train for the **Death Ride,** a one-day, 124-mile "Tour of the California Alps" that takes in five passes above 8,300 feet. This grueling (and some say "hair-raising") marathon has been an annual event since 1983. Serious contenders make their training a year-round effort, and so if the roads are clear of snow and the weather is even marginal, you can count on seeing bicyclists all around town.

You can also count on seeing plenty of people carrying swimsuits. Most will be heading west on Hot Springs Road (Forest Service Road E1) to **Grover Hot Springs State Park.** The large, swimming pool–like baths are open year-round, and can be an especially appealing on a summer's evening when the moon is full, or a winter's afternoon when snow is all around. The state park campground is also open year-round, but snagging a site can be tricky.

Before leaving Markleeville, be sure to climb up School Street to look in on the Alpine County Historical Complex, which consists of a new structure housing a delightful collection of artifacts from Alpine County's past, and an historic schoolhouse and jail, both beautifully restored and furnished with period artifacts. Of note is a large collection of landscapes painted by a Markleeville artist named Walt Monroe. Unschooled in classical technique, Monroe was quite sure of his brushwork. His childhood efforts can be seen on a wall inside of the schoolhouse.

MONITOR PASS (el. 8,314 feet)

Heading south out of Markleeville on Highway 89, after five miles you will need to decide whether to head eastward or westward, but either way, you're going to be ascending to the roof of East Carson River country.

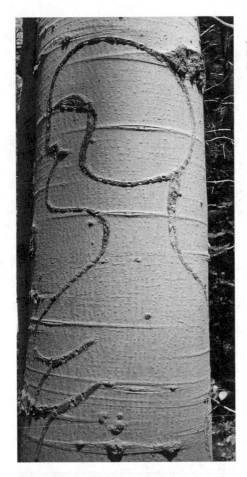

A Basque sheepherder carved his favorite "lady of the evening" into the bark of an aspen.

The eastbound route is the continuation of Highway 89; keep your eyes peeled for the sign indicating the abrupt left turn toward Monitor Pass. As soon as you turn you will find yourself climbing beside sprightly Monitor Creek through a narrow, twisting, aspen-lined canyon that opens out into high sagebrush meadows. Raptors ride the currents overhead. The colors here are mostly the grayish greens characteristic of the eastern escarpment, which is not surprising, since Monitor Pass is entirely to the east of the Sierra crest. In early summer the sagebrush is gorgeously decorated with the bright yellow blossoms of mule ears, and the white crepelike flourishes of prickly poppies. In autumn, the aspens are a shimmer of gold, and the dry leaves of the mule ears rattle in the wind.

A granite monument sitting within a dense grove of aspen marks the pass. The trees here offer a rich trove of arborglyphs, etchings made by early- to mid-20th-century Basque sheepherders who carved their names and fantasies onto the silvery aspen bark. (Look ahead to chapter 4 for more on arborglyphs).

In the Monitor Pass area there are dozens of off-highway vehicle (OHV) trails. To the north, the trails skirt around 8,963-foot **Leviathan Peak,** while east and south they lead through seemingly endless groves of aspen. The destination in most cases is a high rocky ridge offering extraordinary views southward into the wildlife refuge of the Slinkard Valley, and eastward into the Great Basin, the Sweetwater Range, and Antelope Valley, where the West Walker River runs. To explore the beautiful country of the West Walker River, turn to chapter 4.

Highway 4 Through Ebbetts Pass

If you bypass the left turn on Highway 89 to Monitor Pass, you will find that you are on Highway 4 heading west into the heart of the Sierra Nevada. A few miles beyond the Highway 89/4 junction, **Wolf Creek Road** turns south to follow the East Carson River into an arena of 10,000- and 11,000-foot-high peaks. A primitive campground and several trailheads serve hikers setting out to explore the East Carson headwaters and the **Carson-Iceberg Wilderness.**

Highway 4 continues on to the southwest, climbing next to **Silver Creek** and past the scant ruins of **Silver Mountain City,** which for a time held the title of Alpine County seat. The "city" was established as a silver claim in 1858, a year before the Comstock Lode was discovered. By 1885 the town was deserted and the buildings that had not yet collapsed were hauled off to Markleeville.

EBBETTS PASS (el. 8,730 feet)
On the dramatic switchback ascent toward Ebbetts Pass, Highway 4 suddenly narrows and loses its painted centerline, giving the feeling that you are entering a more remote country. The sculptural forms of ancient

Sierra junipers stand guard on the steep volcanic landscape, and thick stands of aspen crowd into the creek bed below. East of the pass, colorful **Highland Peak** (el. 10,034 feet) rises up with its distinctive sandcastle-like flutings. North of the pass is massive Raymond Peak (el. 10,014 feet), but the stone fingers of **Reynolds Peak** (el. 9,690 feet) are what make northward views so striking.

About a mile beyond the pass, a road heading south off the highway provides access to the fishermen's haunt of **Highland Lakes.** My favorite guidebook to California campgrounds gives the Highland Lakes campground very high marks, but it was here, one intensely moonlit summer's night, that I learned that I should never choose campgrounds that are large and on bodies of water. These places should be left to the avid anglers, boaters, and late-night partiers. However, I found that the cacophonous serenade of dueling boom boxes, bell-ringing cows, and a rambunctious chorus of coyotes provided a great opportunity to practice the Buddhist art of acceptance. As Highway 4 makes its western descent from Ebbetts Pass, it comes to a brief meeting with the **North Fork Mokelumne River** at a pretty, but ravaged place called **Hermit Valley.** This is the terminus

Sierra Juniper (*Juniperus occidentalis*). Photo by Erlda Parker

of the 4WD road from Blue Lakes, mentioned in the preceding Highway 88 trip.

Heading west out of Hermit Valley, Highway 4 makes a steep climb to a second crest at **Pacific Grade Summit** (el. 8,085 feet), passing fractured granitic slabs and twisting around huge boulders and massive conifers. Here, the dark volcanic forms of Reynolds and Raymond peaks again rule the view.

Once past the second summit, the narrow highway descends past **Mosquito Lakes.** The demure little lakes attract many visitors, and if you choose to join them, you'll find day-use parking at the west-end campground, which is across the road from the lakes. Another attraction is the easy two-mile hike south to **Heiser Lake.** From the outcropping of jointed boulders at the west end of the lake there is an incredible view southward over a bold granitic landscape with the striking brown palisade of the Dardanelles in the background. To the west is the deep green canyon of the Mokelumne River. On the way back to the road, watch for a short spur trail leading eastward to a spot offering a view of **Peep Sight Peak** (el. 9,727 feet), a feature with a distinctive natural bridge. On the September afternoon when I made this hike I found the sun glinting off the gossamer streamers of a million baby spiders just launched on their maiden voyage. A rough-legged hawk rode in lazy spirals above them.

LAKE ALPINE (el. 7,400 feet)

From Mosquito Lakes down to Lake Alpine and Bear Valley along Highway 4, the midsummer scene is as much about people-watching as it is about enjoying nature. On summer afternoons, the crowds parade around Lake Alpine. Recreation opportunities include scrambling, swimming, or boating out to reach the granitic slabs and boulders that form enticing islands and peninsulas in the lake. In the evenings, those not entertaining themselves at the lakeside campgrounds flow into **Bear Valley** (el. 7,073 feet), where the **Bear Valley Music Festival** is a summer highpoint.

In winter, the draw is the popular **Bear Valley Ski Resort,** along with a plethora of winter recreation services. On one visit, I stumbled onto a dogsledding event, noting with amusement that you don't need an Arctic breed pedigree to run with the pack in front of the sled; quite a few of the dogs waiting patiently for their turn were of the retriever persuasion.

Lake Alpine's islands lure swimmers and boaters on a hot summer's day.

(Note: There are several places known as Bear Valley in the Sierra Nevada.)

A short distance down Highway 4 is **Tamarack** (el. 6,960 feet), frequently noted as the snowiest spot in the Sierra. It was here, in the winter of 1906–7, that 73.5 feet of snowfall was recorded in a single season. (A more typical snowpack in March might be 17 feet at this location.) In 1847, an empirical notation of the snowpack, made by a member of the Mormon Battalion traveling the Mormon Emigrant Trail (see earlier in this chapter), indicated there was at least enough to bury a donkey. (This donkey was rescued by means of its impressively long ears, which were seen poking out above the snow.) Measurements became more scientific around 1870, and the data began to show that many spots above 5,000 feet on the western slope receive snowfall far in excess of donkey depth.

In order to get a closer look at the snowpack in this area, I signed up for a winter ecology course with Mountain Adventure Seminars (MAS), based in Bear Valley. Stylishly shod in a rented pair of red plastic snowshoes and clad in full waterproof coating, I followed the MAS guide through the serene forest of red fir and lodgepole pine, learning how nature gets on here in winter. We found the treetops aflutter with LBJs feasting on insects. (In birders' parlance, the term LBJs — "little brown jobs" — refers to any number of small brown bird species.) We noted the methodical trail of a weasel in the soft snow along the bank of a stream. It appeared to have tacked back and forth to pick up the sound and scent of a mouse running through tunnels beneath the snow. As we carved out snow ledges and covered them with our jackets to make a comfortable picnic spot, we learned that any animal moving about in this winter setting was seeking a vital meal. I munched on my favorite winter mountain lunch of dates, cashews, tangerines, and cubes of Parmigiano-Reggiano while contemplating what might constitute a meal of an all-local nature.

As we trekked out, a most useful lesson unfolded when a fellow participant dropped into a snow pocket, becoming buried up to his armpits. Fortunately, our guide was carrying a collapsible shovel, an indispensable piece of backcountry safety equipment in winter. MAS is best known for its Telemark ski school and annual Telemark festival, but they also offer guided tours, all-season mountaineering workshops, and courses in how to ski safely in avalanche country. Anyone intending to go out in the wilderness in winter should have the right equipment and learn as much as they can about avalanches and winter safety. Schools such as this are a good place to start.

CALAVERAS BIG TREES STATE PARK (el. 4,800 feet)
Twenty miles down Highway 4 from Tamarack, you will come to the main entrance of a gorgeous state park, one of several sanctuaries in the Sierra Nevada preserving multiple groves of giant sequoias. While Sequoia National Park gets better billing, there is no reason to bypass Calaveras Big Trees State Park if you have the time for a visit. The North Grove offers well-tended trails for every level of effort, including one accommodating wheelchairs. Kids delight in climbing over and even right through some of the fallen giants, although parents are warned that rattlesnakes are present. More-ambitious hikers often prefer the natural setting of the South Grove five miles distant. The park is a great place for cross-country skiing and snowshoeing, with one of the campgrounds kept open all winter.

I count myself among the few devoted sequoia admirers who visit the big trees in winter. That is when it is easiest to speak to these silent watchmen of the universe in utter confidence. I never seem to pick the right moment in spring to see the understory of mountain dogwood in bloom, but I've come many times in autumn when the dogwood's changing leaves create a delicate crimson translucence.

The big trees are very tall, some reaching well over 300 feet in height.

Now only pedestrians and park vehicles can pass through the tunnel, but early motorists often made a detour to get a photograph of their Model T parked under this giant sequoia.

But what startles the mind is their massiveness; a mature tree might span 25 feet at its eye level diameter. A giant sequoia can live for more than 3000 years if doesn't grow unbalanced and topple over at a younger age, as many of them do.

When the Calaveras North Grove was discovered in the 1850s, some entrepreneurs saw the trees as a bonanza in building materials. They soon found, however, that the sequoia's size and brittleness make it difficult to harvest. Several trees at the grove were felled anyway for pure curiosity. One stump was made into a dance floor; another became the foundation for a small hotel. The entire bark sheath of one tree was stripped off and sent around the Horn for reassembly in New York City, so Easterners could marvel at the size. Having died an unnatural death, that tree remains standing—a ghostly snag unique to the grove—while its naturally departed brethren lie as moss-covered sculptures on the forest floor.

Note: Poisonous reptiles and arachnids are quite at home in the Sierra, but the incidence of rattlesnake and spider bites is very low compared to the number of serious injuries and deaths caused by recreational accidents. Keep your eyes and ears open and know what the venomous creatures look like and where they hang out. But chances are you will never encounter them.

From Calaveras Big Trees State Park, it's but a few miles drive southwest on Highway 4 to Arnold, where travelers will find plenty of services. The Gold Country town of Angels Camp is only another 20 miles beyond Arnold, at which point Highway 4 takes off across the Central Valley. However, this book is about the Sierra Nevada, so at Angels Camp, we'll take Highway 49 for the 17-mile drive to Sonora, where we can take Highway 108 back up into the mountains.

Highway 108 Through Sonora Pass

Highway 108 provides an appealing trans-Sierra route for cheapskates like myself who don't want to pay a fee for the privilege of driving through Yosemite, even when Yosemite's Tioga Road might provide a more direct route. Highway 108 climbs northeast out of California's Central Valley to its junction with Highway 49 at Sonora (el. 1,826 feet) in the Sierra foothills, and then passes through a series of tiny communities at the 3,000- and 4,000-foot elevations. When you come through the town of Sugar Pine (el. 4,471 feet), start looking at the trees, and you may find you can pick out the sugar pines, which tower in magnificent profusion at this elevation. Sugar pines dangle their crops of gigantic cones from the tips of their gracefully lanky branches. A good way to get an up-close look at the pinecones is to continue past Long Barn (el. 4,963 feet) and take a right turn on Forest Service Road 31. The sugar pine's magnificent cones can be found strewn along the ground at many points along this road. Should you be tempted to take one of these prizes home, bear in mind that it's illegal to remove anything from national forest lands.

The countryside appears more sparsely settled with each mile of the climb on Highway 108, and one can start to envision the deep wilderness that greeted the emigrants crossing the Sierra crest in the opposite direction in the 1840s. Backpackers heading east from Pinecrest into the heart of the 118,000-acre **Emigrant Wilderness** will find various sites marked in honor of the emigrants' passage

PINECREST (el. 5,680 feet)

Pinecrest Lake is very popular for summer relaxation and recreation. In winter, families flock to Dodge Ridge Ski Resort, a little ski and snowboard haven much loved for its low-key ambience, lack of lines at the lifts, and its many long and leisurely runs through the Stanislaus National Forest.

A mile farther along on the highway from Pinecrest is the tiny community of **Strawberry,** where travelers have stopped for food and lodging since the days of the stagecoach. On one visit, I enjoyed a meal while looking down on the South Fork Stanislaus River from the tree house–style deck of the local resort hotel. For the community's cheeky Steller's jays, the deck is practically an all-you-can-eat buffet. As diners get up to leave, the birds swoop in to help themselves to the leftovers, snatching up dollar bills left as tips as well and taking them back to their nests to use as lining material.

GARGOYLES

A few miles beyond Strawberry, a sign on the southeast side of the highway at Herring Creek Road announces "Gargoyles." Don't expect to find any Gothic architecture here — the Gargoyles are a geologic feature formed of eroded lava flows, ash deposits, and lahars (mudflows that result when volcanic ash mixes with water). Seeing gargoyles within these formations requires a bit of imagination, but the forms are fascinating nonetheless, and the desire to get a closer look can be the perfect excuse to take a break during a long trip over the mountains. Natural history buffs should plan ahead and stop at the **Summit Ranger District Station** in Pinecrest for a "Trail of the Gargoyles" brochure, which offers interpretation along the marked trail to the formations. To find the Gargoyles, watch for the sign at Herring Creek Road. Turn east and drive six miles, · watching for another sign announcing the Gargoyles. Turn left and drive another quarter mile to a dirt parking area on the edge of an amphithe-

The "Gargoyles" formed in a process of erosion through soft volcanic mudflows, ash deposits, and lahars.

ater of cliffs. The trail can be found by looking for a worn footpath on the north side of the parking area.

DONNELL VISTA POINT (el. 6,600 feet) AND THE DARDANELLES

For years I drove right past this rest area and lookout point without stopping. As it turns out, even a brief stop is well worth the time. It was here that I first learned how to identify a Douglas fir — a large one stretches its tousled branches across the overlook platform. Below is the dramatic chasm of the Middle Fork Stanislaus River Canyon, now partly filled by Donnell Reservoir. The walls and stair steps of this granitic canyon rival nature's architecture at Yosemite, and it's a bit frightening to imagine the even greater depths that lie beneath the reservoir's surface. The well-designed quarter-mile-long trail to the platform also offers a good opportunity to contemplate the brown palisade of the **Dardanelles** lava flow.

A few miles east of Donnell Vista Point you will come upon Clark Fork Road, a route leading up the Clark Fork Stanislaus River into the heart of the Carson-Iceberg Wilderness. The road ends at the Iceberg Meadow trailhead, from which one might launch a hike around **the Iceberg,** a granitic monolith for which the Carson-Iceberg Wilderness is named.

After passing Clark Fork Road, Highway 108 ascends steeply alongside Deadman Creek, where rocky ledges offer enticing picnic spots, but where pull-off opportunities are few and far between. A small vista point near **Kennedy Meadows Resort** affords an excellent view toward **Relief Valley** (now a reservoir). According to an 1858 issue of *Hutchings' Illustrated California Magazine,* Relief Valley "takes its very appropriate name from the fact that it was here that relief was brought to the emigrants in their almost starving condition, from the generous-hearted citizens of Sonora and Columbia."

Hutchings was speaking of the Clark-Skidmore party, which started up the West Walker emigrant route from the eastern Sierra in late September 1852. At Emigrant Pass the party met an early snowstorm and sent a group ahead for supplies as they struggled on. Relief arrived as the party was camped in a valley at 8,000 feet in the Stanislaus River headwaters. Now called Relief Valley, it sits in the western shadow of 10,808-foot Relief Peak. Even today, backpackers with modern equipment following maintained trails will spend several days on this emigrant route from Leavitt Meadows to Pinecrest Lake.

The Dardanelles.

SONORA PASS (el. 9,625 feet)

Less than a mile before Sonora Pass, a spacious parking area on the north side of the road serves those who would tread the northeast-trending trail to **St. Mary's Pass,** a gap at 10,420 feet on the southwest flank of 11,459-foot Sonora Peak. The trail is a remnant of a wagon road used heavily in the 1860s by travelers heading east to the Aurora and Bodie mines or west to Sonora. Now, it is only a steep footpath, but the way is lined most delightfully with red and mauve volcanic boulders joined in summer by remarkable fields of wildflowers that seem to explode in a whole new array with every 100 feet of altitude gained. At the pass, the blue flax grows flattened to the ground by the effects of wind and snow.

Sonora Pass is an excellent place to investigate a portion of the **Pacific Crest Trail.** The climb southward toward **Leavitt Peak** (el. 11,569 feet) into Yosemite National Park traverses a high ridge offering spectacular, wide-open views.

From Sonora Pass, Highway 108 descends east through a steeply glaciated terrain. Quite suddenly, the braiding silver ribbons of Sardine Falls appear to the south as they cascade off a high ledge in open view. The hike to the falls from Sardine Meadow is relatively easy. The trailhead sign has a habit of disappearing, but you can improvise a starting point from the meadow, which is located two and a half miles east of the pass before the Soda Creek crossing. Along the meadow trail, skeletal lodgepole pines show off their spiral growth patterns. Higher up, stunted aspen form a shimmering green canopy over the trail in summer, while wildflowers burst forth in wild abandon along the waterway.

LEAVITT MEADOWS (el. 7,000 feet)

As you continue your descent on Highway 108, watch for the **Leavitt Falls Vista Point** on the right. From this inviting cliff-side lookout, your gaze is likely to stray from the falls to the aspen-rimmed expanse of Leavitt Meadows below — an extraordinary scene when the aspens turn gold in autumn.

Leavitt Meadows is one of many places in the Sierra that has been loved nearly to death. Serenity was in somewhat short supply in October 2001 as I hiked through the meadows accompanied by a thundering herd of sheep that appeared to be tended only by a donkey. Overhead, heli-

After the lodgepole pine dies and loses its outer covering of bark, its spiral growth structure is revealed. Photo by Mark Middlebrook

copters were taking troops from the nearby Mountain Warfare Training Center into terrain that simulated what they might be about to encounter as they attempted to rout out the Taliban in Afghanistan.

From this end of Highway 108, a traveler is well positioned to begin discovering the wonders along U.S. 395 in Mono County. Head east, turn south, and flip to chapter 4.

Practical Matters

With elevation changes of more than 8,000 feet, these routes present a variety of seasonal conditions. In winter, all four routes provide access to winter sports areas, but some routes are closed for trans-Sierra travel. Spring is ideal for wildflower viewing at the lower elevations. Spring snowmelt can make river areas exciting, but dangerous to explore. Remote sights at the higher elevations may remain snowbound into June. Summer can be hot at lower elevations, but ideal in the high mountain regions, with wildflowers in bloom throughout the season. Watch out for summer thunderstorms in high spots, and always be prepared for cold weather in the higher elevations. Autumn visits can be spectacular when the aspen are changing in first half of October. For more on Sierra weather and climate statistics for Woodfords, Sonora, and Bridgeport, see the introduction.

ROADS

This chapter covers U.S. 50, and highways 88, 89, 4, and 108. Only U.S. 50, Highway 88, and the Highway 89 connection between U.S. 50 and Highway 88 are kept open in winter, when traffic to ski resorts can be considerable. Chains are required in snowy conditions. Winter closure of Highway 89 over Monitor Pass, Highway 4 over Ebbetts Pass, and Highway 108 over Sonora Pass begins with the first significant snow accumulation in autumn and continues until sometime in April or May, depending on snow levels.

WHERE TO STAY AND EAT

Inns, motels, B&Bs, and resorts can be few and far between in the extensive national forest regions that these highways traverse. In the lower elevations, the best selections will be along Highway 49: at Placerville (off U.S. 50), Jackson (off Highway 88), Angels Camp (and uphill at Murphys and Arnold on Highway 4), and at Sonora and Jamestown (off Highway 108). In the upper elevations there are great resort options in the Carson Pass and Hope Valley areas of Highway 88, in Markleeville on the Highway 89 connection between Highway 88 and Highway 4, and at Strawberry and Pinecrest on Highway 108. On the east side of the range, lodging is pretty much limited to South Lake Tahoe and Bridgeport (near the eastern end of Highway 108). The best dining options will be found in the same places listed above for lodging.

CAMPING

Along these routes there are dozens of campgrounds in the Eldorado, Stanislaus, and Humboldt-Toiyabe national forests.

U.S. FOREST SERVICE

Eldorado National Forest, (www.fs.fed.us/r5/eldorado/): **Headquarters,** 100 Forni Road, Placerville, 530-622-5061, Visitor information: 530-644-6048; **Carson Pass Information Center,** Highway 88 at Carson Pass, 209-258-8606; **Pacific Ranger District,** 7887 Highway 50, Pollock Pines, 530-647-5415; **Placerville Ranger District,** 4260 Eight Mile Road, Camino, 530-647-2324.

Stanislaus National Forest, (www.fs.fed.us/r5/stanislaus/): **Headquarters,** 19777 Greenley Road, Sonora, 209-532-3671; **Calaveras Ranger District,** Hathaway Pines (Highway 4), 209-795-1381; **Mi-Wok Ranger District,** 24695 Highway 108, Mi-Wuk Village, 209-586-3234; **Summit Ranger District,** #1 Pinecrest Lake Road, Pinecrest, 209-965-3434.

Humboldt-Toiyabe National Forest, (www.fs.fed.us/r4/htnf/): **Bridgeport Ranger District,** U.S. 395, Bridgeport, 760-932-7070.

VISITORS BUREAUS

Alpine County Chamber of Commerce and USFS Visitors Center, www. alpinecounty.com, 3 Webster Street, Markleeville, 530-694-2475.

El Dorado County Chamber of Commerce, www.eldoradocounty.org, 542 Main Street, Placerville, 530-621-5885.

REGIONAL GUIDES

Schaffer, Jeffrey. *Carson-Iceberg Wilderness.* Berkeley, Calif.: Wilderness Press, 1992.

Schifrin, Ben. *Emigrant Wilderness and Northwestern Yosemite.* Berkeley, Calif.: Wilderness Press, 1990.

Sprout, Jerry. *Alpine Trailblazer.* Markleeville, Calif.: Diamond Valley Company, 2004.

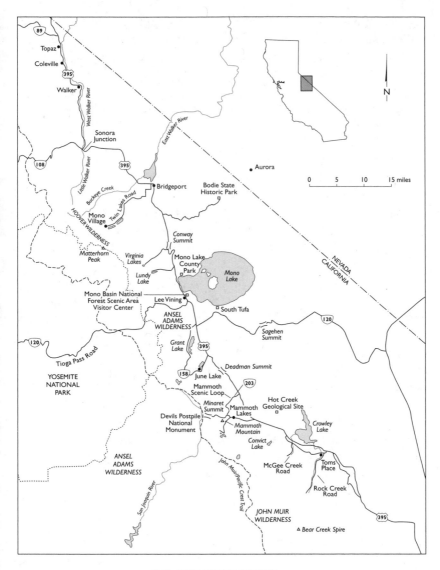

U.S. 395: MONO COUNTY

4

U.S. 395: Mono County

This is El Camino Sierra . . . a major interregional route for long
distance travel and freight, and the Eastern sierra's Main Street.

—Tom Hallenbeck, Caltrans District 9 Manager

Along the Sierra's eastern escarpment, the sun shines brightly through
bone-dry air, glinting off the snowfields that linger high up along the
Sierra crest. Icy creeks tumble down steep slopes through aspen and sagebrush, rushing into the alkaline sinks and shrinking lakes of the Great
Basin. But before these waters meet their salty ends, they cross under U.S.
395, a gray ribbon of road that for a time connected Canada to San Diego.
Travelers who make their way through this enchanted land know this
lonely desert highway well.

Antelope Valley and the West Walker River

This tour begins in the Antelope Valley (el. 5,000+ feet) land of the beautiful West Walker River, where U.S. 395 meets the southern terminus of
Highway 89 coming in from Tahoe over Monitor Pass. The Antelope Valley was once the home of Paiute, Shoshone, and Washoe, but today it is a
region of alfalfa fields and pasturelands. In October 1841, the valley briefly
hosted the first party of overland emigrants to California. The Bartleson-
Bidwell Party began their ascent of the Sierra from here, and it was also in
this area that Frémont abandoned a howitzer cannon, which became the
subject of many subsequent treasure hunts. By the 1860s, ranchers settled
in the valley and the little supply towns of Topaz, Coleville, and Walker
grew up along the stage route.

South of Walker (el. 5,400 feet), the road twists and climbs through

This view of West Walker River high country is from near Monitor Pass. Antelope Valley is off to the left. Photo by Erlda Parker

hills covered with sagebrush, Sierra juniper, and pinyon pine before it enters a narrow canyon. Here the rounded pinyon gives way to skyward-pointing conifers, and the water tumbles brightly over smoothly rounded river rocks. A small campground and day-use area beckon a stop at this small but splendid sample of eastern Sierra wilderness scenery, but takers appear to be mainly fishermen who must know how to tune out the traffic as they tune in the trout.

At the south end of the canyon, views open out on a terrain of big rolling hills and the soaring 11,000-foot peaks from which the West Walker gathers its headwaters. U.S. 395 meets Highway 108 at Sonora Junction, then makes a sudden bend to the east.

U.S. 395 continues eastward into the willow-filled bed of a little hot creek. Here, individuals bent on a hot soak at any cost can lie in a ditch and dream of times past when **Fales Hot Spring** was a developed resort. In winter, steam billows up from the springs and ducks navigate through the frosted reeds, enjoying their own private spa facilities. This stretch of road has a haunting lonely quality I can't quite explain. It seems uninhabited except by the long-tailed black-billed magpies that perch singly in the tops of trees or willow rushes.

About three-quarters of a mile beyond Sonora Junction, a campground sign indicates the three-mile dirt road to the small and peaceful **Obsidian Campground,** set at 7,840 feet at the confluence of the **Little Walker River** and Molybdenite Creek. The creek provides the only source of running water for the campground. Campers seeking solitude will find it here, except perhaps in deer season, when bow hunters in full camouflage can be a startling sight first thing in the morning. Trails from this road lead through a branching forest of dense aspen up to icy, high-altitude lakes in the **Hoover Wilderness.**

Bridgeport Valley (el. 6,468 feet)

There is no need to check your watch in the town of Bridgeport. The bell atop the handsome **Mono County Courthouse** chimes the hours, just as it has since 1881, when this working courthouse was built. Bridgeport became the county seat in 1864 after it was determined that the silver-mining town of Aurora, then the county seat and now nearly vanished, was in fact located in Nevada. Confusion over the exact placement of California's eastern boundary had persisted for 14 years after the adoption of the California Constitution, due to a certain difficulty in surveying the territory. Article XII states:

> The boundary of the State of California shall be as follows: Commencing at the point of intersection of the 42d degree of north latitude with the 120th degree of longitude west from Greenwich, and running south on the line of said 120th degree of west longitude until it intersects the 39th degree of north latitude; thence running in a straight line in a southeasterly direction to the river Colorado.

The problem is that the intersection of the 120th degree of west longitude and the 39th degree of north latitude lies out in the middle of Lake Tahoe. The difficulty of surveying from a drifting boat presented a knotty problem for the surveyor general, and for a time, citizens living in the borderlands were left wondering whether they lived in California or Nevada. In 1861, James W. Nye, the newly appointed territorial governor of Nevada, began drawing county lines into the disputed areas and proclaimed Aurora as the seat of Esmeralda County, Nevada. The citizens of Aurora, in true miner's style, seized the opportunity to hold elections for both the California and the Nevada districts in the spring of 1863. When full slates of Union Republicans were elected in both districts, a small Civil War battle was reported to have ensued in the streets of Aurora. Peace was gradually reestablished when a more definitive survey was completed a few months later, and Aurora was determined to be in Nevada . . . only.

The Mono County records were moved to Bridgeport, a small settlement beside a footbridge over the East Walker River. Unlike doomed Aurora, Bridgeport was not economically dependent on mining. As early as 1860, the fertile prairie grasses of the Big Meadow, as the Bridgeport Valley was then called, were being irrigated from Sierra creeks to the southwest. Bridgeport grew to become an important hub of the local ranching industry, which it remains. One still sees the names of the original homesteading families high over the entry gates of working cattle

A typical summer gathering at the Bridgeport Inn. Photo courtesy of the Bridgeport Inn

ranches in the Big Meadow, and on a Saturday night, the ranchers often can be found at the **Bridgeport Inn** tucking into platefuls of prime rib. When it was built in 1877, the Bridgeport Inn was called the Leavitt House, and served as a stage stop. The establishment has retained its way-station ambience, along with a wing of historic rooms. Winter guests are likely to be ushered into the plush parlor, where a fire rumbles in the antique stove, and the town's past is illuminated in old photos on the walls. In summer, red-shirted members of the Bodie chapter of E Clampus Vitus (ECV), might be bending their elbows all along the row of coveted swivel-stools on the front porch while engaging in their annual debate over which Mono County historic site they should honor with a plaque in the coming year. They may also be pursuing the perennial question of whether ECV is a historical drinking society or a drinking historical society. Ask any one of these fellows (or any other Clamper you meet in the course of your travels) about the origins of E Clampus Vitus, and you will learn that it is an ancient order, which found its great glory during the tumultuous days of the California Gold Rush. Like their forebears, modern-day Clampers attempt to uphold the traditions of fellowship, good spirits, and fun. Their tenets also require that they remain "dedicated to the care and protection of the 'widders' and orphans . . . but especially the widders."

TWIN LAKES ROAD

At the **Hunewill Ranch,** located west of Bridgeport on the Twin Lakes Road, the original Hunewill family has been running cattle since 1861. The ranch has also run dudes since 1930, but some of these guests are highly skilled in the saddle. Guests have been known to pay good money here to help rope cattle, mend fences, or go on the annual cattle drive 60 miles east to Smith Valley, Nevada, with the real cowboys. Most guests are content to lope across acres of prairie or ride into the Sierra or the Sweetwater Mountains where they might share the meadows with herds of mustangs.

At the end of Twin Lakes Road beyond the Hunewill Ranch, the Twin Lakes (el. 7081–92 feet) nestle gracefully below the rugged Sawtooth Ridge. The little resort town of Mono Village at the top of Upper Twin Lake becomes a thicket of satellite dishes and lawn furniture in summer.

Fishermen and packs of kids roam excitedly along the waterways, and whole families make the four-mile hike to **Barney Lake** for a picnic. The trail begins at the end of the meadow above Mono Village.

Stepping into a fragrant forest of Jeffrey pine, hikers find themselves in the company of scurrying chipmunks, pensive mule deer, and raucous Steller's jays, all made bold by handouts from the campground. Further along, the trail traverses groves of aspen alternating with open sagebrush fields, where a profusion of birds bursts forth from the shrubbery. Lizards and chipmunks hightail it across the trail in front of human intruders, while black bears, mountain lions, and coyotes remain largely out of view.

On the steep switchbacks to the lake, the trail crosses the creek bed, which in summer is a showcase for yellow monkey flower, rosy-purple wild onion, red columbine, spotted orange alpine lily, blue monkshood, droll clumps of fuzzy white ranger's buttons, and little pink elephant heads — look closely to see the tiny ears and trunks. At Barney Lake, hikers look up to see 11,346-foot Crown Point and down at its image reflected on the calm water of this pretty little lake.

BUCKEYE CREEK CANYON

On the return to Bridgeport from Twin Lakes, a visitor with ample time, and the vehicle and disposition to handle a bumpy road, could take an

---

ON MATTERHORN PEAK

Matterhorn Peak, an impressive sharp-pointed "horn," stands at 12,279 feet, above Twin Lakes along the jagged, granitic walls of the Sawtooth Ridge. Fans of Gary Snyder and Jack Kerouac might recognize Matterhorn Peak as the destination of the characters in Kerouac's 1958 novel *The Dharma Bums.*

So we unpacked our packs and laid things out and smoked and had a good time. Now the mountains were getting that pink tinge, I mean the rocks, they were just solid rock covered with the atoms of dust accumulated there since beginningless time. In fact I was afraid of those jagged monstrosities all around and over our heads.

'They're so silent!' I said.

'Yeah man, you know to me a mountain is a Buddha. Think of the patience, hundreds of thousands of years just sitting there bein perfectly perfectly silent and like praying for all living creatures in that silence and just waiting for us to stop all our frettin and foolin.'

Cattle grazing in Bridgeport Valley beneath the Sawtooth Ridge. Photo by Erlda Parker

alternate route back to town. Turn north at Doc and Al's Resort onto For-est Service Road 017, a washboard gravel road that leads into the secluded canyon of Buckeye Creek. From Buckeye Campground, a trail sets out along the rushing creek into the Hoover Wilderness. After the camp-ground turnoff, the road crosses the creek and continues northeast, pass-ing Buckeye Hot Springs, which is easy to spot because of all the bathing-suited people clambering up and down the steep hillside. Once past the hot springs, the road contours along the slope, offering splendid views down into the lush meadows of Bridgeport Valley.

Bodie State Historic Park (el. 8,375 feet)

From Bridgeport, U.S. 395 heads south along Virginia Creek, arriving seven miles later at a site identified as Dogtown. Dogtown was a general term miners used for a cluster of shacks erected at a gold strike, but this particular one bears note as being the first miners' settlement in the east-ern Sierra. It was inhabited for a mere two years, from 1857 to 1859. The site now serves as a signpost for the turnoff to Bodie, 13 miles to the east.

Bodie State Historic Park preserves one of the region's most enduring miners' settlements and the West's largest unrestored mining-era ghost town. It ranks up with Yosemite and Tahoe in popularity. But few visitors ever appreciate the isolation of a Bodie winter, where overnight temperatures are often the lowest recorded anywhere in the state. The road to Bodie is closed the moment snow makes it impassable, leaving the park staff to keep company with the swallows, the ghosts, and an occasional party of cross-country skiers. It was a blizzard in November of 1859 that took the life of the town's namesake, William S. Bodey (or Body). Bodey froze to death while returning on foot to his mining camp from the now vanished town of Monoville just north of Mono Lake. The weather apparently did not deter the wave of miners who heard of the wealth of Bodie's mines. The town grew by leaps and bounds, and by the time its population peaked at around 10,000 in 1880, the rowdy and the wicked had worked their way with the town's reputation. Residents continued to mine (or entertain tourists) as late as 1947, and it is that lingering human presence that accounts for the fact that the town still remains so well intact despite ravaging fires, crushing snows, and powerful windstorms.

Today, the extensive ruins of Bodie represent 10 to 20 percent of the structures that were present in the 1880s. The ruins are being preserved

Bodie Ghost Town. Photo by Erlda Parker

**A Bodie kitchen.
Photo by Erlda
Parker**

in a state of "arrested decay" to remain in the same 1962 condition when the site became a California state park. While the town once poured local brew and spirits at more than 50 saloons, today there are no refreshments to be had, save a swig of spring water available at the museum/bookstore. But the lack of modern comforts adds to the alluring ambience. As you wander Bodie's long and dusty streets, gazing at wooden buildings weathered a rich and uniform brown, the town offers up generous shades of its vibrant past. Peer into windows, and you will see articles of daily life still sitting on countertops as if the residents had only just left on a

Goin' nowhere at Bodie. Photo by Erlda Parker

brief errand, although calendars on the walls show that the errands have taken a half-century or more. Off in the town's graveyards is a record of souls who left more emphatically. The daily toil in an 1880s gold and silver mine is effectively illustrated with a tour of the Standard Mill, the prominent metal-clad building on the southern side of town. Docent descriptions of the din caused by the stamp mill present an utter contrast to the peaceful ambience of a summer afternoon in high tourist season.

CONWAY SUMMIT (el. 8,138 feet)

Beyond the Bodie turnoff, U.S. 395 climbs southward toward Conway Summit. This high spot on the highway is not a likely stop for most travelers, but those in search of a good fishing lake or magnificent eastern Sierra wilderness might be inclined to turn west toward Virginia Lakes. The well-maintained Virginia Lakes Road winds up past 12,374-foot Dunderberg Peak and into a piece of high country that remains splendidly wild in spite of the campgrounds and resorts. Trails from the road end traverse the magnificent Hoover Wilderness. Backpackers often continue over the crest into the Yosemite backcountry.

During my first winter of dedicated research on this book, I felt the urge to stop right on Conway Summit. The library in my car trunk held a newly acquired copy of *Speaking through the Aspens,* J. Mallea-Olaetxe's discourse on Basque sheepherders' arborglyphs. The tables cataloguing the most prolific arborglyph sites did not list Conway Summit, but I was looking at an impressive stand of aspens, and the urge was upon me. Donning my red plastic snowshoes, I tromped off into the grove to see who might have passed that way in years gone by. A few recent names and dates were carved awkwardly into a tree right by the road, and along the little creek, tracks in the snow provided fresh evidence of busy rabbits and mice. I was looking for carved Basque symbols or some elaborately etched depiction of a soaring bird, and in my heart, I was hoping to find one of the indiscreet fantasies carved by a lonely young sheepherder. Deep in the grove I found a large dead aspen bearing a Basque name: Pyerre (last name no longer legible) 5 Julyo 1918, a very early date among Mallea's listings. As I was heading south toward the Owens Valley, I thought about how recent this carving would be in comparison to the petroglyphs etched 4,000 years ago into the tuff of the volcanic tableland north of Bishop. And yet, the arborglyphs seem just as compelling. These records last only as long as the aspens on which they are carved — a mere 80 years — a lifespan similar to that of the young man who might have carved upon it.

Just south of Conway Summit, and before U.S. 395 begins its descent into the Mono Basin, there is a good turnout on the downhill side. From this fortified ledge, there is an incredible sweeping view of the Mono Lake Basin. Since there is so much to see in the Mono Basin, there will be plenty of times to speak the name "Mono," so why not learn to say it correctly right now before you get there. It is *moe-no,* not *mah-no.*

LUNDY CANYON

As U.S. 395 descends into the Mono Basin, watch for a turnoff to the west marked Lundy Lake Road. The reservoir called Lundy Lake is at 7,808 feet, four miles up this paved road. Although the lake and the quaint resort at its upper end are a pleasant destination, the best scenery in the canyon is located farther up along the dirt road to the main trailhead.

There are those who will always see the hand of a divine creator in the sublime scenery of the Sierra Nevada, but in Lundy Canyon, the beavers have done much of the work. The semi-aquatic rodents living here on Mill Creek (the northernmost feeder of Mono Lake) have turned an already exquisite glacial canyon into a marvelous set of terraced water gardens surrounded by high ridges and endless acres of flickering aspen. Behind the complex wickerwork of the beavers' dams, the creek spreads out into wide pools, where the waters project mirror images of the drowned trees on their stilled surfaces.

The first in the string of beaver ponds is right beside the road to the trailhead, but it is well worth the effort to hike from the trailhead to see more of the beavers' work. If you continue beyond the ponds, you will climb over a high rock bench to reach an area of luxurious meadows and young aspen forests. Most day hikers continue to the waterfalls that tumble down from Shepherd Crest, but more-ambitious hikers climb to the upper lakes and Lundy Pass. To hike to the old May Lundy Mine, you will need to drive back down to Lundy Lake, where the mine trail takes off from the southern shore.

Into the Mono Basin

During the ice ages, the Great Basin, which covers most of Nevada and Utah, was filled with lakes. Some were very large, such as Lake Bonneville and Lake Lahontan, and others were smaller, like Ice Age Lake Russell, the ancestor of Mono Lake. (Remember, *moe-no*, not *mah-no.*) As the ice ages ended, the waters receded and these magnificent lakes shrank. Most of them disappeared, leaving behind great stretches of sand and flat white pools of salt, as Mono Lake is likely to do as well, regardless of human intervention

Around the perimeter of the Mono Basin, high terraces mark the receding shores of Ice Age Lake Russell. The lower bathtub rings, however, were formed between 1941 and 1994, when the Los Angeles Department of Water and Power (LADWP) was diverting most of the Sierra snowmelt from Mono Lake. A series of lawsuits by the Mono Lake Committee and its allies finally convinced the State Water Resources Control Board to modify the license that allowed the LADWP to divert the water, and now Mono Lake is refilling, no longer doomed to becoming another salt flat in the very near future. (For more on the LADWP controversy, turn to the Owens Valley chapter of this book.)

As you explore the Mono Basin, more of the dramatic geological story unfolds. As recently as the recession of glacial water at the end of the last ice age, cauldrons of fiery rock welled up under this Great Basin perimeter, and those fires have not yet gone out. Starting 40,000 years ago and continuing into the present, a chain of volcanic vents has produced the **Mono-Inyo Craters,** a series of plug domes located south of the lake. **Panum Crater,** at the north end of these, is barely 700 years old. Black Point, located just north of the lake, is 13,000 years old, and black Negit Island, sitting out in the lake, shows evidence of flows in the early 18th century. At that time, Paoha Island was rising up in the middle of the lake like a big bubble covered with white lake-bottom sediment. Paoha has never fully erupted, but steam vents and fumaroles on the island suggest it might at any moment. (Anyone wishing to test the watched-pot theory could stand here and stare at Paoha for a few years and then report back to the rest of us.)

At many points around the lake, some curious-looking shapes can be seen huddled near the shoreline. These knobby white towers of calcium carbonate have formed (and are continuing to form) as a result of fresh-water springs, which bubble up under the lake. Calcium in the spring water reacts with carbonates in the lake water, and the combined miner-als then precipitate to form the masses of rock called *tufa* (pronounced *too-fa*). Many of these towers were exposed during the height of the LAD-WP's stream diversion, but now they are being slowly submerged as the water level rises.

Perched high on the west shore of the lake is the town of **Lee Vining** (el. 6,781 feet), named for the prospector who arrived over Sonora Pass with his brother, Dick, to take his chances at the Mono diggings in the mid 1850s. Upon their arrival, the Vining brothers might have found the Kuzedika Paiute preparing their favorite food, *kutsavi,* beside the lake. A neighboring tribe, the Yokuts, told the white prospectors and explorers that these Paiute were "mono" or "fly-eaters," because it appeared they were eating flies. In fact, the Paiute were preparing bread or stew using the flavorful and nutritious larvae of *Ephydra hyans,* the alkali fly. I find it

Tufa towers on Mono Lake. Photo by Erlda Parker

interesting to think that, in a way, these Paiute were human interlopers in the simple but remarkable food chain of this alkaline lake.

Holding down the bottom of the chain are the lake's green algae, a favorite food of the ubiquitous flies and of the four trillion or so brine shrimp that swarm in foamy swirls or plumes just below the surface of the water. (A brine shrimp, according to Mark Twain, looks "like a bit of thread frayed out at the edges.") There are no fish able to live in these alkaline waters, and so huge numbers of plovers, phalaropes, eared grebes, and California gulls are attracted to the feast of flies and shrimp. Some of these birds nest on the islands. A rallying cry from the National Audubon Society in the fight to save Mono Lake focused on the ravaging of this avian population when the dropping lake level made the nesting ground on Negit Island accessible to four-legged carnivores, adding a new and fatal link to the top of the food chain. The Society's concern was not just for the local ecology. When the delicate balance of life here at Mono Lake is disrupted, it has an influence on migratory bird populations in distant parts of the globe.

Your first stop on arriving at the lake from the north might be the northwest shore's **Mono Lake County Park,** where a peaceful stroll out the boardwalk path takes you past clumps of wildflowers, tufa towers, and markers showing the dropping shore levels of the LADWP diversion period. When the water is high, the walkway ends near a maze of reedy canals replete with waterfowl.

The second stop would be the **Mono Basin National Forest Scenic Area Visitor Center,** on the east side of the highway just north of Lee Vining. The extensive exhibits cover the natural history of the Mono Basin. Several interpretive trails traverse the sagebrush on the high ground of the lake's west shore.

On entering the town of Lee Vining, watch for the headquarters of the **Mono Lake Committee**, in the center of Lee Vining at the corner of U.S. 395 and 3rd Street. The Committee has a fabulous bookstore staffed by knowledgeable volunteers, plus displays describing the ecology and history of the lake and a bird-watcher's log. Among the Committee's educational outings is an early-morning canoe trip on Mono Lake. Participants get a close-up look at the biota and the tufa (including tufa in construction) along with insight into the lake's political history. The trips embark

As seen from Sagehen Summit southeast of Mono Lake, an April snowstorm on Mount Dana.

from **South Tufa,** which is a great place to go, even without a guide, to admire the tufa towers (and the flies and the shrimp). To get to South Tufa, continue five miles south of Lee Vining on U.S. 395 and turn east on Highway 120. This route crosses Pumice Valley, climbing into the Mono Craters. (**Panum Crater** is fascinating to explore on foot.) At around the five-mile point, signs indicate the turnoff to South Tufa. Highway 120 continues east to **Sagehen Summit** (el. 8,139 feet) — a vantage point for remarkable views of the Mono Basin and of **Mount Dana** (el. 13,053 feet) and **Mount Gibbs** (el. 12,764 feet) on the Sierra crest to the west. Numerous dirt roads through the volcanic terrain south of the highway lead up to the rim of the Long Valley Caldera, where the Owens River begins its journey south.

As of this writing, those desiring to dine by the shores of Mono Lake don't have to settle for fly larvae or brine shrimp. The upscale **Mono Inn Restaurant,** located on U.S. 395 north of Lee Vining, is housed with the **Ansel Adams Gallery,** operated by Sara Adams, granddaughter of Ansel Adams, the Sierra's most noted photographer. And then there's the legendary **Tioga Gas Mart** (a.k.a. the Gourmet Gas Station) at the intersection of U.S. 395 and Tioga Road (Highway 120). From the end of April to the beginning of November, when the gas station's Whoa Nellie Deli is open, many people in nearby campgrounds forgo the campfire cooking routine altogether and come here for espresso drinks, mango margaritas, fancy fish tacos, and inspired specials. Seating is indoors or outdoors, where there's a fine view of the lake, especially captivating at sunset with a mango margarita.

June Lake Loop

Five miles south of Lee Vining, just before the Highway 120 east turnoff, is the northern end of the June Lake Loop (Highway 158), which ranges into some surprisingly wild high country along a chain of lakes. The largest of these, **Grant Lake** (el. 7,130 feet) sits in a sere Great Basin sagebrush environment at the north end of the loop. Development is confined to a campground and boat launch. One April day I found the landscape utterly transformed with the effects of a splendid snowstorm that was laying down a couple of fresh inches of white over the decaying shreds of the winter's snowpack. As I peered upward at the steep slope beside Grant Lake, the budding aspen appeared neon green while the strong spring sunlight burned through clouds of glowing, blowing snow.

Midway around the loop is **Silver Lake** (el. 7,215 feet), where a strenuous but rewarding hike begins from the Silver Lake Campground. Follow the marked trail across Alger Creek and climb southward up the steep, dry slope. The trail crisscrosses the tracks of a tramway built to supply the hydroelectric project at Agnew and Gem lakes. These deep green lakes are surrounded by rock ledges providing perches for a well-deserved rest stop on the climb to **Agnew Pass** (el. 10,000 feet), where there are views of the Ritter and Cathedral ranges. Along the talus switchbacks to the pass, the rocks are painted vivid green, orange, and black with crustose lichens. Down below, the aspens' foliage refracted on the surface of the lakes is a sight to behold in autumn.

The June Lake Loop's eponymous lake and town (el. 7,640 feet) are located at the busy and wooded southern end of the loop, as are several lodges, five more campgrounds, the tiny aquatic body known as Gull Lake, and the **June Mountain** ski and snowboard resort. Skiers get a great view of the area from the June Mountain summit (el. 10,090 feet).

The Lands of the Long Valley Caldera

On leaving the June Lake area in a southwesterly direction on U.S. 395, you will be passing directly through the pumice- and obsidian-strewn chain of **Inyo Craters,** notable for the fact that they are very young (less than 2,000 years old). One, a steep-sided cone named Wilson Butte (el. 8,509 feet), sits directly beside the highway, where on a white, wintry day, there are likely to be road signs warning drivers to keep moving so as not to get caught in an avalanche. Upon passing Wilson Butte, you will be looking south at the dark form of **Obsidian Dome** (el. 8,610 feet), which rears up from a sea of conifers like a jagged crown on a green-coiffed head. A signed road on the right will lead you to the dome. Up close, the dome's volcanic effluence looks like a gigantic batch of Rocky Road fudge just poured out on the kitchen counter. The shiny black glass is mixed with ropy brown glass, and strewn with red and white cinders. Note: The short road to the Obsidian Dome parking area forks at about a mile in. Bear left to reach the dome parking area, which is spread out within a fragrant forest of Jeffrey pine. The right fork leads to Hartley Springs Campground, where acres of empty campsites are laid out in the tranquil pine forest. (There is no running water and no fee.)

From the Obsidian Dome turnoff, U.S. 395 climbs to 8,039 feet at **Deadman Summit.** I suspect that the snowman I once saw on the summit has moved on. No doubt, he drifted into Deadman Creek and on into the Owens River, hitching a ride in the Los Angeles aqueduct to the big city. During his brief sojourn on the summit he looked out into the Long Valley Caldera, a gigantic collapsed and resurgent dome. The caldera was formed by the eruption of the Long Valley Volcano approximately 760,000 years ago. It spewed out almost 150 cubic miles of molten rock and incandescent ash, an amount far larger than what was produced by Mount St. Helens, Vesuvius, or even Krakatoa. The most extensive formation left from that eruption, the Volcanic Tableland of Bishop Tuff, can be seen in the area north of Bishop, coming up in the next chapter.

About five miles south of Deadman Summit is the turnoff for the **Mammoth Scenic Loop,** which some locals refer to as the "Volcano Escape Route," due to its installation during a time when seismologists were noting heightened seismic activity around the caldera and under Mammoth Mountain. The warnings have been played down, but there is no question that the caldera region will some day see more volcanic activity.

As you turn southwest onto the loop, you will be driving between more of the Inyo Craters. At around the six-mile point, watch on the west side for a sign indicating a mile-long improved dirt road to a sight labeled simply "Inyo Craters." The attraction here is a set of 500-year-old craters that have formed deep pits (instead of cones) holding tiny lakes of an appealing milky green color. It's an alluring sight, but the problem will be finding the right footpath to get there. The craters are only a third of a mile walk from the designated parking area, but I found it hard to choose the most direct path within the unsightly maze of off-highway-vehicle (OHV) trails in this area. As I peered into the craters, my reverie was broken when two extraterrestrials on dirt bikes came roaring up, very nearly flinging themselves into the craters by accident. One heavily outfitted creature said to the other, "What's this?" Then without wasting another moment to find an answer for the question, they were off. A few days after this happened I was chatting with a Bridgeport innkeeper and bemoaned the destructive nature of Mammoth-area OHV recreation. He commented, "That's why we have Mammoth." I continue to consider the concept of "share and share alike" in relation to our public lands, but I question why any natural area warrants being treated in this manner. I want to place my prayer here, asking that more eyes will be opened to the beauty and fragility of our few remaining wild places.

MAMMOTH LAKES AREA INFORMATION

The Mammoth Scenic Loop reaches Highway 203, west of the town of Mammoth Lakes. Turn east and head through town toward U.S. 395, watching on the north side of the road for the **Mammoth Lakes Recreation Area Visitor Center.** The center offers exhibits on the cultural and natural history of the area and information on this 200,000-acre recreation area, which includes the Mammoth Mountain and June Mountain ski areas, Devils Postpile National Monument, Rainbow Falls, Mammoth City Historical Site, Mammoth Lakes Basin, portions of the Pacific Crest and John Muir trails, and the nearby geothermal springs. Backpackers can obtain a wilderness permit here, and geology enthusiasts can pick up a brochure for the self-guided auto tour of the Long Valley Caldera volcanic features along U.S. 395.

Another useful resource in town is the Booky Joint, in the Minaret Village Shopping Center. This well-stocked bookstore has a good selection of books on Sierra and local subjects, plus plenty of maps. It's a great place to escape the crowds and get tips from the locals on the best ways to enjoy the area.

MAMMOTH MOUNTAIN RESORT

The humongous iron facsimile of a woolly mammoth in the ski area parking lot might reinforce the impression that this area was named after the now-extinct beast, but, in fact, the name was first adopted by a now-defunct local mining company. Regardless, the name suggests bigness, and Mammoth Mountain Resort is big. With 30 lifts serving 3,500 acres, it is one of the largest ski resorts in the country. As with most things, however, the resort started out very small. It all began in 1936 when a hydrographer and snow surveyor named Dave McCoy built a portable rope tow out of a gasoline engine, a rope, and some pulleys, simply to provide some amusement for himself and his friends. The machine proved very popular and so he set up a permanent rope tow on McGee Mountain, at a site now marked by an E Clampus Vitus plaque. Seeing greater potential, McCoy hocked his Harley and built a chairlift on Mammoth Mountain (el. 11,053 feet), taking advantage of some cast-offs from a spate of modernizing at Sugar Bowl in Donner Pass. Then he started a ski school, which in a short time would develop a strong international reputation for training Olympic racers. In late 2005, McCoy sold his interest in Mammoth Mountain Resort for more than $80 million. The purchaser, Starwood Capital Group, paid $365 million, making this the largest ski resort sale in history. Ninety-year-old McCoy was still skiing and biking at the time of the sale.

In addition to being the masterpiece of a visionary, the resort owes its success to an anomaly in the geography of the Sierra that allows east-moving moisture-laden storm systems to dump more snow in this location than in most other spots within the eastern rain shadow. (See the introduction for more on Sierra weather.) The steepness of the eastern escarpment also contributes to the great ski runs. From the very first moments of the ride up the mountain on the aptly named Panorama Gondola, the Ritter Range's twin sentinels, 12,945-foot **Banner Peak** and 13,104-foot **Mount Ritter,** as well as the jagged 12,281-foot **Minarets** make a striking appearance.

The day I chose to ride the gondola for the view, high winds had closed down the upper portion, so I came back down to look for excitement by window-shopping at the resort's Sport Shop. There I pondered a little fur-

The Minarets. Photo by Mark Middlebrook

lined Prada ski suit priced at a mere $2,000 (tax included) and a Bogner beaded vest that could be had for slightly less. As I left the mountain, riding the town's wonderful free shuttle bus with young ski bums and entry-level resort workers, I noted plenty of vacation condos that would go well with the Prada suit. Mammoth developers appeared to be bent on bringing the Jackson Hole crowd to the Sierra. Among the town's 4,000 permanent residents, I found quite a few bemoaning the coming of the glitterati to their secluded kingdom. A few even were praying secretly for a small resumption of the local volcanic activity, just enough to mitigate the next wave of development.

DEVILS POSTPILE NATIONAL MONUMENT AND BACKCOUNTRY

A shuttle bus from the Mammoth Mountain resort parking lot whisks day-trippers over the Sierra crest at Minaret Summit to an extraordinary wilderness setting dominated by Devils Postpile, a fascinating geologic oddity created when a flow of basaltic lava cracked into columns as it cooled 600,000 years ago. From its glacier-polished top, the post pile resembles a floor made of hexagonal tiles.

Devils Postpile. Photo by Erlda Parker

Two of the most popular hikers' destinations here along the **Middle Fork San Joaquin River** are Minaret Falls and Rainbow Falls, but this is also a popular place to pick up the John Muir and Pacific Crest trails. Side trails lead into the glacier-rimmed Ritter Range and up to the dark, serrated ridge of the Minarets. These are routes along which to investigate how the forests thin gradually toward timberline. Above 8,000 feet, and the multi-trunked whitebark pine, juniper, and mountain hemlock become compact and contorted, because of the effects of the harsher climate. The most contorted and stunted trees are called Krummholz. Once above timberline, all the flora of the alpine landscape shows the extreme effects of adaptation. Small, but often ancient, the tiny mat-like shrubs and flowers hug the ground, their compact leaves and stems projecting little silvery spikes to resist the elements.

MAMMOTH LAKES: THE TOWN (el. 7,800 feet)
Mammoth Lakes' alpine eateries, Swiss chalets, painted murals of European village life, and decades of ski instructors hailing from the European Alps can cause one to forget that old Mammoth City started out in 1878 as a typical Sierra mining camp. The camp lasted but a mere three years before burning to the ground, and settlers did not return until mapmaker Emmet Hayden built his cabin on Sherwin Creek in 1927. Hayden's cabin, at 5489 Sherwin Creek Road, is now restored and operated by the Southern Mono Historical Society as a museum of early-day Mammoth. Otherwise, Old Mammoth is found in scanty remains on the southwest part of town where the newer condo developments creep like slow lava flows through the volcanic terrain. A few small hand-built log cabins from the early 20th century still hold their ground among the log palaces.

MAMMOTH LAKES: THE LAKES
From Old Mammoth, the Lake Mary Road winds south, climbing to 9,000 feet to reach a string of fine sub-alpine lakes that occupy basins carved out by Ice Age glaciers. These are the lakes from which the town derives its name. (Plain old Mammoth would have suited the original residents just fine, but another mining town already had dibs on it. Ironically, the other Mammoth soon went out of existence.)

In winter, cross-country skiers come to the lakes to enjoy the extraordinary setting and the 45km (28 miles) of groomed trails at the **Tamarack Lodge and Resort.** The resort also houses summer guests, but many people are just as happy to rough it at one of the six campgrounds here. Fishermen, day hikers, and backpackers use the lakes as a base camp or jump-off point to the backcountry. The trail heading southeast from **Lake Mary** runs past several mines, through a string of tiny lakes, and over the crest at **Duck Pass** (el. 10,797 feet) to **Duck Lake.**

Visitors often note the dead trees at the north end of **Horseshoe Lake,** which sits on the southern flank of Mammoth Mountain. The trees are being killed off by extremely high concentrations of carbon dioxide percolating up from the well of magma (molten rock) beneath Mammoth Mountain. When the gas concentrations are too high, the lake area is closed to visitors, but even when the area is open, visitors are advised that they should not lie down on the ground or dig around in it, because of the hazards of gas inhalation. Overexposure to the gases can cause dizziness, unconsciousness, and even death.

HOT CREEK (el. 6,500 feet)

Leaving Mammoth Lakes by its main access road, turn right on U.S. 395 and continue east-southeast, watching for Hot Creek Hatchery Road on the left. Many people turning onto this road will be fly fishermen, happy to observe the area catch-and-release rules on the creek while enjoying a vacation at the historic Hot Creek Ranch. Others will continue on this gravel road to the beloved Hot Creek Geological Site. In this former Paiute dwelling place, the icy snowmelt tumbling down from the Sierra crest runs into the sagebrush lands in the heart of the Long Valley Caldera. As superheated water rises from the volcanic zone below, scalding turquoise pools appear in terraces on the creek's steep banks and hot springs boil up in the middle of the cold, ice-fed current. Cliff swallows swoop into the gorge to nest along the cliffs, keeping company with great horned owls, bald eagles, and American dippers (a.k.a. water ouzels).

Like many geothermal sites, this place is sublime, but bathers should be aware that geothermal pools are unpredictable in their temperatures, and can be hot enough to cause serious injury or even death. Also, be

(opposite) Morning at Convict Lake. Photo by Erlda Parker

The handsome pyramidal form of Mount Morrison looks out over a distant row of quaking aspen and the low-growing community of sagebrush scrub so typical of this Great Basin region.

on the lookout for broken bottles, and leave Hot Creek cleaner than you found it.

CONVICT LAKE (el. 7,580 feet)

From the Hot Creek Geological Site, return to U.S. 395, continuing a little over a mile to reach the south-trending road to Convict Lake. It was near this lake in 1871 that some convicts on the lam from Carson City, Nevada, were gunned down in a bloody battle. Today, the lake draws a law-abiding crowd of sophisticated vacationers, some of whom come specifically to dine on freshly caught local trout at the Convict Lake Resort's renowned restaurant.

Convict Lake formed during the ice ages, when glacial till dammed the creek through Convict Canyon. It sits beneath a surreal panorama of ancient, metamorphic rock exposed on the faces of Laurel Mountain (el. 11,812 feet), Bloody Mountain (el. 12,544 feet), and Sevehan Cliff. The zone is thought to contain the oldest rocks in the Sierra. The red, white, and blue-gray formations present themselves as a contortion of stripes and folds with intrusions of younger granitic rocks. As you continue south-east on U.S. 395, you can see more of this gorgeous masterpiece in stone in the colorful forms of **Mount Morrison** (el. 12,268 feet), **McGee Mountain** (el. 10,871 feet), **Mount Morgan** (el. 13,005 feet), and **Red Mountain** (el. 11,472 feet).

MCGEE CREEK

Continue five miles on U.S. 395 to **McGee Creek Road.** If you arrive near sunset, turn south and head up the road to McGee Creek Campground, which is set in the wide-open sagebrush just before the road penetrates McGee Creek Canyon. With its eastward-facing cabanas, the campground looks a bit like a stage set for a Hollywood safari, but as the setting sun casts its rosy glow over Crowley Lake and the White Mountains to the east, the cabanas seem more like box seats arranged precisely for this nightly performance.

You won't want to stick around when the morning sun hits the tent in this wide-open spot, and it is best to get an early start anyway for a hike up McGee Canyon. The trailhead is another two miles up McGee Creek

Road beside the magnificent stands of Fremont and black cottonwood that crowd into the creek bed. As I began my summer hike up the long, hot and dry lower canyon, it became clear why some folks might prefer to contract with the McGee Creek Pack Station for some level of assistance into the cooler realms of the high country. (Packers operating near many of the Sierra's east-side trailheads offer a wide range of services, from simple guided day rides on horseback, to full-service, multi-day horseback excursions with mules carrying the gear. Some customers want only to have the mules transport their gear.) As the trail wanders away from the creek, a hiker with adequate sun protection and water can investigate at great length the fascinating textures of the sagebrush scrub: the showy drama of its wildflower community, the buzzing soundscape of its lively insect population, and the towhees that flutter from bush to bush as if leading the way into seeps where cottonwoods, wild rose, and mountain pink currant cluster. Higher up the slopes, a few sculptural junipers compete as images of grandeur with the ancient, colorful, and folded metamorphic rocks.

Four to six miles up McGee Creek, at 10,000 to 11,000 feet, are several lakes offering good fishing in an arena of 12,000-foot peaks. The trail crosses the Sierra crest at McGee Pass (el. 11,900 feet), between two ancient metamorphic peaks — **Red Slate Mountain** (el. 13,163 feet) and **Red and White Mountain** (el. 12,850 feet).

CROWLEY LAKE (el. 6,781 feet)

Continuing east-southeast on U.S. 395 from McGee Creek Road, you will be skirting around the wide southern shoreline of a 5,000-acre reservoir called Crowley Lake. The lake was named for the beloved "Desert Padre," Fr. John J. Crowley, who shepherded his Owens Valley parish in the early 20th century. As Crowley witnessed the demise of the local farming economy brought on by the LADWP water diversions (see "Into the Mono Basin," earlier in this chapter), he became one of the first to envision tourism as a possible new source of revenue. Through a series of unique publicity stunts, he brought attention to the region's recreational assets. First he arranged for the opening day of trout season to be declared a county holiday, and he presided over the festivities by blessing all fishing equipment. A few years later, he climbed Mount Whitney to become the first priest to celebrate Mass on the summit. Many more than just the faithful mourned when Father Crowley died in 1940 in an automobile accident, and the community placed a marker at the spot where he was killed (south of Owens Lake near the U.S. 395 and Highway 14 junction). Tributes to the Desert Padre continue to this day in murals and publications throughout the valley.

Rock Creek and Little Lakes Valley

As U.S. 395 heads east away from Crowley Lake, it climbs several hundred feet to a spot known as **Toms Place** (el. 7,072 feet). Tom Yerby was a fisherman who operated a resort here in the 1920s. While fishermen still make this a destination, hikers regard Toms Place as the turnoff for Rock Creek Road, where the pavement reaches a greater elevation than it does anywhere else in the Sierra Nevada. The end of the road is at 10,200 feet. From the trailhead at this place, known as Mosquito Flat, hikers access a vast network of high-country trails through the John Muir Wilderness. Backpackers hefting their loads at the trailhead may be aiming their steps toward 12,040-foot **Mono Pass** on a quest to travel the John Muir Trail. (Note: This is not to be confused with another Mono Pass, on the southeast side of Yosemite National Park.) From Mosquito Flat, day hikers can wander up the fairly level trail to the pristine glacial trough of Little Lakes Valley, where the lakes reflect the stunning granitic forms of **Mount Mills** (el. 13,468 feet), **Mount Abbott** (el. 13,715 feet), **Mount Dade** (el. 13,600 feet), and **Bear Creek Spire** (el. 13,713 feet).

My first sight of the Little Lakes Valley came in the mid-1980s during an overnight cross-country ski outing from Rock Creek Lodge. At the time, the lodge maintained a couple of wood-heated yurts in the Little Lakes Valley for those who wanted to spend a night in the backcountry. The weather was ideal. Heavy snow preceded our visit, and the days were bright and typically mild. We skied in shirtsleeves through the deep powder around the lakes.

The following winter we returned to find the eastern Sierra in a deep freeze and nearly barren of snow. The year proved to be worrisome for

Skiers' view of Bear Creek Spire (left) and the Little Lakes Valley. Photo by Mark Middlebrook

California's coastal population and agricultural communities. The Sierra snowpack is key to the viability of Central and Southern California's ever-expanding population, and the pressure to build new dams mounts even as the wisdom behind more dam building is questioned.

Practical Matters

U.S. 395 is kept open year-round, although chains are sometimes required, and extreme winter weather conditions can make the route temporarily impassable. The climate of this area on the rim of the Great Basin is high desert — very dry with large temperature fluctuations seasonally and even daily. Most precipitation falls as snow in the winter months, and side roads into the range may remain snowbound into June, although spring, when the desert regions turn green, can provide stunning vistas. The weather in summer can be glorious, but watch out for sudden thunderstorms. In the high mountain regions, wildflowers bloom all summer long, and the changing of the aspens to gold in early to mid October

(opposite) Bear Creek Spire from the Little Lakes Valley. Photo by Erlda Parker

makes autumn an especially appealing time to visit. For more on Sierra weather, including climate statistics for Bridgeport and Mammoth Lakes, see the introduction.

ROADS

This tour follows U.S. 395 for 110 miles through California's Mono County. Visitors might start out on U.S. 395 from Reno, Nevada, (see chapter 1), or Highway 89 from Lake Tahoe (see chapter 2). Highway 108 (see chapter 3) or Highway 120 (see chapter 8) are possible approaches as well. Travelers coming from Southern California or Las Vegas, Nevada, or those who might want to reverse the itinerary, should begin by reading chapter 5. The closest commercial airport to this region is Reno, Nevada.

WHERE TO STAY AND EAT

In the northern part of this route, a handful of lodging and dining options can be found at Bridgeport, Lee Vining, and a few of the smaller towns. In the June Lake and Mammoth Lakes areas, there is a profusion of lodging and dining options. Convict Lake and the Rock Creek Road area have memorable resort lodges.

CAMPING

Several roadside campgrounds can be found in the area of the Highway 108/U.S. 395 junction, but drive even a short distance up into the mountains, and there are far more to choose from. Most are located on the following roads: Twin Lakes Road (Bridgeport); Virginia Lakes Road (Conway Summit); Lundy Lake Road (northwest of Mono Lake); and Tioga Pass Road (Highway 120 into Yosemite). The larger June Lake and Mammoth Lakes areas offer a huge choice of campgrounds, from vast lakeside spreads to rustic sites hidden away in the forest. Nearly a dozen campgrounds can be found between Toms Place and Mosquito Flat on Rock Creek Road. Wilderness permits, available through Forest Service ranger stations, are required for camping outside of established campgrounds. National forests in this region are the Humbolt-Toiyabe National Forest (north of Mono Lake) and Inyo National Forest (south of Mono Lake). Wilderness areas accessed from U.S. 395 in the Mono County region include: Hoover Wilderness (near Mono Lake), Ansel Adams Wilderness (near Mammoth Lakes), and John Muir Wilderness (Mammoth Lakes and south.)

U.S. FOREST SERVICE

Humboldt-Toiyabe National Forest (www.fs.fed.us/r4/htnf/): **Bridgeport Ranger District,** U.S. 395, Bridgeport, 760–932–7070.

VISITORS BUREAUS

Mammoth Lakes Visitors Bureau, www.visitmammoth.com, Highway 203, Mammoth, 888–466–2666, 760–934–2712.

Mono Basin National Forest Scenic Area Visitor Center, Lee Vining, 760–647–3044.

REGIONAL GUIDES

Clark, Ginny. *Guide to Highway 395 — Los Angeles to Reno.* Lake Havasu City, Ariz.: Western Trails Publications, 1997.

Leadabrand, Russ. *Exploring California Byways VI.* Ward Ritchie Press, 1972.

Schlenz, Mark A. (Photography by Dennis Flaherty). *Exploring the Eastern Sierra — California and Nevada.* Bishop, Calif.: Companion Press, 2003.

Smith, Genny, ed. *Sierra East, Edge of the Great Basin.* Berkeley and Los Angeles: University of California Press, 2000.

OWENS VALLEY REGION

5

U.S. 395: Owens Valley

Owens Valley is a land of both superlative geographic statistics and infamous environmental controversies. For some, this landscape can seem harsh and desolate, but others sense only mystery and grandeur in the myriad muted shades of the rocks, the finely wrought shape of each tiny stem, leaf, and flower that reaches toward the blinding sun, and the pulsing, soothing hum of a soundscape nearly devoid of human interference. Here is the experience of tranquility and connection to nature that brings so many of us to the Sierra in the first place. Those who stay a while in the Owens Valley, or who climb from here into the roadless High Sierra, cannot help but feel a vast expansion of the soul.

Ice Age Owens Valley

When prehistoric humans first looked in on the Owens Valley, around 10,000 years ago, the surrounding 14,000-foot-high peaks were reflected on the icy waters of a vast lake that filled the Owens Basin at that time. This Ice Age lake was but one of a string of stair-step, or paternoster lakes fed by runoff from the waning Pleistocene glaciers. Geologists surmise that the raging flow of ice melt down the course of the Owens River may have ended in a gigantic lake in the location of what is now Death Valley. Pleistocene era artifacts found at various sites along this former lake chain include stone choppers, scrapers, and projectile points, plus one of the most impressive displays of prehistoric rock art found anywhere in North America.

Today, if we were to stand in a spot where a prehistoric hunter might have knapped obsidian into arrowheads on the shore of Ice Age Lake Owens, we will be high above the present lake's 3,600-foot surface elevation, looking down at the reflection of the sky rippling in shallow salty pools on the dry lakebed below. Most visitors will not be thinking about the prehistoric hunter, however. More likely, they will be recalling scenes from the classic Hollywood film *Chinatown* or Marc Reisner's book *Cadillac Desert*. Both provide interesting accounts of how Owens Lake went dry before its time, as its tributary waters were diverted to the faucets of a growing Los Angeles metropolitan area.

The Los Angeles Aqueduct runs along part of that Pleistocene stair step of lakes, taking the precious mountain water a total of 223 miles through channels, conduits, pipelines, and tunnels from the Mono Basin to Los Angeles. At its head, the aqueduct taps the eastern Sierra snowmelt from four of the seven creeks that flow into Mono Lake. From there it continues into the Owens Valley, picking up most of the water flowing into the Owens River just south of Big Pine. The Los Angeles Department of Water and Power (LADWP) began this stunning heist in 1905 with a systematic buy-up of the land parcels through which the tributaries run, convincing many landowners along the eastern escarpment that the project would benefit the local agricultural interests. The farmers found out otherwise. Today, the landscape looks barren, but it is important to ask ourselves what the Owens Valley would look like now had the water not been diverted. Owens Lake would still be a great alkaline pool like Mono Lake, instead of a dry salt flat, but the entire valley might be covered in a great urban sprawl like . . . say . . . Los Angeles. Instead, this arid land has become the entryway to an unparalleled recreation area, with intriguing remnants of several lost cultures and small pockets of living ones in widely spaced oases along this long-distance trucking route.

Down the Sherwin Grade

U.S. 395 begins its 3,000-foot descent into the Owens Valley at Sherwin Summit (el. 7,000 feet), running between Rock Creek and the Owens

The Los Angeles Aqueduct on Bishop Creek Road. The town of Bishop and the White Mountains can be seen in the distance.

River into the relatively lush **Round Valley,** where alfalfa grows today, thanks to a few ranchers who held out against the LADWP a century ago. Ahead to the west and south are Wheeler Ridge, Pine Creek Canyon, and lofty **Mount Tom** (el. 13,652 feet).

To the east is the **Volcanic Tableland of Bishop Tuff,** a 500-foot-thick blanket of rhyolitic ash that flowed rapidly as a *nuée ardente* (burning cloud) from the Long Valley Caldera eruption about 760,000 years ago. The Owens River runs through a deep gorge, which was carved out of the tuff as glacial waters spilled over the lip of the Long Valley Caldera in a raging torrent during the Pleistocene era.

The Bishop tuff. Photo courtesy of U.S. Geological Service

Today, the gorge is a mecca for rock climbers, while those with an interest in anthropology are more likely to be drawn to the tableland's eastern edge, where buff-colored cliffs contain a prehistoric record of early human activity carved into the rock as petroglyphs. The images of bear, deer, bighorn sheep, lizards, birds, and human beings are accompanied by geometrical designs that may represent maps or calculations of various sorts. Regardless of their meaning, one senses in these images a vastly different human interaction with the natural world. Signs pointing to these impressive rock art sites have been removed because of an ongoing concern over vandalism of this precious repository. Those who visit these sites must take great care not to disturb or alter them in any way.

Before heading into Bishop, take a short side trip north and east on U.S. 6, crossing the Owens River into the tiny community of Laws (el. 4,113 feet). It is here at the **Laws Railroad Museum and Historic Site** that the memory of the valley's beloved Slim Princess is best preserved. The Slim Princess was the familiar name for the Carson & Colorado Railroad, a narrow-gauge passenger and freight line that ran from Carson City, Nevada, (east of Lake Tahoe) south to Keeler (on Owens Lake) from the 1880s into the mid-20th century.

Bishop (el. 4,147 feet)

With a population pushing the 3,500 mark, Bishop is second in size only to Mammoth Lakes on the U.S. 395 California corridor. But unlike Mammoth Lakes, with its sprawl of condos and strip malls, Bishop maintains its rugged Old West persona. The ranching and packing industries are well represented throughout the summer at the Tri-County Fairgrounds, with the packers' famous Mule Days celebration on Memorial Day weekend, the Tri-County Fair on Labor Day weekend, and several rodeos in between. By mid-September, crowds move west to Millpond County Park for the popular Millpond Music Festival.

Many visitors arrive in Bishop (as I did one hot summer's day) with a desperate yearning to wash the dust and sweat of the trail from their clothing and person. At several Bishop laundromats visitors can take care of the two tasks simultaneously. Once these basic needs are fulfilled, hikers generally find their way to North Main Street to restock their Sierra-subject book collection and recreational gear, check their email, and wash down Lithuanian pastry with some cappuccino.

Petroglyphs on the eastern edge of the Volcanic Tableland of Bishop Tuff, with the White Mountains in the background. Photo by Erlda Parker

Fremont cottonwoods (*Populus fremontii*) reaching their autumn splendor in the Owens Valley near Bishop. Photo by Erlda Parker

UP BISHOP CREEK CANYON

The stoplight at West Line Street (Highway 168) in the center of town marks the only intersection holding much significance for visitors. A turn to the west on West Line leads into the Bishop Indian Reservation, where one can become better acquainted with the rich heritage of the Owens Valley's Native American populations at the **Paiute Shoshone Cultural Center and Museum.**

As Highway 168 continues west it becomes Bishop Creek Road, and the sloping sagebrush wilderness again opens out in its unrelenting expanse below the fractured Sierra skyline. On the south side of the road, an historical marker pokes up out of the sage, drawing attention with its base of brightly colored local rocks: chunks of a brilliant turquoise-colored ore, milky quartz, red-and-white-swirled travertine, fossils from the Coso shale, and black obsidian glass. The bronze plaque gives recognition to the 1862 battle of Bishop Creek, a land dispute between white settlers and the resident Paiute-Shoshone.

As the good paved ribbon of Highway 168 makes its southwesterly climb into the folds of the high mountain kingdom, unpaved Buttermilk Road (7S01) splinters off due west into the dry, boulder-strewn hills of the

Buttermilk Country. If the name presents some puzzlement, given this sere landscape, it might help to imagine this landscape before the LADWP creek diversions. Settlers here grazed their cattle on the lush grasslands of McGee and Horton creeks, producing exceptional dairy products. Today, the terrain of giant-rounded boulders draws the attention of the large local rock climbing community.

Highway 168 switches back into the bed of Bishop Creek, and then follows the creek's north fork to 9,128 feet at **Lake Sabrina** (pronounced *Sabry-na,* not *Sa-bree-na*). Fishermen head from the lake to myriad smaller lakes fed by perennial snowfields of the Evolution group of 13,000-foot peaks to the west. About a mile before Lake Sabrina, the dirt road to **North Lake** climbs out of the canyon to the north, leading to more enticing little lakes and the five-mile trail to 11,423-foot Piute Pass, gateway to the extraordinary Humphreys Basin (see chapter 7).

Several miles back on Highway 168, South Lake Road takes off due south through the aspen-lined canyon of Bishop Creek's south fork. The first time I made this trip, I arrived with my backpacking companions at **South Lake** (el. 9,755 feet) when its vast amphitheater of towering granite had just been washed by a series of summer thunderstorms, and tattered shreds of storm clouds and a dusting of new snow still clung to the high peaks. With the dark **Inconsolable Range** on our left, we headed toward 11,972-foot **Bishop Pass** with some trepidation about the stormy weather, hurrying past patches of monkshood and colonies of Belding's ground squirrels that whistled a warning to each other of an alien presence. We climbed the switchbacks through a glacial moraine studded with white columbine, and dropped over the pass into the shallow, granite-lined bowl of upper **Dusy Basin.** There we set up camp beside a stream running through a fractured slab of leopard-spotted granite. We camped in this garden of glaciated delights for several days, making excursions to **Knapsack Pass** and to **Thunderbolt Pass,** where the menfolk contemplated an assault on 14,003-foot **Thunderbolt Peak,** a black granitic giant charged through with bold, gray intrusions. During our stay, we observed yellow-bellied marmots, yellow-legged frogs, yellow-throated warblers, and a variegated stream of humans, including flocks of climbers, a famous photographer, two biology majors studying the frogs, and Sam, a packer from Rainbow Pack Station. Sam introduced us to his beloved coworkers, the mules, and told us about his education at **Deep Springs College,** an institute of higher learning that is also a working cattle ranch run by the students. The college is located in the White-Inyo Mountains on the opposite side of the Owens Valley, east of Westgard Pass on Highway 168.

Bishop to Big Pine

Along the 15-mile stretch of U.S. 395 from Bishop to Big Pine, there will be few enticements to deviate from the main highway, except perhaps to go for a soak at **Keough Hot Springs** or to get a close-up look at the big dishes of the Caltech Owens Valley Radio Observatory to the east. You might take advantage of the lull to ponder the origins of this sublime landscape.

Like the Lake Tahoe Basin, the Owens Valley is a graben, a block of the earth's crust that has dropped while the mountain ranges on either side

Seen from left to right, Mounts Agassis, Winchell, and Thunderbolt; North Palisade; and Isosceles Peak, as seen from Dusy Basin. Photo by Kit Duane

of it have risen. In the Owens Valley, movement along the complex series of parallel faults is both vertical and horizontal. Many 10- to 20-foot-high embankments can be found along the fault scarps, but even more illustrative of the earth movement are the jagged courses of many Owens Valley creeks; with each horizontal slip of the fault block, the creeks must search anew for their errant channels.

The long ridge to the east of Owens Valley is one range with two names, the **White and Inyo Mountains**, often contracted into White-Inyo Mountains. The highest point along this range, White Mountain Peak, reaches up to 14,246 feet, rivaling the highest peaks of the Sierra Nevada to the west. Like the Sierra, the White-Inyo Mountains have a batholith of granitic rock at their core. However, the eastern range looks quite different, primarily because it was not as deeply carved during the glaciation of the ice ages. Its granitic rock lies beneath a thicker layer of ancient host rocks, many of them of sedimentary origin: sandstone, slate, limestone, and dolomite. It is the dolomite that provides the perfect growth medium for the uniquely magnificent Western bristlecone pine.

Many speak of a visit to the **Ancient Bristlecone Pine Forest** as a transcendent experience, and, indeed, there is something sublime about being at timberline (around 10,000 feet in this locale) and in the presence of trees that are as old as 4,000 years, said to be the oldest living things on earth. As young trees, the bristlecone pine are unremarkable, but as they age their gnarled and twisted roots, trunks, and branches form fantastic sculptures in shades of off-white, gold, russet brown, and black, joined in old age with increasing portions of silvery-gray dead wood. The living branch tips are lined with short bundles of stiff, dark-green needles in clumps of five. In this arrangement of needles, we can see the tree's kinship with the foxtail pine found across the valley in the Sierra Nevada.

To visit the bristlecone pine forest, you will need to go at a time when the region is not cut off by snow. Turn east on Westgard Pass Road (Highway 168) north of Big Pine and drive about 13 miles in the direction of Westgard Pass. Before reaching the pass you will turn north on White Mountain Road and take a long and winding 10-mile drive to reach the **Schulman Grove Visitor Center.** On arriving at this welcoming cluster of buildings, some visitors are surprised to find that there is no running water or gasoline available, so it is important to plan accordingly. Also, be

aware that you have ascended from 4,000 to 10,000 feet in a very short time. Watch for any symptoms of altitude sickness (see the introduction), and consider taking the four-mile **Methuselah Walk** to the grove's oldest trees in the cool hours of morning to avoid heat exhaustion on a hot summer's day.

On returning via White Mountain Road to Highway 168, be sure to stop at the **Sierra View Overlook** for the marvelous views west toward the Sierra Nevada and the Owens Valley. Even if you do not take the time to stop at the lookout, there are many opportunities to observe from the car window the dirty patches of snow clinging high up on the northeast flanks of a group of Sierra peaks known as the **Palisades.** One of these snow patches is the **Palisade Glacier,** the largest glacier in the Sierra Nevada. While it might be romantic to think that this is a remnant of the great glaciers that reshaped the Sierra in the ice ages, the Palisade Glacier is actually much younger, perhaps no more than 200 years old, and was formed in a recent cool period.

For those who feel the urge to touch the glacier, it is easy enough to drive to within day-hiking distance of the Palisade Glacier. A night at one of the campgrounds on **Glacier Lodge Road** would provide a good, early start. But visitors who choose to explore the glacier should do so with knowledge and the right equipment, as this type of mountaineering poses unique challenges. As I have no desire to find myself at the bottom of a crevasse, a long summer's afternoon spent exploring the water gardens below one of the perennial snowfields would be quite sufficient.

From Big Pine to Independence

South of Big Pine is a stark volcanic landscape pocked with red cinder cones and fields of black basaltic lava rock. According to the Paiutes, this is where the sun got dumped into a pit after losing a contest with the moon. A stony eminence standing just east of the Sierra crest, **Mount Tinemaha** (el. 12,561 feet) is named for a legendary leader of the Paiutes. The chief gazes southeast across the valley toward his brother, the brave **Winnedumah,** an 8,389-foot-high, thumb-like monolith atop the Inyo

(opposite) An ancient bristlecone pine tree in the White Mountains. Photo by Erlda Parker

The Palisade Glacier as seen from the White Mountains. Photo by Erlda Parker

Mountains. The Paiutes say that Winnedumah was turned to stone so that he could keep watch over his people.

While driving between the two stone chiefs, you might catch sight of the local herd of **tule elk** waiting out a hot afternoon among the tall grasses of the marshy riverbed or corralled into an irrigated field. This elk species is not native to the Owens Valley. They were introduced from the San Joaquin and Sacramento valleys, where vast herds of them once grazed on the grasses of the marshy channels, called *tulares*. The explosion of the human population at the time of the California Gold Rush brought rampant hunting of the elk and draining of the marshes for agricultural use, leading the species to the brink of extinction. Small herds now are being nurtured in a couple of Central Valley preserves, but the Owens Valley herds represent a significant portion of the total population.

Along the 28-mile stretch of U.S. 395 between Big Pine and Independence are two fish hatcheries, two tiny communities, and roads leading to the trailheads for three notably grueling climbs to the Sierra crest. The northernmost of these three trailheads is on Taboose Creek Road, west of the tiny town of **Aberdeen** (el. 3,906 feet), the site of the Los Angeles

JOHN MUIR INVESTIGATES A GLACIER

Cautiously picking my way, I gained the top of the moraine and was delighted to see a small but well characterized glacier swooping down from the gloomy precipices of Black Mountain in a finely graduated curve to the moraine on which I stood. The compact ice appeared on all the lower portions of the glacier, though gray with dirt and stones embedded in it. Farther up the ice disappeared beneath coarse granulated snow. The surface of the glacier was further characterized by dirt bands and the outcropping edges of the blue veins, showing the laminated structure of the ice. The uppermost crevasse, or "bergschrund," where the névé was attached to the mountain, was from 12 to 14 feet wide, and was bridged in a few places by the remains of snow avalanches. Creeping along the edge of the schrund, holding on with benumbed fingers, I discovered clear sections where the bedded structure was beautifully revealed. The surface snow, though sprinkled with stones shot down from the cliffs, was in some places almost pure, gradually becoming crystalline and changing to whitish porous ice of different shades of color, and this again changing at a depth of 20 or 30 feet to blue ice, some of the ribbon-like bands of which were nearly pure, and blended with the paler bands in the most gradual and delicate manner imaginable. A series of rugged zigzags enabled me to make my way down into the weird underworld of the crevasse. Its chambered hollows were hung with a multitude of clustered icicles, amid which pale, subdued light pulsed and shimmered with indescribable loveliness. Water dripped and tinkled overhead, and from far below came strange, solemn murmurings from currents that were feeling their way through veins and fissures in the dark. The chambers of a glacier are perfectly enchanting, notwithstanding one feels out of place in their frosty beauty. I was soon cold in my shirtsleeves, and the leaning wall threatened to engulf me; yet it was hard to leave the delicious music of the water and the lovely light. Coming again to the surface, I noticed boulders of every size on their journeys to the terminal moraine—journeys of more than a hundred years, without a single stop, night or day, winter or summer.

The sun gave birth to a network of sweet-voiced rills that ran gracefully down the glacier, curling and swirling in their shining channels, and cutting clear sections through the porous surface-ice into the solid blue, where the structure of the glacier was beautifully illustrated.

—from *The Mountains of California*, John Muir

Aqueduct's uptake of the Owens River. From this trailhead, it's a climb of 8.75 miles with nearly 6,000 feet of elevation gain to reach **Taboose Pass** at el. 11,366 feet. Three miles south of Aberdeen, at the end of Division Creek Road, is the trailhead for **Sawmill Pass** (el. 11,347 feet); the climb to the pass is 13.5 miles with an elevation gain of 6,749 feet. Prospects are no easier farther south at North Oak Creek Road (near the Mount Whitney Fish Hatchery), where the hike to **Baxter Pass** (el. 12,320 feet) is 14.2 miles long with 6,299 feet in elevation gain.

Liberating myself of the notion that I needed to go on foot through each of these passes in order to gain the right to write about them, I grabbed my most enthusiastic hiking partner and headed for Baxter Pass. Starting out at 6,040 feet from the **Oak Creek trailhead,** we traversed a glacial moraine decorated with the spider-like skeletons of dead sagebrush before dropping down into the groves of aspen and California black oak that line the creek bed. We had traveled a full mile up the trail before the oak trees finally gave way to pinyon, white fir, and a scattering of beavertail cactus. At a pretty creek crossing, we made the acquaintance of a little yellow bat. He came in for a daytime drink as we filtered out our own fresh beverage from the creek. On ahead, we marveled at the fine banquet awaiting the bears in a dense thicket of elderberry, currant, gooseberry, and bitter cherry, and having brought only some dried prunes and cheese sticks, we were sorely tempted to ravage the bears' feast. However, since we do not look kindly on the bears when they raid our own food, we decided it was only fair to leave the berries for the bears, and so as not to go hungry, we decided to turn back. On our return to the car after the three-hour hike, we checked the map to find that we had made it barely a quarter of the way to the pass. It seemed abundantly clear why backpackers and mule packers alike might prefer the high trailhead at **Onion Valley** (el. 9,200 feet) through 11,823-foot **Kearsarge Pass** farther south.

To reach that trailhead, turn west onto Onion Valley Road at the center of the tiny town of **Independence.** The well-paved route follows Independence Creek for 15 miles to Onion Valley, achieving its destination by a most impressive switchback ascent. The Forest Service campground at the popular Onion Valley trailhead is perhaps the most beautiful in the Sierra. Here I have spent enchanted days in a grove of young aspen, elegant white fir, and tousled foxtail pine, with waterfalls crashing down from stony gray ramparts on either side of the valley. The broad wedge of sky to the east fills with golden dawn in the morning, and the smaller high wedge above Kearsarge Pass turns magenta as dusk transforms to velvety, star-spangled night.

On the first steps up the trail to Kearsarge Pass, the aroma of wild onions plunges up the nostrils, while a moment later, the soothing scent of yarrow or sage rights the senses. Many of the foxtail pines on the rocky ledges have twisted into fantastic sculptures reminiscent of the foxtail's kin, the bristlecone pine in the neighboring White-Inyo Mountains. The lush vegetation dwindles as the trail threads through

Morning sun on the south palisade above Onion Valley.

a huge glacial moraine with a magnificent assortment of granitic boulders — some a dazzling white, peppered with large black oblong laths of amphibole, others a chaste pink, rich in feldspar. The cleft surfaces of some rocks are glazed with sugary green olivine or waxy serpentine. Others are shot through with inclusions and dikes that create jaunty patterns of spots and stripes. One feels the urge to take these treasures home, but there are two perfectly good reasons not to: the weight will make the hike miserable, and it is against the law to remove public property from its natural setting.

One day as I happened by, a Forest Service trail-building crew was prying a huge boulder out of the steep slope. As it was released from its age-old bed, this boulder rolled down perhaps 100 feet, crash-landing almost precisely where the crew intended to place it as a part of their new retaining wall. This same hard-working band had just finished refurbishing a nearby trail in an area set aside to protect the regal and reclusive **bighorn sheep.**

While hiking the trails around Onion Valley, I imagined myself on the very mountain "streets" that the writer Mary Austin spoke of in her book of essays entitled *The Land of Little Rain,* which she wrote in 1903 while living in Independence. A marker in front of her home at 253 West Market Street still bears her welcome, although she is no longer there: "But if ever you come beyond the borders as far as the town that lies in a hill dimple at the foot of Kearsarge, never leave it until you have knocked at the door of the brown house under the willow tree at the end of the village street, and there you shall have such news of the land, of its trails and what is astir in them, as one lover of it can give to another."

Visitors who have fallen in love with the eastern Sierra as a whole will want to visit the **Eastern California Museum,** located on the western edge of Independence at the corner of Grant Street and West Market (the Onion Valley Road). The museum was established in 1928 for the purpose of preserving a history of Indian cultures and pioneer life in this region. Look for artifacts and photographs from Mary Austin's era, when El Camino Sierra (the Sierra Road — predecessor of U.S. 395) was first being constructed.

Manzanar National Historic Site

Memories of one deeply troubled moment in the region's past are preserved six miles southeast of Independence at the site of an abandoned orchard that was turned into an internment camp during World War II. At that time, the U.S. government concluded that Japanese Americans and resident Japanese aliens posed too great a danger to society to leave them unmonitored, and so thousands of people were incarcerated in internment camps. Ordinary businessmen, shopkeepers, teachers, and even little children were torn from peaceful, productive lives to wait out the war in confinement. The 800-acre Manzanar National Historic Site offers visitors a three-mile driving tour of the camp's grounds. All that is left are the camp's concrete foundations, ruined water system, and cemetery, but some visitors to this site still come seeking memories from their own childhoods.

Lone Pine and Surrounds (el. 3,733 feet)

According to *Historic Spots in California,* an engaging history guide first published by Stanford University Press in 1932, the eponymous lone pine tree of Lone Pine blew down in a storm in 1876. For years before that, the tree served as a landmark and meeting spot for white settlers and Indians alike. The demise of the tree followed on the heels of the destruction of the original adobe settlement in an earthquake on March 26, 1872. The tremor registered 8.3 on the Richter scale, making it the strongest earthquake in California's recorded history. Twenty-seven people died as Lone Pine's adobe buildings collapsed and the Owens Valley graben dropped 20 feet. The fault scarp along the western edge of town and some adobe fragments preserved just off Main Street still give testimony to the dramatic event, but these are not what most folks go looking for on their initial visit to Lone Pine.

MOUNT WHITNEY (el. 14,505 feet)
The universal obsession with Lone Pine newcomers is to discover which of the many tall spires clustered on the western horizon is **Mount Whitney,** the highest spot in the contiguous United States. Arranged in a spread of approximately 12 miles on either side of it are **Mount Langley** (el. 14,022 feet), **Mount Russell** (el. 14,086 feet), **Mount Tyndall** (el. 14,019 feet), and **Mount Williamson** (el. 14,373 feet), along with dozens of peaks that reach above 13,000 feet. For some years, a big arrow pointing to Mount Whitney could be found painted on the sidewalk at the southwestern corner of Main Street and Whitney Portal Road (better-known as the intersection with the only stoplight in Lone Pine). This public works project might have appeared condescending to the greenhorns, but any Lone Pine regular will tell you that Whitney is not all that easy to pick out from the group of high pointy places to the west. The famous mountaineer and geologist Clarence King mistakenly climbed other mountains twice before he finally stood atop the windswept giant in 1873. Even then, King was unable to claim the first ascent, since a couple of fishermen out on a lark had bagged it a month earlier.

Thousands of people come to Lone Pine every summer to mark an ascent (or even a sighting) of Mount Whitney in their personal record books. Though a climb is usually done as a multi-day backpacking trip, it has become quite popular of late to go up the crowded 11-mile trail and back down (that makes 22 miles) all on the same day. Given the 6,000-foot elevation gain, it is not uncommon to see unacclimatized day hikers

Whitney Portal Road makes a switchback ascent to the Mount Whitney trailhead. From this east-side perspective, Mount Russell (the high point on the right) appears to be taller than Mount Whitney (the two horns to its left).

retching from altitude sickness near the top. But even these pitiful souls will usually say it is worth it, just to say they did it. The view from the top is astounding, but then, so are the views from many Sierra peaks.

ALABAMA HILLS
Slung low in the foreground of Mount Whitney is a reddish terrain of granitic rock that juts up from the earth in rounded and stacked lobes, slabs,

BAGGING MOUNT WHITNEY, CIRCA 1864

The impressive height of the Sierra rooftop was only a matter of speculation until the summer of 1864, when the California State Geological Survey moved its study into the High Sierra. The survey was commissioned in 1860 under the direction of Josiah D. Whitney, but by 1864, Whitney had left the direction of the survey's fieldwork to a very able natural scientist named William H. Brewer. Brewer's loyal team of assistants included Charles F. Hoffmann, Clarence King, James T. Gardner, and a packer named Richard Cotter. Together, this band rambled all over the state for four years, sampling, charting, and generally exploring its prominent features.

The project was plagued with a perennial lack of funding, which, combined with the primitive and unwieldy nature of the party's equipment, made the endeavor more a labor of love than a means for employment. For Clarence King it would become a passionate adventure as he became one of the Sierra's foremost early mountaineers, competing with those attempting to bag the first ascents.

Brewer kept a journal during his years on the Survey, which came to be published under the title *Up and Down California in 1860–1864*. On June 20, 1864, after surmounting 9,594-foot Shell Mountain in an area on the west side known today as the Jennie Lakes Wilderness, he wrote: "The view was grand—on the west the whole slope of the Sierra and the great plain, ending in haze— around us the roughest region imaginable—along in front the crest of the Sierra, its more prominent points not less than twelve thousand feet high, with rocks, precipices, pinnacles, canyons, and all the elements to make a sublime landscape."

From this vantage point, Brewer would have been looking east, at the Great Western Divide, where the peaks, in fact, exceed 13,500 feet. Two weeks later, he would make the first recorded ascent of the 13,570-foot giant that would be given his name, Mount Brewer, and from there he would see the higher crest of fourteeners. One of these peaks would have been Mount Whitney, at 14,494 feet the highest peak in the contiguous United States. Brewer might even have seen the White-Inyo Mountains across the Owens Valley to the east. If the day had been less hazy, he might have seen the Coast Range to the west. "Such a landscape! A hundred peaks in sight over thirteen thousand feet—many very sharp—deep canyons, cliffs in every direction . . . sharp ridges almost inaccessible to man, on which human foot had never trod—all combined to produce a view the sublimity of which is rarely equaled, one which few are privileged to behold."

It is interesting that Brewer underestimated the height of the highest peaks, as misjudgment continued to plague the attempts of his assistant, Clarence King, to identify and climb the Sierra's highest peak. King's pursuit of this goal began on July 4, 1864, as he and his companion Richard Cotter took off from the surveying party to explore the cluster of high peaks. They returned five days later, having made the first recorded ascent of 14,019-foot Mount Tyndall. From the top of Tyndall they identified what they believed to be the highest peak of the group, and named it Mount Whitney in honor of the Survey's chief. A few days later, they returned with the intention of scaling Whitney, but were unable to find a route to the top. Seven years later, King made another attempt. As he stood in storm clouds at his destination, declaring himself to be the first to reach the Sierra's highest peak, he was in fact at the top of 14,022-foot Mount Langley. It would be another two years before he would learn of his mistake and then it would be too late to claim the laurel of making the Whitney first ascent, as a group of fishermen had preceded him there. Today, thousands hike to the top every year following a relatively easy trail up the south ridge.

Sniffing out the scene in the Alabama Hills.

and blocks, with spreading, north-south–trending joints that form end-less, perplexing, narrow corridors. The spot looks like the set for a Holly-wood Western, and indeed it is. The Alabama Hills have served as a film-ing location since the 1920 silent film *The Roundup,* with Fatty Arbuckle. In the heyday of the Hollywood Western, the likes of John Wayne, Gene Autry, and Errol Flynn rode among the boulders. Businesses in Lone Pine that served the industry, like the charmingly kitsch **Dow Villa Motel**, at 310 South Main Street, appear frozen in time, still exuding the rambunctious naiveté of Hollywood's depiction of the Old West.

As if in conspiracy to further the popular misunderstanding of the region's history, tourism promoters once called the Alabamas "the Earth's oldest hills." In fact, they are only as old as the Sierra Nevada (which they are a part of), but they have weathered differently than their lofty overlords as a result of their low, desert location. According to Thomas Keough's report in the *Sierra Club Bulletin* (January 1918), the name Alabama came into use in this district in the closing year of the American Civil War. On June 19, 1864, a Union ship, the USS *Kearsarge*, sank a Confederate ship, the CSS *Alabama*, off the coast of France near the town of Cherbourg. That summer, a group of men with Union sympathies were building trail near Onion Valley. They discovered an ore deposit and decided to give the new mining district the appellation Kearsarge as a way to taunt some Rebels working a mining district nearby. The Rebels, in turn, named their district Alabama.

One hot July day at high noon, my companions and I donned our wide-brimmed sun hats and drove the car into the Alabama Hills to investigate. Our holsters full of water bottles, our feet clad in heavy hiking boots against rattlesnake, scorpion, and cactus spines, we relied on the rudimentary map put out by the Lone Pine Chamber of Commerce to navigate the bumpy dirt roads in search of Lone Ranger Canyon. Once in the middle of this enchanted landscape we forgot all about the movies and Lone Ranger Canyon as we communed with the rocks and the sere desert flora in whatever place we happened to be. Among the gorgeous things we found were beautiful rosette arrangements of pink-hearted hedgehog cactus; long-jointed green straws of Mormon tea; a strange-looking wild buckwheat called the desert trumpet, which has an inflated pod and goes by the appropriate Latin name of *eriogónum inflatum*; and of course, the ubiquitous, aromatic sagebrush. We had an uneventful encounter with a rattlesnake, and then wandered between the stone corridors of a narrow wash, finding stranded pools of water in small sandy basins. Looking up at the gathering thunderclouds, we knew this was not the place to be as the heavens threatened to break loose with an afternoon torrent.

(above) Beavertail cactus (*Opuntia basilaris*).

(below) Hedgehog cactus (*Echinocereus engelmannii*).

Owens Lake (el. 3,600 feet)

From Whitney Portal Road in the Alabama Hills, Horseshoe Meadows Road runs south, zigzagging up the barren east face of 10,371-foot Wonoga Peak past firecracker penstemon and exquisite yellow blazing star. A stop at one of the road's broad switchbacks affords a view down into the southern end of Owens Valley, where the most visible effect of the Los Angeles Aqueduct plays out in the bed of dry Owens Lake. A few meager remnant pools of mineral-steeped water, stained red with halophilic bacteria, reflect strands of cloud that streak the vast blue sky. The wind sends up puffs of toxic dust from the lakebed, a situation only recently recognized, which the LADWP is being forced to mitigate by allowing more water into the lake.

It is now hard to imagine that at one time two steamships plied the waters of Owens Lake, taking supplies to the Cerro Gordo silver mine, which is perched at 8,500 feet in the Inyo Mountains above the eastern shore. For two brief decades, the region positively boomed with mining-associated commerce, starting with the first silver claim in the late 1860s. The long slide into obscurity was well under way by the mid-1880s, and became mingled with the general demise of the lake in the early 1900s. The spirit of mining-era civilization in Owens Valley passed away for-

Wild horses at Little Lake, a former resort spot south of Owens Lake.

The fossilized Ice Age riverbed at Fossil Falls.

ever with the dismantling of the Slim Princess (described earlier in this chapter).

Up at the end of **Horseshoe Meadows Road,** three nice campgrounds lure car-camping families to while away summer days in idyllic meadows filled with Indian paintbrush, buttercups, and Sierra shooting stars. But the area is just as likely to lure horseback riders or backpackers headed over 11,200-foot Cottonwood Pass to the Pacific Crest Trail or up into the lake-filled cirques below New Army Pass (el. 12,320 feet). Army Pass (el. 11,475 feet), constructed by U.S. soldiers in the 1890s, was chronically snow choked and difficult to maintain.)

Fossil Falls

At the south end of Owens Lake's dry bed, the highway and the Los Angeles Aqueduct thread in tandem for miles through black, basaltic lava flows pocked with red cinder cones; 500,000- to 20,000-year-old outliers of the volcanic Coso Range to the east. A little more than 20 miles south of the town of Olancha, watch for Red Hill — a prominent red cinder cone on the east side of the highway — and a dirt road that leads toward a quarry on the cone's flank. A spur road turning south from the quarry will be marked for Fossil Falls, a short drive ahead. This is a place where one expects no flowing water, and, indeed, there is none. But the marvelous lacquered bowls and chutes in the black lava rock at Fossil Falls provide evidence of a once-raging torrent. The fossilized streambeds of this Pleistocene epoch river are now dry, but archaeological evidence shows human occupation from 5,000–10,000 years ago along this once verdant waterway. How strange it seems, as we travel through this land where the harsh hand of human progress has remolded the waterways to its own devices, that nature, as if capriciously, has at times done the same.

Practical Matters

Visit the Owens Valley at any time of year. Spring can be spectacular as the desert flora comes into bloom. Summer can be very hot in the valley, but the dry desert conditions make the heat feel quite tolerable. Temperatures are lower in the high mountain regions, and wildflowers there are in bloom throughout the summer. Watch out for thunderstorms, and always be prepared for cold weather in the higher elevations. Autumn can be spectacular, especially when the aspens are changing, but always be prepared for snowfall in the higher elevations. Winters can be brisk, and side trip destinations in the high mountain locations will be inaccessible to automobiles from October through May. For more on Sierra weather, including climate statistics for Bishop and Independence, see the introduction.

ROADS

This tour covers approximately 125 miles on U.S. 395, from the Sherwin Grade in the north to Fossil Falls in the south. There are side trips on Highway 168 into both the Sierra Nevada and White Mountains. Travelers coming from the north should consult the previous chapter for access. Travelers coming from Southern California or Las Vegas, Nevada, will be reversing the itinerary described here. There are no airports with commercial service along this route.

WHERE TO STAY AND EAT

Motels and inns can be found at Bishop, Big Pine, Independence, and Lone Pine. Resort lodges can be found in the high mountain locations of

Bishop Creek and Glacier Lodge Road. The best dining options will be found in the same places.

CAMPING

Along the length of the Owens Valley, campgrounds are found in intriguing spots just off the highway, some in eerie volcanic areas or along willowy creek beds, and many more along the roads leading to the numerous trans-Sierra trailheads. Campsites in the Bishop Creek Road area, and anywhere near Mount Whitney, can be at a premium in summer.

U.S. FOREST SERVICE

Inyo National Forest (www.fs.fed.us/r5/inyo/): **Headquarters,** 351 Pacu Lane, Suite 200, Bishop, 760–873–2400; **White Mountain Ranger Station,** 798 North Main Street, Bishop, 760–873–2500; **Mount Whitney Ranger Station,** 640 South Main Street, Lone Pine, 760–876–6200; **Ancient Bristlecone Pine Forest Visitor Center,** Schulman Grove, White Mountain Road, 760–873–2500.

VISITORS BUREAUS

Eastern Sierra Visitors Center, www.395.com, 163 North Main Street, Bishop, 866–873–9275, 760–873–9275.
Eastern Sierra InterAgency Visitor Center, U.S. 395 at Highway 136, Lone Pine, 760–876–6222.

REGIONAL GUIDES

Clark, Ginny. *Guide to Highway 395 — Los Angeles to Reno.* Lake Havasu City, Ariz.: Western Trails Publications, 1997.

Leadabrand, Russ. *Exploring California Byways VI,* Ward Ritchie Press, 1972.

Schlenz, Mark A. (Photography by Dennis Flaherty). *Exploring the Eastern Sierra — California and Nevada.* Bishop, Calif.: Companion Press, 2003.

Smith, Genny, ed. *Sierra East, Edge of the Great Basin.* Berkeley and Los Angeles: University of California Press, 2000.

6

The Southernmost Sierra

Twenty miles south of Mount Whitney, Olancha Peak presses its pale head 12,123 feet into the blue southern Sierra sky. Surrounded by mere 9,900-foot peaks, this lone southern outpost of the Sierra rooftop casts its watch another 80 miles to the south, down the descending granitic backbone of the great range into a softly undulating terrain of desert scrub. The Garlock Fault, where the Sierra batholith comes to its southern end, does not announce itself with any grandeur.

Yet through this descending landscape, the great Kern River rages, fed by the snowfields of the Sierra's highest reaches in Kings Canyon National Park and the Golden Trout Wilderness. South of the Kern River's watershed, only fleeting rains dampen the thirsty ground. The dense conifer forests and stream-threaded meadows of the north give way in the south to brown mounds of weathered rock sprouting ancient and expanding rings of creosote bush and the weirdly wonderful Joshua trees. Gathered in their spindly forests, the Joshua trees reach their bristled arms skyward.

There are few wilderness explorers here in the southernmost Sierra. Rather, one meets a host of bird-watchers, anglers, white-water rafters, hunters, and OHV (off-highway vehicle) enthusiasts, all intent on pursuing their pastimes.

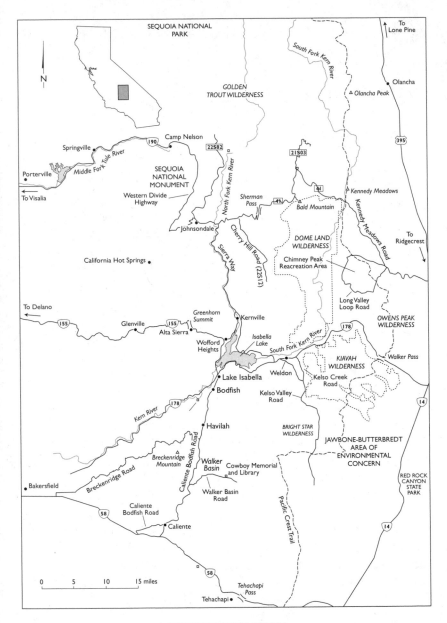

SEQUOIA NATIONAL
PARK

South Fork Kern River

To
Lone Pine

GOLDEN
TROUT WILDERNESS

Olancha

△ Olancha Peak

N

Camp Nelson
190

22582

21503

395

Springville

Middle Fork Tule River

SEQUOIA
NATIONAL
MONUMENT

Kennedy Meadows

Porterville

Western Divide
Highway

41

Sherman
Pass

To Visalia

Johnsondale

North Fork Kern River

Bald Mountain

To
Ridgecrest

California Hot Springs

Cherry Hill Road (22S12)

Sierra Way

DOME LAND
WILDERNESS

Chimney Peak
Reacreation Area

Kennedy Meadows Road

To Delano

Greenhorn
Summit

Kernville

Long Valley
Loop Road

OWENS PEAK
WILDERNESS

155

Glenville

155

Alta Sierra

178

Wofford
Heights

Isabella
Lake

South Fork Kern River

Walker Pass

Lake Isabella

Weldon

KIAVAH
WILDERNESS

Bodfish

Kelso Creek
Road

14

Kern River

178

Havilah

Kelso Valley
Road

Breckenridge
Mountain

Walker
Basin

Cowboy Memorial
and Library

BRIGHT STAR
WILDERNESS

JAWBONE-BUTTERBREDT
AREA OF
ENVIRONMENTAL
CONCERN

Bakersfield

Breckenridge Road

Caliente Bodfish Road

Walker Basin
Road

RED ROCK
CANYON
STATE
PARK

58

Caliente
Bodfish Road

Caliente

Pacific Crest Trail

14

0   5   10   15 miles

58

Tehachapi
Pass

Tehachapi

SOUTHERNMOST SIERRA

Joshua trees in Walker Pass.

From Tehachapi Pass to Isabella Lake

A visitor seeking the southernmost point on the Sierra crest is not likely to be awestruck by natural beauty at **Tehachapi Pass** (el. 4,064 feet). The pass is on a major thoroughfare between Bakersfield at the south end of California's Central Valley and Barstow in the Mojave Desert, and the most remarkable features around are manmade. A field of wind turbines stands to the east of the pass. To the northwest is the Walong railroad loop, where train enthusiasts come hoping to get a shot of a freight train looping over itself. The natural feature that defines the Sierra's southern border, the Garlock Fault, is not readily visible to the untrained eye.

Spanish missionaries moved through the brown, barren-looking Tehachapi Pass region as early as 1776, and by the 1830s, Americano hunters and trappers, including the great trapper/explorer Jedediah Smith, were regularly entering and exiting Alta California via this snow-free southern zone. Traffic through the area picked up significantly a few decades later with the discovery of valuable mineral deposits east of the Sierra.

Most travelers coming from the Bakersfield area enter the southernmost Sierra via Highway 178 along the Kern River. The route offers many enticing picnic spots on the river's tree-shaded banks overlooking the swift green water. Fishermen and river rafters are drawn here throughout the long warm weather season.

As appealing as the river drive can be, our tour into the heart of the southernmost region begins on Highway 58 east of Bakersfield and follows a rugged historic stage route northward for 35 miles before converging with Highway 178.

Like so many back roads through the Sierra, the Caliente Bodfish Road served as a thoroughfare in the mining era, and true to form, its memories drift into a deeper sleep with each passing decade. A few clues to the region's past can be found in historic structures that have been preserved or re-created, and also in the continuity of certain ranching families.

From Highway 58, turn north on Bealville Road, which shortly will merge with Caliente Bodfish Road at the tiny community of Caliente (el. 1,298 feet). Continue north through the switchbacks of Oiler Canyon to the **Walker Basin.**

Although it is much smaller than the Tahoe Basin or the Owens Valley, the Walker Basin is, like them, a graben, a downshifted fault block.

Entrance to the Cowboy Memorial.

The active Breckenridge fault runs along the basin's western border, connecting into a system of other north-south–trending faults that have created the southern Sierra's unique topography and abundant hot springs. Geologists regard the Walker Basin as a significant piece of the Sierra Nevada's puzzle of basins and faults, and as a result, study tours often visit this region. Contact the Bureau of Land Management in Bakersfield to learn about these tours.

Ranchers Walker Rankin and Lavinia Lightner settled in the Walker Basin in 1863. Their descendants still run the **Quarter Circle U Rankin Ranch,** accommodating cattle and sheep, as well as guests who would like to sample the ranching life. The southern Sierra is generally arid, but this lowered plain collects moisture from the surrounding hills, allowing grazing animals to thrive on the basin's grasses.

From the ranch, take a short drive east on Walker Basin Road up Ranchería Creek to a unique, but perhaps ephemeral attraction: the **Cowboy Memorial and Library,** which can be found huddled against the dry hills on the north side of the road. On my visit in March 2003, octogenarian Paul de Fonville was still operating the shrine with his beautiful and equally aged wife, Virginia. This authentic cowboy once broke horses, roped calves, rode the range, and slept under the stars until he was discovered by Hollywood and became part of the cowboy myth. At the Cowboy Memorial, tales of the past can go on long into the starry southern Sierra night.

Return to Caliente Bodfish Road and continue north past the Piute Meadows Trading Post. Travelers with the time to spare might turn west at Breckenridge Road just ahead and drive up the winding mountain road to the top of Breckenridge Mountain (el. 7,548 feet), where there is a lookout tower above a nice campground.

Approximately 10 miles north of the Walker Basin is **Havilah** (el. 3,150 feet), a tiny hamlet with a name from the Good Book: "Havilah, where there is gold; and the gold of that land is good . . ." (Genesis 2:11). In 1866 when Kern County was founded, the thriving settlement of Havilah was made the county seat, but by 1874, Central Valley agriculture had ascended as the true commodity of the region, and so the seat was moved to Bakersfield. Havilah's reconstructed Kern County Courthouse is now a museum.

A reproduction of the old Kern County Courthouse in Havilah. Photo by Erlda Parker

From Havilah, Caliente-Bodfish Road makes a picturesque climb over Hooper Hill and Ball Mountain to arrive at Bodfish (el. 2,680 feet). Continue north to the town of Lake Isabella, which sits beside Isabella Lake, or turn west on Old Kern Canyon Road to descend to the Kern River at one of its most inviting spots. Follow Old Kern Canyon Road southwest down the river, past the Borel Powerhouse, and two miles farther, past the Sandy Flat and Hobo campgrounds. Just beyond is **Miracle Hot Springs,** once a resort, but now a secluded natural sanctuary for clothing-optional bathing. The Forest Service campgrounds make a stay slightly less than primitive, but watch out for the virulent poison oak that flourishes as massive shrubbery.

To continue on to Isabella Lake, return to the powerhouse, take Borel Road across the river to Highway 178, and head northeast on the highway.

Around Isabella Lake (el. 2,581 feet)

Lake Isabella, to hereby dispel further confusion, is the name of the town located at the egress of the Kern River from the reservoir known as Isabella Lake. Here the Kern River plunges over two dams into an impressive gorge to continue its journey to Bakersfield. The first dam was built in 1953, and since that time, the town of Lake Isabella has grown up into a commercial clutter. However, this is *the* place to stock up on supplies, since they will be hard to find in the remote countryside ahead. Lake Isabella (town), with its ranger district office and visitor center housed together near the dams, is also the information center for the region. There are numerous campgrounds right in town, although the more picturesque campgrounds can be found along the west shore and scattered at various points around the lake.

To tour the lake, head north on Highway 155 as it climbs above the west shore, affording a high view over the branching reservoir. At the community of Wofford Heights, seven miles north of the dams, Highway 155 provides a winding escape over the **Greenhorn Mountains** to the Central Valley and the Bakersfield area. Located atop the Greenhorns' ridge are the family-friendly Shirley Meadows Ski Resort and many roads and woodland trails offering endless day hiking to pretty creeks and summit lookouts. It's a surprisingly steep descent back down Highway 155 to the lake, and drivers need to take care to prevent their brakes from overheating.

KERNVILLE (el. 2,706 feet)

Continuing north on Burlando Road along the lake's western shore, watch for signs indicating the site of Old Kernville (once known as Whiskey Flat). Before the dam was built, the town sat here on the west bank of the North Fork Kern River. A few of the original buildings were moved three miles upstream as the site was about to become inundated, and these vintage structures became the anchors for the new village of Kernville. The new town is very tourist-friendly and projects an appealing Old West ambience. Stop into the **Kern Valley Museum** at 49 Big Blue Road to learn more about the town, the valley, the Hollywood Westerns that were filmed here, and the Tubatulabal Indians, whose descendants still live in this region. Shops, restaurants, motels, and resorts are numerous here, with several more resorts upriver to the north.

At Kernville, turn south on Sierra Way for a quiet drive above the lake's largely undeveloped northeastern shores. From high vantage points along this route, the low weathered mountains look like piles of boulders stacked up by a prehistoric giant. Vistas encompass miles of cliffs, coves, and beaches. Colorful sailboats can be seen negotiating past the snags and submerged fences that still mark the former riverbanks of the South and North Kern confluence.

Highway 178 Through Walker Pass

At the western tip of Isabella Lake, Sierra Way crosses over the ingress of the South Fork Kern River to meet Highway 178 in a stunningly lush riparian forest of Fremont cottonwood and willow. Here at Audubon's 3,462-acre **Kern River Preserve** is a world reminiscent of California's Central Valley before all the water diversions and farming began. The habitat is hugely attractive to migrating turkey vultures and supports a stunning diversity of wildlife, with 340 species (nearly 200 nesting) on the preserve's bird list. At the visitor center, which is a little over a mile east of the Sierra Way junction, at 18747 Highway 178 in Weldon, you can pick up a schedule of educational events and workshops held throughout the year at the preserve. Highlights of the program are the annual spring Bioregions Festival and a fall festival in honor of the turkey vulture migration.

Highway 178 continues east along the South Fork Kern on the way to Walker Pass, a trans-Sierra route used in 1834 by explorer Joseph Reddeford Walker, and not rediscovered until the advent of the mining excitement. In fact, the existence of the Kern River proved to be a source of great confusion in 1845, when Walker accompanied John C. Frémont on his famous Third Expedition. Walker mistakenly believed that the Pathfinder already knew of this southernmost river, and so he suggested the junction of the Kern's south and north forks as a place to reconvene after the party split up at Walker Lake in Nevada. As Frémont went west over Donner Pass to Sutter's Fort, Walker went south along the Sierra's eastern escarpment. In his company were an able mountaineer named Richard Owens, for whom the valley, lake, and river would be christened, and a cartographer, Edward M. Kern, for whom the river would be named. The party explored the Owens Valley and moved on to the junction of the

Kern River's forks just after Christmas, at which time they expected to meet Frémont. Instead, Frémont and company were exploring the North Fork Kings River, climbing to a ridge of 11,000 feet to better survey the territory in search of Walker's contingent. "Each was familiar with his own river and knew nothing of the other," wrote Francis P. Farquhar in his *History of the Sierra Nevada*. As mining spread throughout the entire Sierra Nevada region, traffic to and from the Cerro Gordo Mines on the east side of Owens Lake ensured that these routes would become well-defined roadways through the southern Sierra.

Today, the highway through Walker Pass is a modest thoroughfare, with human residents appearing almost as sparse as the vegetation. Historic sights that struggle to survive on tourist services often lose the ability to sustain themselves, and so visitors find places listed in guidebooks, such as the old general store at Onyx, reverting to private establishments. Some of the historic ranches appear to be surviving through the generations, but the land does not offer itself for many commercial uses. By the end of the 20th century, OHV use was proliferating. Fortunately, a few key areas were set apart as protected federal wilderness or areas of critical environmental concern. Kelso Valley Road and Kelso Creek Road, which join heading south from Weldon on Highway 178 near the wildlife center mentioned above, lead into the **Kiavah Wilderness,** the **Bright Star Wilderness,** and the **Jawbone-Butterbredt Area of Environmental Concern,** places where curious travelers might observe the rich desert ecosystem in a state that is only marginally disturbed by human use.

CANEBRAKE CREEK

Highway 178 departs from the South Fork Kern, climbing along Canebrake Creek through a forest of Joshua trees. Watch for the north-tending turnoff for Canebrake Road among the sage scrub. The road leads up some impressive switchbacks beside the Spanish Needles and Lamont Peaks, which point their dark fingers up toward 8,000 feet. This is the back route into the **Chimney Peak Recreation Area.** With its long dirt loop road and campgrounds at two gorgeous creek-side locations, the recreation area is a perfect place for a spring or autumn bicycling adventure.

WALKER PASS (el. 5,280 feet)

At Walker Pass, the Joshua trees register hardly a tremor of their bristling spiky leaves as the incessant wind pulses through the corridor. Pacific Crest Trail hikers leaving the pinyon forests of the **Kiavah Wilderness** to the south cross the highway to continue north into the **Owens Peak Wilderness.** Their next lookout point will be **Morris Peak** (el. 7,215 feet), four and a half miles ahead.

From the pass, Highway 178 descends to Highway 14 through Freeman Canyon, hardly a canyon in appearance, but more of a soft undulation in the spreading terrain. The most notable feature is **Robbers Roost,** a pair of granite "horns" that rise up from the scrub to the south. During the gold era, this was the roost of none other than Tiburcio Vásquez, a bandit who worked the region between Los Angeles and the Cerro Gordo Mines from the early 1850s until 1874, when he was apprehended and then hanged for his crimes. These days, the most dangerous character hanging around the rocks might be a Mojave rattlesnake. Falcons and owls nest here from February through June, and so the Bureau of Land Management restricts access during those months.

The Spanish Needles prick the sky on the south side of the Chimney Peak Recreation Area.

Robbers Roost.

Highway 178 leaves the Sierra Nevada at Freeman Junction in Indian Wells Valley. Travelers bound for Los Angeles should turn south on Highway 14. To the north, Highway 14 meets U.S. 395, which goes north to the Owens Valley or east toward Death Valley.

The Kern Plateau and Route 41

The land north of Highway 178 is known as the Kern Plateau, although the ruggedness of the terrain does not give the appearance of an elevated tableland, as a dictionary definition of plateau would suggest. The Kern River's parallel forks flow southward through this plateau, dropping more than 10,000 feet from the highest headwaters to the confluence in a reservoir known as Isabella Lake. Once past the lake's earthen dams, the Kern makes a mad dash southwest, leaving the mountains to meet an unimpressive end in a dry lake near Bakersfield.

Within a few of the Kern's upper branches, a certain shining treasure swims in its native habitat — the beautiful golden trout, California's state fish. Seen in the water, the fish is a darting sliver of red and gold. Though the golden trout has been introduced to many creeks in the Sierra, it was in the Kern Plateau, in Little Kern River, Golden Trout Creek, and the South Fork Kern River, that this unique trout evolved to its golden hue.

I can liken it to nothing more accurately than a twenty-dollar gold piece, the same satin finish . . .
it melted and glowed as though fresh from the mold . . . I thought then, and have ever since, that
the golden trout . . . is one of the most beautiful fish that swims.

—from *The Mountains,* Stewart Edward White, 1903

This evolution occurred in the Tertiary period (30 million to 3 million years ago), when a few of the trout's rainbow ancestors were stranded in high spots by the uplifting of the range. This venerated fish now presides over a federally protected kingdom of its own, the **Golden Trout Wilderness.** Scores of fishermen come here to pay tribute, but they learn quickly that they must adhere to a specific set of regulations detailing where, when, how, and which size of fish they might take from this wilderness. The regulations even apply to gear, so it is best to contact a fishing or sport shop in the area to get the details. Fines for infractions are heavy.

The **South Fork Kern** arises from within the snows at 11,000 feet in the crest region south of Horseshoe Meadow (see chapter 5). In spring, while these high regions are shedding their white winter cloak, the river runs in raging torrents, attracting a few intrepid kayakers who care more for fast water than warm weather. But the flow cuts out early in the season, because the watershed of the South Fork Kern is small and robbed of moisture by the rain shadow of the Great Western Divide (a sub-range just west of the main Sierra crest that nearly rivals it in height).

The **North Fork Kern,** on the other hand, arises in the long-lasting snowfields of a glacial cirque at the very roof of the Sierra Nevada, where the Great Western Divide, the Kings-Kern Divide, and the Mount Whitney group reach heights of 13,000 to 14,494. The North Fork Kern runs swiftly all summer through a long, deep, and remarkably straight canyon carved along an ancient north-south trending fault. Foot and pack trails into the glacier-scoured bowls of the headwaters and along the brushy **Kern River Canyon** are long and rugged (see the High Sierra Trail, in chapter 7), but every year, a few kayakers and rafters carry their craft for 21 miles from Whitney Portal over a 13,777-foot pass to **Junction Meadow** for the class v, 37-mile wilderness run down to **The Forks** (see later in this chapter). (The pioneer of this route was Royal Robbins in 1981. Yes, that's the same Royal Robbins who makes the classy outdoors clothing.)

From the Johnsondale Bridge and south along **Sierra Way** to Isabella Lake, the North Fork Kern becomes accessible to mere mortal, and its boulder-strewn shores are lined with campgrounds and resorts. The fantastic shapes of water-sculpted boulders and cliffs high above the summer river level are testament to the power of the Kern's cold, swift currents. *This is a river that has claimed many lives.* If you don't believe me, listen to Merle Haggard's "Kern River."

U.S. 395 TO SHERMAN PASS

There are no trans-mountain roads through a huge swath of the middle to southern Sierra. Hikers heading southeast on the Pacific Crest Trail can be certain of walking 250 miles from Tuolumne Meadows on Tioga Road (Highway 120) in Yosemite National Park before encountering any trans-Sierra automobile traffic. Their luck will run out upon encountering Route 41 east of Sherman Pass.

The road through Sherman Pass is not heavily used for trans-Sierra travel. Snow keeps the way closed in winter, and a traveler will need to do some serious map study to pick a route through from Sherman Pass to the Central Valley. Services are few and far between throughout the Kern Plateau region.

From the east on U.S. 395 north of Pearsonville, Route 41 begins its climb up the Kern Plateau as Nine Mile Canyon Road. On the way up Nine Mile Canyon, creosote scrub gives way to large stands of Joshua trees, which then give way to a thin forest of juniper and pinyon pine. Crag-topped peaks loom above while the roadway cuts through pink and green metamorphics and past granitic cliffs shot through with bold white intrusions.

At Kennedy Meadows (el. 5,934 feet), Nine Mile Canyon Road becomes Kennedy Meadows Road amid sparse forests of juniper, Jeffrey pine, manzanita, and oak. Kennedy Meadows is a big recreation hub, serving South Kern fishermen and river rats, Pacific Crest Trail through-hikers, campers going out on horseback, and the area's few residents.

DOME LAND WILDERNESS

From Kennedy Meadows, a fleeting view to the south reveals some of the eroding granitic spires and domes of the Dome Land Wilderness. This will be about the only opportunity to look in on this 130,000-acre wilderness from a roadway. Visitors go in on foot or horseback from north, south, east, and west, but not without ample planning for a few days of rugged travel.

On this northeastern corner of the Dome Land Wilderness, the river and the Pacific Crest Trail come in through Kennedy Meadows. The trail deviates east to traverse the secluded wilds of Chimney Peak Recreation Area (described earlier), while the river glides placidly through the Rockhouse Basin before raging through a series of slot canyons in the increasingly arid and trailless lands to the south. Trails from the northwest enter the wilderness high up near Sirretta Peak and Bald Mountain (see below), fanning east and south through a series of meadows linked by meandering creeks and into sparse pinyon and juniper woodland.

On a visit in 2001, I found the dome lands still gripped by the devastation of the Manter fire the year before. But a brilliant flush of wildflowers had already sprung up from the blackened ground, giving testimony to the passion with which nature renews herself.

INTO THE GOLDEN TROUT WILDERNESS

About 10 miles to the northwest of Kennedy Meadows, Route 41 makes a sharp turn to the south. However, hikers and fishermen might want to turn north onto Forest Service Road 21S03, which runs northward past the Blackrock Ranger Station to the southern border of the roadless Golden Trout Wilderness. Take this for two miles bearing left as the road forks, and continue five miles until the road ends at the Blackrock Campground and trailhead. From here, a steep north-trending trail follows Nine Mile Creek to **Casa Vieja Meadows,** a big grassy bowl surrounded by several of the soft, forested mounds that pass for peaks in these parts.

A decrepit log cabin in the meadow gives a sense of human habitation, but I found the meadows deserted, with only a coyote keeping watch over my passage through its realm. In 1861, John Jordan of Visalia blazed a trail through these meadows, intending to promote it as a trans-Sierra toll road for use by the prolific mining traffic. He was swept away by the swift Kern River waters the following year. The road was never built, but Jordan's name remains on a trail that follows many of his blazes. If you were to head east from here on the Old Jordan Trail, you would arrive at the South Fork Kern in Monache Meadows. If instead you head north-westward, you would approach the North Fork Kern along Nine Mile Creek. On the way, you might be tempted to stop for a few hours of bliss at **Jordan Hot Springs.** The hot springs were a popular, developed resort destination for over a century, but with the establishment of the Golden Trout Wilderness in 1978 and the expiration of the concessionaire's lease in 1990, the resort was closed and it has now become a ghost spa. The Forest Service has not determined a way to turn off nature's spigot, how-ever, and so the heavenly hot water still runs into the cold creek. With patience and care, you might find a perfect rock-lined pool where the water temperature is just right. While planning a day trip to the springs from the Blackrock trailhead, you might want to remember that it's a steep five-mile climb back to the parking lot.

A complete description of this trail, and many others in the southern-most Sierra, can be found in the highly recommended two-volume hik-ing, biking, and driving guidebook, *Exploring the Southern Sierra* (see the end of this chapter).

BALD MOUNTAIN (el. 9,382 feet)

As you drive along the 15-mile stretch of Sherman Pass Road (Route 41) between 21S03 and Sherman Pass, a few brief breaks in the forest cover reveal an awesome view of the High Sierra to the north. However, you might look in vain for a good turnout from which to admire the view. Instead, plan ahead and watch for the sign to Bald Mountain Lookout, which is on a dirt road (numbered 22S77) that takes off from the east side of the highway. It's a bumpy two-mile drive up to the parking area and from there, a steep but short hike to the tower, but the splendid view from the lookout will make it all seem worthwhile. The following is what you might see on a clear day.

Directly to the south, the Dome Land Wilderness stretches out as a dry landscape of intriguing granitic domes and chimneys interspersed with pinyon and juniper. The San Gabriel Mountains form a distant southern backdrop 140 miles away. To the east, sitting at a distance of 75 miles on the edge of Death Valley, is the pointy spire of 11,049-foot

Telescope Peak. Approximately 20 miles north-northwest and appearing almost close enough to touch is **Olancha Peak** (el. 12,123 feet), which pokes its tawny pointed head above the forested Kern Plateau. Directly north, approximately 40 miles distant, are the bare stone spires of the Mount Whitney group. Five of these peaks exceed 14,000 feet: Mount Langley (el. 14,022 feet), Mount Whitney (el. 14,494 feet), Mount Russell (el. 14,086 feet), Mount Tyndall (el. 14,019 feet), and Mount Williamson (el. 14,373 feet). They look like a jawbone full of jagged white teeth about to bite down against the darker metavolcanics of the Great Western Divide to the northwest.

This view would be reason alone to visit, but Bald Mountain is also noted as an unusual island of botanic diversity. The richly nutritive-growing medium derived from the mountain's 135-million-year-old metasedimentary sandstone, slate, and dolomite supports more than 170 species of plants. One modest member of the rose family, the Bald Mountain Potentilla, is found nowhere else. The array of conifers includes five different species of pine, two species of fir, and the western juniper.

SHERMAN PASS (el. 9,200 feet)

The view from the Sherman Pass pullout pales beside the panoramic experience at Bald Mountain Lookout, so it might be more worthwhile to press on. As you zigzag down the western-slope switchbacks ahead, the craggy knob making a striking appearance to the north will be 9,909-foot Sherman Peak. Looking down, you will be peering into the sagebrush-covered trough of the Kern River. Broader views extend west across Sequoia National Monument and over the lands of the Tule River. Approximately 10 miles from the pass, watch on the south side of the highway for Cherry Hill Road (22S12).

HORSE MEADOW (el. 7,600 feet)

Cherry Hill Road heads south-southeast, regaining elevation as it converges on the path of Salmon Creek. About seven miles ahead, a sign for Horse Meadow campground appears on the right. The campground is arranged on a saddle of land at about 7,600 feet, among a pretty garden of manzanita and Jeffrey pine. It is nicely furnished with large granitic boulders, on which you might sit to admire the striking views both east and west. **Salmon Creek** trundles by, drawing hikers down the 4.5-mile trail to its splendid falls.

From Horse Meadow, Cherry Hill Road continues on to Big Meadow, where trails take off east into the Dome Land Wilderness and north to 9,977-foot Sirretta Peak. If you choose to explore this region, it is imperative (as it is everywhere) to have a good map, since the area offers a bewildering tangle of forest roads and trails.

WEST END OF ROUTE 41

Sherman Pass Road (Route 41) ends at the Johnsondale Bridge over the North Fork Kern. Here you can take Sierra Way south along the river to Kernville and Isabella Lake, or continue west on County Route sm99 past the showy South Creek Falls and on to Johnsondale.

At Johnsondale, a paved Forest Service road marked 22s82 leads north to Lloyd Meadows, from which 20s67 heads east to reach the trailhead and campground for the **Forks of the Kern,** a popular spot with river runners. Also known as simply The Forks, this is both the put-in point for the gorgeous 14.5-mile class IV+ run to the Johnsondale Bridge and the take-out point for the mythic 37-mile class v run from Junction Meadow

Spring on the Kern River. Photo by Erlda Parker

west of Mount Whitney through the long Kern Canyon. Those who are not up for such excitement might be content simply to drive a couple of miles north on 22s82 from Johnsondale to picnic on the huge slabs of granitic rock at **Long Meadow Creek.**

During snow-free seasons, you can continue west out of Johnsondale to reach the Central Valley. In about five miles, there will be the choice of either a southwest-trending route via the town of California Hot Springs, or a north-trending route via **Western Divide Highway.**

If you go north, you will be traversing the **Sequoia National Monument,** an area set aside in 2000 by President Bill Clinton to preserve a region hosting many groves of giant sequoias. The monument is not the same as Sequoia National Park, which is described in the next chapter.

As Western Divide Highway meets the South Fork Tule River, it becomes Highway 190 and descends toward Lake Success (el. 652 feet). If you continue along this highway, you will come to **Porterville (el. 459 feet),** where there are several interesting historical sights and various lodging and dining options. From Porterville, you can take Highway 65 north to reach Highway 198, the southern entryway to Sequoia National Park and the High Sierra.

Practical Matters

Warmer temperatures in this lower, southern region of the Sierra make it ideal for fall-through-spring visits, but services will be fewer than in summer, and access to the Kern Plateau and Sherman Pass Road may be limited by snow.

ROADS
Most visitors to this region arrive from Southern California. Highways 190, 155, and 178 provide access from the Central Valley. Highway 58 follows the Sierra Nevada's southern border from Bakersfield through Tehachapi Pass to the Mojave Desert. Highway 14 and U.S. 395 skirt the region closely on its east side. East-side access is on Route 41 through Sherman Pass (closed in winter) and Highway 178. Most routes through the area converge at Isabella Lake. Many side trips described in this chapter follow county and Forest Service roads, and these are generally main-

tained and in good condition (when seasonally accessible). There are commercial airports in Bakersfield and Fresno.

WHERE TO STAY AND EAT

The majority of the region's lodging and dining options are found around Isabella Lake — at the town of Lake Isabella, south of the lake, or in Kernville to the north. Some unusual lodging options are available through the Sequoia National Forest, which has several refurbished historic fire lookouts and guard station cabins along the western slope that can be rented by the public for overnight stays. Call the district offices below for more information.

CAMPING

There are dozens of campgrounds accessible from Highway 190 out of Porterville. Other clusters can be found along the Kern River from Johnsondale to Isabella Lake, along the western shore of the lake, in the Greenhorn Mountains off Highway 155, and along Highway 178 south of the lake. Also, isolated campgrounds can be found in the Sherman Pass, Chimney Creek, and Walker Basin areas.

NATIONAL FORESTS

Inyo National Forest Headquarters, 351 Pacu Lane, Suite 200, Bishop, 760–873–2400.
Sequoia National Forest (www.fs.fed.us/r5/sequoia/): **Headquarters,** 1839 South Newcomb Street, Porterville, 559–784–1500; **Kern River Ranger District,** Kernville Office, 105 Whitney Road, Kernville, 760–376–3781; Lake Isabella Office, 4875 Ponderosa Drive, Lake Isabella, 760–379–5646; **Tule River/Hot Springs Ranger District,** California Hot Springs Office, 43474 Parker Pass Drive, California Hot Springs, 661–548–6503, Springville Office, 32588 Highway 190, Springville, 559–539–2607; **Bakersfield Visitor Center,** 3801 Pegasus Drive, Bakersfield, 661–391–6088.

VISITORS BUREAUS

Kern County Board of Trade, www.visitkern.com/, Bakersfield, 800–500–5376, 661–861–2367.

REGIONAL GUIDES

Jenkins, J. C., and Ruby Johnson. *Exploring the Southern Sierra: East Side.* Berkeley, Calif.: Wilderness Press, 1992.

——. *Exploring the Southern Sierra: West Side.* Berkeley, Calif.: Wilderness Press, 1995.

7

The High Sierra

For a span of more than 140 miles, between Sherman Pass on the Kern Plateau and Tioga Pass in Yosemite National Park, no roads cross the Sierra crest. Long dusty fire trails snake upward for endless miles through the western forests and a few swaggering paved roads switch back and forth down the steep flanks on the east. The traveler who wants to cross the Sierra in this rugged region must abandon his car, shoulder a pack, and continue upward on foot or horseback to narrow passes at 10,000, 11,000, or upward of 12,000 feet. Above these rocky trails, 11 windswept peaks rake the sky at more than 14,000 feet.

This is the High Sierra, defined by a superlative set of statistics, yet unquantifiable. In my mind, the High Sierra is the mystical state of being that comes about in the thin air above timberline. A glance down the long trail ahead and an August breeze that whispers of coming snow do little to dispel the urgent desire to linger in the moment, in the endless sweep of sky and rock, or beside a dwarf thicket of ancient willow where glacial melt trickles down through stair-step meadows.

I have heard the term "High Sierra" used to refer to the range as a whole, and will grant that a mystical experience can come about at any elevation, and even from a car window. But here, in the highest Sierra, one feels a distinct sharpening of the senses — a feeling that deepens with each day and each turn of the trail, becoming imprinted in the bones.

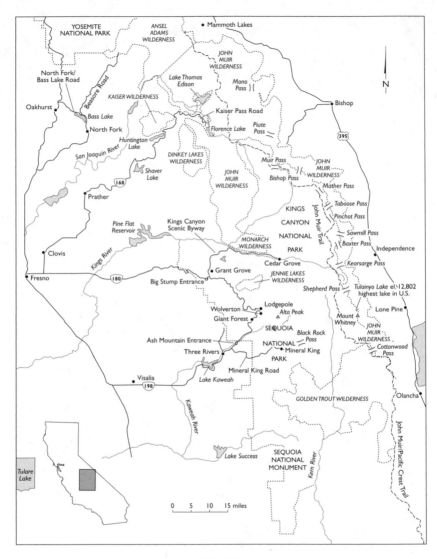

HIGH SIERRA

Highway 198 to Sequoia National Park

California Highway 198 begins near the California coast in the Salinas Valley southeast of Monterey Bay. It crosses the Diablo Range and then continues east into the Central Valley, over the bed of what was once a vast tule-filled lake. Measured in 1849 at about 570 miles square (22 miles north to south and 26 from east to west), Tulare Lake gathered the waters of three Sierra rivers — the Tule, the Kaweah, and the Kings. A northern outlet of the lake spilled into the San Joaquin River to begin a journey north into the Sacramento-San Joaquin River Delta. Tulare Lake was gradually drained as the valley's gold era settlers began turning the marshy expanse into the prime agricultural land it is today. Dams built on the Tule, the Kaweah, and the Kings now regulate the release of water via a series of canals through the farmlands. The dams also create exceptional recreational opportunities at Lake Success (Tule River), Lake Kaweah (Kaweah River), and Pine Flat Reservoir (Kings River). In very wet winters Tulare Lake has been known to arise as a ghost lake to fill part of its former bed.

On the rare day when agricultural dust is not being borne eastward out of the valley, a visitor headed into Sequoia National Park can admire a splendid view of the High Sierra from **Lake Kaweah,** which is located at 894 feet about 20 miles northeast of Visalia. On leaving the lake to continue the ascent on Highway 198, watch to the right for a river joining the Middle Fork Kaweah. It will be the **South Fork Kaweah,** coming down from Hockett Meadows in Sequoia National Monument.

A few miles above this confluence, the **North Fork Kaweah** joins the Middle Fork at the town of **Three Rivers,** a thriving ranching community offering a good assortment of visitor services. One service here is unique — the chance to mail a letter from an historic post office. On the highway, watch for the State Historic Landmark sign pointing left up North Fork Drive. Three miles up this road is a plaque in front of a tiny wooden cabin that serves as the **Kaweah Post Office.** The working post office is a vestige of the **Kaweah Co-Operative Commonwealth** (generally referred to as the Kaweah Colony), an epic experiment in utopian socialism that attracted worldwide attention during its brief existence

Atop Hands and Knees Pass on the Great Western Divide. Photo by Mark Middlebrook

from 1886 to 1892. The commonwealth intended to harvest Sierra timber as its primary resource, but was stymied by disputes to its claims. The dream ended altogether in 1890 when Congress signed the legislation establishing Sequoia National Park. During those six years, however, the colony managed to build a sawmill and a road up to the timber claims. The remarkable 18-mile road made a 4,000-foot vertical elevation gain and was used for many years as the primary access from this region into the national park, with the sawmill serving as the park's entrance station. The road is still in service as a fire road.

MINERAL KING (el. 7,830 feet)

About five miles past Three Rivers, Mineral King Road splinters off to the east from Highway 198, heading up the **East Fork Kaweah River.** The steep and winding road (open May through October) leads to two campgrounds, the Atwell sequoia grove, the Silver City Mountain Resort, and a visitor center before reaching 7,800 feet in the verdant valley of Mineral King.

The valley saw a little mining activity in the 1870s and narrowly escaped being turned into a ski kingdom by Disney Enterprises in the 1970s. The only engineering going on there now is by a mutant strain of

The Kaweah Post Office and a newspaper called the *Kaweah Commonwealth* are living reminders of the utopian community that operated here from 1888 to 1892.

yellow-bellied marmots that specializes in disabling cars left overnight by backpackers. Apparently, the marmots here have developed the ability to drink antifreeze without dying, and they will gleefully gnaw through car hoses to get to it, possibly taking out your wiring at the same time. They also go after more common trailhead delicacies, such as salty, sweat-soaked hiking gear and backpacks stuffed with camp rations.

As a backpacker leaving from Mineral King, I found the marmots to be the least of several challenging situations. My husband and I followed our hiking guidebook's advice and spent our first night acclimating to the high elevation at a Mineral King campground. This was a good thing, as our level of conditioning was barely up to the first day's test of hiking over the Great Western Divide. We climbed over 11,700-foot Sawtooth Pass and down into the stark granitic cirque of Columbine Lake (at 10,970 feet). The whiteness of the rock here was intensified by ice on the lake and hail pelting down on the tiny tarp that was to serve as our tent for the entire expedition. From a little pond beside the trail, a chorus of frogs added a cheerful note to the scene in its direst moment. The next day, we climbed over 11,630-foot Black Rock Pass to reach Big Five Lakes, where we battled clouds of mosquitoes and where my husband almost crippled

A yellow-bellied marmot (*Marmota flaviventris*) contemplates the day's possibilities. Photo by Bob Greensfelder

Big Five Lakes Basin. Photo by Mark Middlebrook.

himself while throwing a rock over a limb in an effort to put up the bear bag. The summer ranger there, who was keeping a log of illegal military training flights over the area, told us about a marathon runner who had been airlifted out the summer before because of pulmonary edema (an extreme form of altitude sickness). I spent a sleepless night monitoring my vital signs for any indication that pulmonary edema was about to set in. Needless to say, I survived to write this book. The marmots did not eat our car hoses, and the trip remains one of our all-time favorites because of the extraordinary scenery.

ALONG THE GENERALS HIGHWAY

About a mile past Mineral King Road, Highway 198 reaches an elevation of 1,700 feet at the **Ash Mountain Entrance Station** to Sequoia National Park. Here, the road becomes the Generals Highway as it begins a tour through the northwestern corner of Sequoia National Park. Those inclined to linger in this splendid rolling foothills landscape of chaparral, grass, and oak might want to stop a mile east of the entrance station at the **Foothills Visitor Center,** where museum exhibits focus on the foothills ecosystem.

At 1.6 miles from the entrance station, look to the north side of the road for **Tunnel Rock.** The tunnel was excavated in 1938 by the Civilian Conservation Corps to allow passage for automobiles coming and going to the national park. When Generals Highway was widened in 1997 the tunnel became obsolete.

About four miles past Tunnel Rock, the road begins a twisting climb of more than 5,000 feet in elevation, leading past one astounding vista after another along its jagged route. Poised high above the switchback ascent are two regal stone monuments, **Castle Rocks,** with its craggy points touching the thinning air at 9,180 feet, and **Moro Rock** (el. 6,725 feet), which are reminiscent of Yosemite's granitic masterpieces.

Once past the main switchbacks on this ascent, visitors anticipating the eponymous tree of this national park will be rewarded as the road narrows and splits to pass between three big trees that seem to be poised as a natural welcome station to the sequoia belt. Sequoia National Park, along with Sequoia National Forest and the Sequoia National Monument, comprise the most extensive group of giant sequoia groves in the Sierra. There are more than 50 groves scattered throughout this region, many with excellent systems of trails allowing visitors to wander for hours among the enigmatic giants.

The Sierra is full of magnificent trees of many species, and it is not uncommon to be stopped in one's tracks by the sight of a regal old ponderosa pine or red fir. But the age and mass of the sequoias in these groves are what make them noteworthy. According to the Sequoia and Kings Canyon National Parks Information Service:

> The largest of the sequoias are as tall as an average 26 story building, and their diameters at the base exceed the width of many city streets. As they continue to grow, they produce about 40 cubic feet of wood each year, approximately equal to the volume of a 50-foot tall tree one foot in diameter. The ages of the General Sherman, General Grant and other large sequoias are unknown, but it is estimated that these giants are between 1800 and 2700 years old. They have seen civilization come and go, survived countless fires and long periods of drought, and continue to flourish, inspiring yet another generation of admirers.

It's hard to portray the size of a giant sequoia in a photograph. One way is to focus on just one small part of it. This part, however, is hardly small. A person could easily walk inside of the crevice on the right, although they would be breaking park rules by doing so.

GIANT FOREST (el. 6,409 feet)

The General Sherman and General Grant trees (numbers one and three respectively on the park's list of the 30 largest) are found in the Giant Forest on the Generals Highway. At the center of the area is the **Giant Forest Museum,** where exhibits focus on both the natural history and the human history surrounding these trees.

Another highlight of the Giant Forest section is **Crystal Cave,** one of over 200 caves that can be found in the park. A visit to the cave requires some time and advance planning, because tickets are not sold at the cave and must be purchased at the Foothill or Lodgepole visitor centers. The drive out Crystal Cave Road is long and winding, and once you reach the parking lot, there is still a steep half-mile hike to the cave entrance.

Before leaving the Giant Forest section, drive out the three-mile-long **Moro Rock–Crescent Meadow Road,** which heads eastward from the Giant Forest Museum. Along the way are two popular sights — the Tunnel Log, a fallen and hollowed-out sequoia that cars can drive through the length of, and the Auto Log, a fallen sequoia that once accommo-

The Great Western Divide. Photo by Mark Middlebrook

dated cars along its length before it became too rotten. Located midway between the two logs is **Moro Rock** (el. 6,725 feet). The stairs to the top of the rock number more than 400 steps and afford a glorious view of the Great Western Divide.

At the end of Moro Rock–Crescent Meadow Road is **Crescent Meadow,** a great place for a picnic amid the midsummer wildflowers. The most ambitious visitors arriving here are likely to be backpackers using the meadow to launch or land a Mount Whitney expedition. They go via the **High Sierra Trail,** which wends out of Crescent Meadow via the south-facing slope of the Middle Fork Kaweah River canyon. Eleven and a half miles out of Crescent Meadow, the High Sierra Trail passes through **Bearpaw Meadow,** where (for a goodly price) hikers can enjoy a tent cabin resort and two gourmet meals a day. (Some hikers make this their final destination.) The High Sierra Trail continues, crossing the Great Western Divide at **Kaweah Gap** (el. 10,700 feet) before descending into **Big Arroyo.** Climbing over the **Chagoopa Plateau,** the trail then drops into the **Kern River Canyon,** where a reward is a soak in the **Kern Hot**

Springs. From there, the trail runs north up the bottom of the Kern Canyon and turns east to reach a junction with the John Muir Trail for the last leg up to Mount Whitney.

WOLVERTON (el. 7,200 feet)

Located north of the Giant Forest section on Highway 198 is Wolverton, a former ski bowl that now serves primarily as a trailhead. Not a few ambitious hikers set out from here with their sights on 11,204-foot **Alta Peak,** 6.9 miles and 4,000 feet up the trail. On a clear day, the view from Alta Peak might reach as far as the California Coast Range. A less ambitious destination, at a mere 1,000-foot climb and 2.7 miles from the trailhead, is **Panther Gap,** where the 8,200-foot-high saddle affords a view of the Middle Fork Kaweah running in its canyon nearly 5,000 feet below. Across the canyon is the Castle Rocks formation seen so prominently on the drive up from Visalia. To the east is the Great Western Divide with its wall of snow-draped peaks towering well above 13,000 feet.

When I came through the gap one sweltering July day, the thunder gods were tuning up their kettledrums for an afternoon concert as the big clouds boiled into formation. The standing ghosts of several red fir

---

CROSS-COUNTRY SKIING IN SEQUOIA NATIONAL PARK

Determined to explore the park on skis the easy way, I headed up Highway 180 (Kings Canyon Scenic Byway) from Fresno to the Montecito-Sequoia Lodge, a friendly and accommodating four-season resort set at 7,500–8,500 feet amid red and white fir and Jeffrey pine. I arrived just in advance of a February storm that was getting some impressive publicity.

The place was packed with skiers testing their mettle in the Chimney Rock Classic, one of many cross-country ski races held each year throughout the Sierra. Ignoring the racers, I set out at a leisurely pace to investigate some of the 80km (50 miles) of ski trails the resort keeps so nicely groomed. Within an hour, I had five inches of snow piled up on my hat, so I went back to the lodge to see what other types of recreation might be available.

The next morning, the weather had cleared, and I looked out my window to see the high, snow-swept Great Western Divide against the eastern sky. Heading out on skis again, I headed up toward Baldy Ridge, where I was able to catch a splendid view west toward Fresno and the Great Central Valley, then full of orchards in passionate spring bloom. As I retreated from the ridge, I realized I had ventured out a little too far onto a dangerous cornice. The view could have cost me my life, but I lived to tell about it and have tucked the lesson into my list of things never to repeat. *Never proceed into unmarked terrain in the Sierra winter without knowing how to read the snow.*

---

trees made it clear that this was not a prime seat from which to enjoy the performance.

Another popular destination, 6.7 miles from Wolverton, is **Pear Lake,** described in the park's hiking brochure as "a shimmering surface of light and motion in a world of rock." During the snowy season (often from November through April), cross-country skiers with adequate skill and preparation might make a challenging overnight trip to the lake, where they can stay overnight in a little hut. Some skiers arrive here from the east on a trans-Sierra tour, perhaps following the route over 12,055-foot **Shepherd Pass** pioneered in 1931 by Otto Steiner.

LODGEPOLE VISITOR CENTER (el. 6,720 feet)

A few miles northeast of Wolverton, the Generals Highway reaches beautiful Tokopah Valley, where the Marble Fork Kaweah River tumbles through a region of domed granitic rock. The valley holds the Lodgepole Visitor Center, a complex of visitor services, including the large and lovely Lodgepole Campground. The camper comforts available to anyone lucky enough to snag a site include showers, a laundromat, flush toilets, and a deli. Trails take off from here to points near and far.

FROM LODGEPOLE TO HIGHWAY 180

The last stretch of the Generals Highway offers several beautiful lodges, resorts, and campgrounds within range of the main attractions. Among the sights is the world's largest sequoia grove, tucked away in an area called Redwood Canyon. Here, decades of prescribed burns have rejuvenated the sequoias' growth, demonstrating the vital role played by fire in a healthy ecosystem.

Highway 198 ends at its junction with Highway 180. Here, a left turn leads down to the orange groves above Fresno and a right turn leads toward Kings Canyon.

Kings Canyon National Park

Highway 180, in the guise of the Kings Canyon Scenic Byway, makes its approach to Kings Canyon National Park through **Grant Grove,** where there is a store, a visitors center, several campgrounds, and yet another stunning grove of sequoias. Grant Grove is home to the **General Grant Tree,** which was designated as the nation's Christmas tree by President Calvin Coolidge in 1926. The grove's elevation of 6,600 feet makes it a cooler place to camp in midsummer than Kings Canyon.

Eight miles north of Grant Grove, you will find the Hume Lake Road turnoff from Highway 180. The road leads to **Hume Lake,** an idyllic place to linger on a hot summer's day. Besides the Forest Service campground at this fine lake, there's a sizable Christian camp, where multitudes spend weeks finding the hand of God in the exquisite scenery. The presence of such a reliable population in this remote setting benefits even unaffiliated campers looking for supplies, since the Christian camp offers a gas station and a well-stocked general store. Just don't send your teenager into the store alone to buy cookies — the community has some tough rules on when unescorted minors can shop and what they can buy.

Heading back to Highway 180 on Hume Lake Road, you will be treated to views to the north that offer a stunning preview of the Kings River Canyon country ahead. Once on Highway 180, you will be making a spectacular twisting descent toward the river and the park proper. This approach offers some extraordinary views, so don't rush.

The Highway 180 pull-off at **Junction Vista Point** (el. 4,488 feet) is a good place to contemplate the desolate and remote country at the confluence of the Kings River's middle and south forks. To the northwest and 2,232 feet below, the forks meet, appearing as slim silver threads coming through the deep folds on either side of **Monarch Divide,** a rocky spine that soars up to 11,433 feet at Kennedy Mountain.

Not so much as a faint footpath can be seen traversing the steep, chaparral-covered slopes flanking the Middle Fork Kings River, and, indeed, few hikers make it up into that remote, rattlesnake-infested region, where features bear names such as Tombstone Ridge, Gorge of Despair, Burnt Mountain, Lost Canyon, and Swamp Lakes. The first mountaineer to explore the Middle Fork Kings region was Frank Dusy, whose name is immortalized at Dusy Basin (visited in the Owens Valley chapter). He went there with L. A. Winchell, the mountaineer who made the first successful ascent of 13,568-foot **Mount Goddard,** which we will see on our journeys ahead. One of the surprises the two uncovered in 1869 was the marvelous **Tehipite Valley.** They photographed the 7,708-foot-high emi-

A young visitor claims this cabin in Giant Forest as his new home. Mom does not agree to the relocation.

nence of **Tehipite Dome,** adding evidence to John Muir's claim that the splendid, glacier-carved monuments of Yosemite Valley are not unique; here was a valley where nature had wrought beauty of equal stature.

As Highway 180 descends toward the South Fork Kings, it passes Convict Flat Campground, which has six sites and no piped water. It seemed like the world's loneliest campground on a weekday morning in July, when there was not even a bear eating the ripe blackberries that rambled

(opposite) This family jumped the fence in order to make an informal measurement of the General Grant Tree. Fortunately for them, there were no park officials nearby to cite them for this infringement of park rules. Please stay on the paths.

Marina at Hume Lake.

around the edges of the oak-shaded campsites. Less than a mile beyond the campground turnoff is an unmarked overlook that I found identified on one map as Horseshoe Bend Viewpoint. Here the sheer canyon walls, glazed with green lichen and mineral stain, rise up nearly face-to-face.

Soon the highway finds the south bank of the river, and the drive becomes more inviting as the South Fork Kings tumbles along in the opposite direction. At many spots, there are turnouts wide enough for a car to pull over, but signs warn of the dangerously swift current and icy cold waters that have swept a few visitors away. The road crosses over to the north bank at a bridge beside the entrance station to **Boyden Cavern** and then continues on into the more populated portion of Kings Canyon National Park.

Confluence of the Kings River's middle and south forks.

CEDAR GROVE TO ROAD'S END

At **Cedar Grove Village** (el. 4,635 feet), there is a main lodge and four campgrounds, but these are not often in high demand, because Kings Canyon does not see any significant crush of visitors. Along the 20-mile stretch of highway from the park entrance to Road's End, the south fork's wide, U-shaped glacial valley shows off only a few majestic stone monuments through the dense forest of pine, fir, cedar, oak, and cottonwood. To experience Kings Canyon to its fullest in summer, you will need hiking boots, a hat, and a sizeable water bottle.

The gem of Kings Canyon is **Roaring River Falls,** located three miles east of Cedar Grove Village and up an oak-shaded walkway on the south side of the canyon. Here Roaring River comes thundering out of a granitic chute, falling into a deep green pool surrounded by a jumble of boulders. Agile rock hoppers might like to explore the setting further, but they should take great care, as the water is swift and cold. From the falls, hikers can start down the River Trail to Zumwalt Meadow and then on to Bubbs Creek.

By car or by foot, **Zumwalt Meadow** is a mile and a half east of the falls. Either way, it will be necessary to walk in order to see the scenery. Those who choose to drive to the Zumwalt Meadow parking area can enjoy a mile-and-a-half-long interpretive nature trail around the meadow. It's mostly level terrain, but a portion negotiates some sizable steps through a rocky cliff area.

Setting out through the pines from the Zumwalt Meadow parking lot on the north side of the river, hikers will find themselves passing some large flat rocks pocked with grinding holes where the Monache women once ground seeds and acorns into meal. I found it easy to imagine the women chattering away as they worked accompanied by the raucous laughter and rhythmic tapping of acorn woodpeckers in the trees overhead.

The path crosses the river on a graceful footbridge and then rejoins the River Trail before climbing among the talus piled up below the 8,504-foot granitic dome named **Grand Sentinel.** From the rocky passageways, there are many good views across the canyon to **North Dome** (el. 8,717

(opposite) Roaring River makes a dramatic escape through the south wall of Kings Canyon.

feet) and down into the expanse of Zumwalt Meadow, which in mid-summer is lush green, spangled with purple shooting stars, and painted on occasion with the vivid yellow and orange plumage of the Western tanager. Cattails, herbs, and skinny-jointed common horsetails rim the meadow's marshy border, echoing the milky greens of the enticing pools along the riverbank.

The River Trail continues east from Zumwalt Meadow, following the river's south bank. A footbridge a mile down the trail allows hikers to cross back to the parking area at Road's End, but on a hot day, the sandy bank beside the pool below the bridge seems a better place to spend the

Coming through "the Incinerator" to the confluence of the South Fork Kings and Bubbs Creek, below the formation known as the Sphinx.

hours than in a sizzling car. The end of the road (el. 5,035 feet) offers little for the visitor who is not planning to hike. There are three main trails from **Road's End**. The most popular trail follows the South Fork Kings River to Paradise Valley (see below). The others are a steep 5,000-foot climb up the Monarch Divide via Copper Creek to Granite Pass (el. 10,673 feet), and the more-traveled route up Bubbs Creek to Kearsarge Pass. While consulting William Brewer's journal, *Up and Down California,* I wondered if these might be the routes followed by his little band of surveyors in July of 1864: "We camped at the head of this valley by a fine grassy meadow where the stream forked," Brewer wrote. "On both sides rose grand walls of granite about three thousand feet high, while between the forks was a stupendous rock, bare and rugged, over four thousand feet high. We luxuriated on trout for the next two meals. The rattlesnakes where thick — four were killed this day."

After dispatching the rattlesnakes, the party climbed up Monarch Divide, where they picked out and christened many High Sierra peaks. They were moved especially by the prominent black mass of Mount Goddard to the north. At the end of their stay they traveled up Bubbs Creek and made their way over Kearsarge Pass to the Owens Valley, following what for centuries had been an important trade route for the Monache of the Kings River region and the Paiutes of the Owens Valley. Western Sierra acorns, deerskins, and tule reed arrow shafts were a common exchange for the pinyon pine nuts, salt, and obsidian of the eastern Sierra.

TO PARADISE VALLEY

Most day hikers set out from Road's End with the goal of visiting **Mist Falls.** Since the falls are but a reasonable four miles up the South Fork Kings River, this is doable for most, but on a hot day, the first two miles of canyon bottom can be trying. Maggie Loverin of the Cedar Grove Pack Station says that the packers call this part "The Incinerator"; it is easy to see the appeal of contracting with the packers for a lift up the river to the cooler climes. Once the trail turns north and leaves the canyon bottom, the grandeur mounts as the canyon narrows between vast jointed walls of granite, some of which have tumbled down into magnificent heaps that the steep trail must negotiate in narrow, twisting passageways. Conifers appear, some fighting for toeholds by twisting their roots into cracks

in the rock, while others soar to great heights, seeking to rival the majesty of the rock walls. Judge E. C. Winchell of Fresno County, who made the first in-depth exploration of Kings Canyon, described it as "a deep, dread, silent, stupendous amphitheatre, twenty miles across, crowded with adamant mountains, pinnacled crests, thunder-scarred cliffs, green lines of forests, snows in eternal sleep, horrid gorges and yawning gulfs."

At Mist Falls, the water thunders past, sending out a mist that can be a godsend to weary hikers. The water spews upwards in clouds of spray and then spreads out in sheets as it runs over the glacier- and water-smoothed slabs, dropping huge distances into deceivingly inviting pools. The currents here are dangerously swift well into the summer.

Beyond Mist Falls, the trail continues north into the gentle flats of **Paradise Valley** before turning east to follow Woods Creek to a junction with the John Muir Trail. At this point, hikers headed southeast will be joining the throngs making the final 40-mile push to Mount Whitney. The junction sits below **Mount Clarence King** (el. 12,905 feet), a massive mountain with stony buttresses that rise in a complex of granitic blocks to a forbidding summit. Mount Clarence King is considered to be one of Sierra mountaineering's greatest challenges.

Along the John Muir Trail

The idea of a crest-line trail from Yosemite Valley to Mount Whitney first appeared in the mid-1890s, when Theodore S. Solomons was writing for the *Overland Monthly, The Traveler,* and *Appalachia.* His explorations of a proposed route came to fruition in 1916 with the opening of the John Muir Trail. The trail extends for 211 miles, from the top of Mount Whitney to Yosemite Valley. Those who walk its full length make their plans and preparations far in advance. They expect to spend a minimum of two to three weeks on the trail, or they travel it a section at a time over a period of years. Several good publications with descriptions of the entire trail are available for those who intend to hike its length. This section presents but a few highlights of the trail within Kings Canyon National Park.

(opposite) The Sphinx (el. 9,146) watches silently over the confluence of South Fork Kings River and Bubbs Creek.

WOODS CREEK TO MUIR PASS

At the beaten-down campground beside the bridge over sprightly Woods Creek, rangers have posted dire warnings about the bold efforts of local bears to relieve backpackers of their precious food supplies. The bears sometimes leave their signatures in long swiping claw marks in the silvery bark of the aspen trees where campers hang their bear bags.

Seven miles north of the campground, the trail crosses **Pinchot Pass** (el. 12,130 feet) and then climbs to the headwaters of the South Fork Kings River in a barren, tundra-like basin below **Mather Pass** (el. 12,100 feet). Watching over this pass is **Mount Bolton Brown** (el. 13,538 feet), named for a Stanford art professor who in 1895 made the first ascent of Mount Clarence King. On his ramblings with his wife Lucy, Brown christened some of the nearby peaks, preferring descriptive names like Striped Mountain, Split Mountain, and Arrow Peak to the convention of choosing names of prominent people.

At Mather Pass, the trail crosses into the headwaters of the Middle Fork Kings River. Stretching northwest along the crest, the dark jagged ridge of the **Palisades** reaches above 14,000 feet with five of its peaks, and harbors the Sierra's largest glacier on its eastern escarpment (see chapter 5). Creeks rushing down the Palisades' western slope flow into lush **Le Conte Canyon,** which bottoms out at a surprisingly low 8,000 feet. The canyon was named for Joseph N. LeConte, a contemporary of Bolton Brown and second director of the Sierra Club (John Muir was the first). LeConte made the first ascent of the 14,242-foot North Palisade.

The winding, glacier-carved western wall of Le Conte Canyon rises up to the long metavolcanic ridge of **Black Divide,** which is crowned to the northwest by the 13,330-foot-high, glacier-encrusted **Black Giant.** The giant is an awesome sight to hikers climbing up out of the canyon through tortuous corridors of colorful fractured rock on their way to **Muir Pass** (el. 11,955 feet) on the **Goddard Divide.**

Muir Pass is a most memorable stop on the John Muir Trail, owing to its charming little beehive-shaped hut of stacked granitic blocks, built in 1932 by the Sierra Club in Muir's honor: "As his work is destined to carry on through the years, so, the hope was expressed, this shelter, dedicated to him, may likewise serve for an untold period of time to offer protection and safety to storm-bound travelers."

The hut atop Muir Pass. Photo by Larry Rich

This spot feels like the roof of the world, and in spite of the fatigue of the climb, there's an urge to ramble out in every direction at once to take in the dramatic landscape. A scramble up Mount Goddard reveals the icy tarns imprisoned in the south-trending **Ionian Basin,** a Homeric stone sea watched over by the imposing black forms of **Scylla** (el. 12,956 feet), **Charybdis** (el. 13,096 feet), and **The Three Sirens.**

In 1896, Solomons introduced the marvelous vista of the Ionian Basin to readers of the *Overland Monthly* in this enthralling passage:

> Immediately below the amphitheaters at the base of the peak, Goddard Creek drains at first a deep valley, the black walls of which — similar to those of the Enchanted Gorge — imprison it relentlessly within the mountain fastness. A strangely incongruous sight it is, and yet one eminently characteristic of the high Sierra . . . a narrow defile of rockthrottled gorge, through which the maddened stream tears its way for twenty miles to the Middle Fork. Thus harshly enclosed is a garden so spacious that a town could be built upon it, and so lovely that it might well be the home of a band

of mountain sylphs. . . . In the middle, through a rich, level lawn the stream winds its sinuous, glassy course, and exactly in the center of the garden is a beautiful lake of forty or fifty acres.

Twelve miles below, opposite the mouth of Disappearing Creek, granite walls rise to the height of Yosemite cliffs, and similar to them in abruptness, in sculpture, and in vegetation. From this point on to the Middle Fork, the right hand wall of Goddard Creek is a continuous precipice of gray granite, the left hand wall a continuous precipice of blackish slate. On one side a glare as of midsummer day, on the other the somber shadow of winter twilight.

HEADWATERS OF THE SOUTH FORK SAN JOAQUIN

Northwest of Muir Pass, the John Muir Trail descends to the **Evolution Basin** on a pathway constructed through a field of talus. It was here that I first came eye-to-eye with a pika. This tiny member of the rabbit order stood bravely on a rock to observe the strange parade of Gore-Tex–clad humans make their way into the basin to find a place to camp for the

At Wanda Lake in the Evolution Basin. Photo by Larry Rich

THE WATER OUZEL

The waterfalls of the Sierra are frequented by only one bird—the Ouzel or Water Thrush. He is a singularly joyous and lovable little fellow, about the size of a robin, clad in a plain waterproof suit of bluish gray, with a tinge of chocolate on the head and shoulders. In form he is about as smoothly plump and compact as a pebble that has been whirled in a pot-hole, the flowing contour of his body being interrupted only by his strong feet and bill, the crisp wing-tips, and the up-slanted wren-like tail.

Among all the countless waterfalls I have met in the course of ten years' exploration in the Sierra, whether among the icy peaks, or warm foot-hills, or in the profound yosemitic cañons of the middle region, not one was found without its Ouzel. No cañon is too cold for this little bird, none too lonely, provided it be rich in falling water. Find a fall, or cascade, or rushing rapid, anywhere upon a clear stream, and there you will surely find its complementary Ouzel, flitting about in the spray, diving in foaming eddies, whirling like a leaf among beaten foam-bells; ever vigorous and enthusiastic, yet self-contained, and neither seeking nor shunning your company.

—from *The Mountains of California*, John Muir

The water ouzel, a.k.a. American dipper or *Cinclus mexicanus*.

night. As the day came to an end, I watched a water ouzel stride right down into the southern headwaters of the San Joaquin River in search of its dinner, while to the northeast, the glorious pale ramparts of **Mount Huxley** (el. 13,086 feet), **Mount Spencer** (el. 12,431 feet), **Mount Darwin** (el. 13,831 feet), and **Mount Mendel** (el. 13,700 feet) reflected the rosy spectrum of sunset.

From Evolution Basin, the trail drops 800 feet into **Evolution Valley,** passing the hulking mound of **The Hermit** (el. 12,328 feet). In the valley, Evolution Creek threads through a series of lush meadows to meet the South Fork San Joaquin River. One spur trail follows the river through **Goddard Canyon** to the river's headwaters west of Mount Goddard, while another leads over one of the Sierra's most colorfully named features, 11,320-foot **Hell For Sure Pass.**

INTO THE HUMPHREYS BASIN

The John Muir Trail exits Kings Canyon National Park at Piute Creek, from which a spur trail heads east over Piute Pass (el. 11,423 feet), dropping travelers into the Bishop Creek drainage above the Owens Valley (see chapter 5). Hikers headed up the 12 miles and 3,000 feet to Piute Pass can look south toward the ice-rimmed Glacier Divide and north into the vast, nearly flat, lake-studded amphitheater of the Humphreys Basin, where the solitary mass of 13,986-foot Mount Humphreys dominates the view. This impressive peak, with its huge blocks of cracked and broken granite, has instilled a particular desire in mountaineers ever since the summer of 1898 when Joseph LeConte Jr. attempted (unsuccessfully) the first ascent. LeConte's frequent climbing companion, James S. Hutchinson, achieved the goal in 1904 and described the climb in an article entitled "First Ascent: Mount Humphreys," published in the January 1905 edition of the *Sierra Club Bulletin*: "Probably no one ever stood where we then were, unless during the Jurassic period, before the mountain was fully sculptured. Then the mariners of that age (if there were any) might have sailed upon the waters of the Pacific close to the base of the mountain, and, there landing, have climbed up its then gently sloping sides."

The High Sierra of the San Joaquin River

North of Kings Canyon National Park and south of Yosemite there lies another vast stretch of High Sierra backcountry that is not traversed by any road. Here in the **John Muir Wilderness** and the **Ansel Adams Wilderness,** the headwater region of the San Joaquin River can be explored by foot or on horseback with access via many good trails from both east-side and west-side road ends. East-side access is described in chapters 4 and 5. Access from the western foothills begins with a bumpy ride up one of the long rutted roads from resort areas around **Bass Lake** (el. 3,420 feet) near Oakhurst at the southern Yosemite border, and **Shaver Lake** (el. 5,370 feet), on Highway 168 from Fresno. Stock up on major supplies and gasoline before leaving these lower lakes. Maps, wilderness permits, and visitor information are available at the ranger stations in nearby Prather and North Fork.

SOUTH FORK SAN JOAQUIN RIVER

My first visit to **Huntington Lake** (el. 6,950 feet) came on the occasion of a blown radiator hose, which apparently is not an uncommon episode on a journey up the steep grade of Highway 168 from Shaver Lake. Fortunately, this woodsy resort community is a friendly enough place to wait out a repair after such an incident. In fact, many people come to Huntington Lake deliberately to fish, ski, camp, tear around on the OHV roads, or just hang out.

Backpackers might head into the adjacent **Dinkey Lakes Wilderness** or the **Kaiser Wilderness,** but most head up the notorious single-lane **Kaiser Pass Road.** The 22-mile drive over rocks and around potholes can be a two-hour ordeal, but at Kaiser Pass (el. 9,184 feet), dramatic views of the Sierra crest make apparent the reason for enduring the arduous road. Eight miles beyond the pass the road forks — the right fork leads to Florence Lake and the left to Lake Thomas Edison. Both destinations offer rustic accommodations for John Muir/Pacific Crest Trail through-hikers looking to resupply, but the resorts also see plenty of folks who regard them as final destinations.

RUMINATIONS AT FLORENCE LAKE (el. 7,328 feet)

I didn't think twice about handing over eight dollars for the ferry ride across Florence Lake, as it shaved four miles off the hike up to the John Muir Trail. But as I strained for a glimpse of the dusty land route among the conifers and granitic domes of the southwest shore, I was seized by the irony of taking the easy way when the ostensible point of backpacking is to enjoy the wild scenery while grunting along under one's own steam. I found myself wondering whether the poor suckers trudging around the lake were having the more elevated experience, or just needed better financial resources. Later in the trip I encountered a unique individual who, given his reasons for backpacking in the wilderness, most certainly would not have taken the ferry. On reaching the middle of his fourth decade, this person had calculated that he could retire and live on his savings if he spent no more than an average of 63 cents a day while waiting for social security to kick in. Given the paucity of opportunities to spend money in the wilderness and the ease of encountering oversupplied backpackers eager to offload a few pounds of excess food, he had managed (more or less) to stay within budget for several years. As he described it, his occasional visits to civilization were made more comfortable through the unwitting generosity of party hosts who didn't notice until morning that he had pitched his tent in their backyards, or simply gone to sleep on the couch. Heaven only knows who might have been willing to put him up for the winter. The key to his existence was that he had no expectations, no itinerary, and no appointments. The ferry ride would have been a pointless expenditure.

The trail from the southeast end of Florence Lake passes through **Blayney Meadows,** where weary hikers can wallow in the primitive, clothing-optional hot mud hole called **Blayney Hot Spring.** Just beyond

PERISH THE THOUGHT

As viewed from the Seven Gables, one of the peaks that rise from the wall, and a mountain of striking and unique form—this upper Bear Creek region is sublimely spectacular. Nowhere in the Sierra have I seen it matched in utter wildness, sternness, and desolation. I can fancy several hotels—perish the thought—pitched in the glacial valley just in front of the wall with the vents. The most-used path of the many that are to lead from these Swiss-like edifices will ascend the Seven Gables, and the register in the monumental cairn built on its summit will be filled with eulogies scrawled in all languages.

Another valley of future hotels—the masses will not come to worship till cushions are ready for their knees—is that of the Middle Branch of the South Fork, where, a thousand feet below the highest alps of the San Joaquin Sierra, trees, grass, and flowers, birds, and bees, offer one of those remarkable contrasts that everywhere delight the traveler in the Sierra.

—from the *Overland Monthly* (May 1896), Theodore Solomons

Seven Gables Peak. Photo By Kit Robberson

the meadows a set of drift fences indicates the grounds of the **Muir Trail Ranch.** A wilderness vacation here can include a modicum of creature comforts along with the pleasures of horseback riding, fishing, hiking, and lounging. The Florence Lake Trail ends at Shooting Star Meadow, where the John Muir/Pacific Crest Trail heads southeast into Kings Canyon National Park or north toward **Selden Pass** (el. 10,870 feet).

INTO THE BEAR CREEK BASIN

Drivers who opt for the north fork of Kaiser Pass Road will pass by **Mono Hot Springs** on the way to Lake Thomas Edison. The resort, built in 1935 and on the National Register of Historic Places, has a long and venerable counter-culture history. Tie-dyed T-shirts are likely to outnumber Hawaiian print button-downs, and it is best not to look for a shop selling a fashionable swimsuit, since swimsuits are not given much regard here anyway. The stone cabins are charming and quite affordable, and the hot mineral baths are clean and soothing.

Just beyond Mono Hot Springs is a 4WD road leading up to the Bear Diversion Dam, a good embarkation point for explorations into the rugged lake-strewn terraces at the headwaters of **Bear Creek.** Watching over the region are 13,075-foot **Seven Gables** and 13,361-foot **Mount Hilgard.** The creek sings a cheerful traveling song in the right ear of the uphill hiker on nearly every branch of the trail's substantial network. Each verse of the song is illustrated with the sight of delightful water gardens where the snow-fed currents find devious routes through jointed granitic slabs.

Boot-shaped **Lake Italy,** located up Bear Creek's **Hilgard Branch,** sits in a rocky crevice in the western shadow of **Bear Creek Spire** (el. 13,713 feet). The path along its southern shore leads over **Italy Pass** to the Little Lakes or Round Valley regions of the eastern Sierra. (See the U.S. 395 chapters.)

MONO CREEK AND LAKE THOMAS EDISON

North of Mono Hot Springs is a large reservoir named for the father of the electric light. When it was created in 1954, Lake Thomas Edison inundated **Vermilion Valley,** a place that enchanted Theodore Solomons, who wrote about its red-hued cliffs. Now, the sharp cries of nesting ospreys mingle with the sounds of human interlopers coming and going from

Along Bear Creek on the John Muir Trail. Photo By Kit Robberson

the pack station, the water taxi, and the Vermilion Valley Resort. A long trail from the lake's east end leads up Mono Creek, passing the **recesses**, as Solomons dubbed these alluring side canyons. This trail continues to Mono Pass, where it crosses the Sierra crest at 12,040 feet before dropping into Little Lakes Basin (see chapter 4).

MIDDLE FORK AND NORTH FORK SAN JOAQUIN RIVER

The northernmost headwaters of the San Joaquin River emanate from a complex divide near the southeastern border of Yosemite National Park. Visitors to this region of 12,000- and 13,000-foot-high peaks are more apt to start their treks from Yosemite (chapter 8) or from the June Lake or Mammoth Lakes regions described in chapter 4. The rare traveler who makes the long, twisting drive west from Bass Lake into the Ansel Adams Wilderness is rewarded with secluded hiking and camping around enchanting pine-rimmed lakes.

Practical Matters

Summer is the ideal time to visit most of the places described in this chapter, since travel on mountain trails is not likely to be restricted by snow. Above the tree line (around 10,000 feet), the temperature might reach 70 degrees on a warm summer's day and then drop to freezing at night. The highway into Kings Canyon National Park opens in April and closes

AN AUTUMN REVERIE

Every autumn as the shadows lengthen, I feel a deepening urge to make a last camping trip before the Sierra is covered in the white blanket of winter. The weather can be glorious, the summer crowds have dispersed, and nature seems caught in a spell, awaiting transformation. Harbingers of winter are all around—the wind rattling through brittle leaves, the wild creatures scurrying around gathering their stores, the chill creeping through the forest shadows. Slanting sunbeams turn the aspen groves to shimmering gold, and liquid crimson seems to spill from the dogwoods making their autumn change beneath the majestic sequoias. It feels like a special blessing to come out of the tent and step onto the first virgin carpet of snow. As I head down the whitened trail leading back to my warm sea-level home, there's a small temptation to follow the tiny tracks leading off the trail toward some creature's cozy mountain burrow. But winter is about to reclaim this high mountain wilderness for her own, and I, a frail human, come here only as a respectful visitor.

in November, but the main sights on the Generals Highway in Sequoia National Park are open year round. For more on Sierra weather, including climate statistics for Huntington Lake, Fresno, and Grant Grove see the introduction.

ROADS

The main routes into the national parks are Highway 198 from Visalia and Highway 180 from Fresno. Winter access is only via Highway 180. There is a fee charged for entrance into the national parks on these highways. Access to Shaver Lake, Huntington Lake, Florence Lake, and Lake Thomas Edison is via Highway 168, also from Fresno. For access from the east, see chapters 4 and 5. There are commercial airports in Fresno and Visalia. There is no public transportation available into the parks. Note: Some people may find that travel to high elevations can bring on symptoms of altitude sickness — headache, dizziness, fatigue, shortness of breath, loss of appetite, nausea, disturbed sleep, and a general feeling of malaise. If these symptoms occur, return immediately to a lower elevation.

WHERE TO STAY AND EAT

Inside the national parks: Cedar Grove, Grant Grove, and Mineral King. Outside the parks: Three Rivers, Shaver Lake, Mono Hot Springs, Lake

Thomas Edison, Huntington Lake, and Bass Lake. The national forests of this region offer several interesting rentals utilizing decommissioned lookout and ranger facilities.

CAMPING
Nearly every road into the High Sierra from the west side has a dozen campgrounds strung along it.

NATIONAL PARKS AND FORESTS
Sequoia Kings Canyon National Park, www.nps.gov/seki/.
Sequoia National Forest Headquarters, 900 West Grand Avenue, Porterville, 559-784-1500.
Sierra National Forest (www.fs.fed.us/r5/sierra/): **Headquarters,** 1600 Tollhouse Road, Clovis, 559-297-0706, 800-735-2929; **High Sierra Ranger District,** 29688 Auberry Road, Prather, 559-855-5355; **Bass Lake Ranger District,** 7003 Road 225, North Fork, 559-877-2218.

REGIONAL GUIDES
Krist, John. *50 Best Short Hikes in Yosemite and Sequoia/Kings Canyon.* Berkeley, Calif.: Wilderness Press, 1993.
Roper, Steve. *Sierra High Route: Traversing Timberline Country.* Seattle, Wash.: The Mountaineers, 1997.
Robinson, Douglas. *Starr's Guide: John Muir Trail.* San Francisco, Calif.: Sierra Club Books, 1982.
Secor, R. J. *The High Sierra: Peaks, Passes, and Trails.* Seattle, Wash.: The Mountaineers, 1999.

8

Yosemite National Park

Why do 4 million people come to Yosemite every year? The answer can be found with every word in this chapter, but still, you must see for yourself. Your second, third, fourth, and fifth visits are likely be those of a lover returning to a beloved.

At Yosemite Valley on a warm spring day, the air seems to tremble as falling water thunders from every direction, coming out of the snow-covered high-country to leap from mythic formations of glittering granitic rock. The stone monuments rise so nearly perpendicular from the flat valley floor that they appear to have emerged from the ground in a cataclysmic moment.

As summer mounts and the gush of snowmelt slows, the waterfalls become wispy shades of their former splendor. But now all roads are open, and crowds fan out into the Yosemite high country, where the sun dances among wildflowers and spills across the high glacier-polished domes. On nights when moonlight floods the meadows, bear and deer run with wild abandon.

The most devoted Yosemite visitors come in autumn, when they might share the Valley's leaf-strewn paths with bobcat and coyote, and in winter, when they delight in a changed valley landscape, making their forays on snowshoes or skis and returning to a roaring fire in an historic lodge. The most intrepid cross-country skiers, unbowed by the snow that bars automobiles from the high country, experience the Yosemite rooftop at its most sublime as the regal snow banners unfurl from the high peaks.

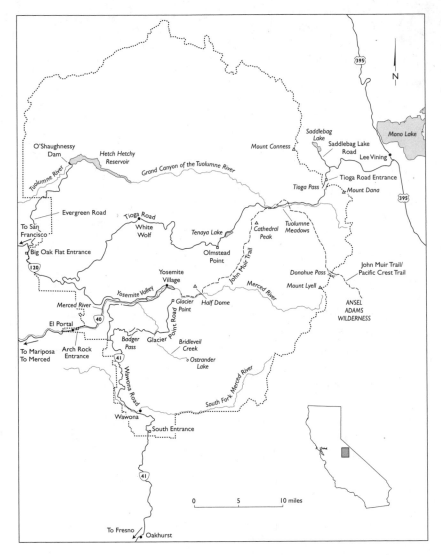

YOSEMITE NATIONAL PARK

A first view of Yosemite Valley. Photo by Erlda Parker

Visitors come to Yosemite National Park in cars and tour buses, on motorcycles and bicycles, and surprisingly, quite a few arrive on foot, walking all the way here from Mount Whitney via the John Muir Trail. Some visitors return again and again, aiming to explore as much as they can of these 1,200 square miles of extraordinary wilderness, while others do nothing more than go around to the major sights of Yosemite Valley.

Yosemite Valley (el. 3,985 feet)

This tour begins at the mouth of Yosemite Valley, with a view that has been immortalized by countless painters and photographers. The first-known written description of that vista was in a journal entry by William Penn Abrams, a member of the Mariposa Battalion (see later in this chapter), who in October 1849 became lost in the wilderness while tracking down a grizzly bear. He writes, "[We] found our way to camp over an old Indian trail that led past a valley enclosed by stupendous cliffs rising perhaps 3,000 feet from their base and which gave us cause for wonder. Not far off, a waterfall dropped from a cliff below three jagged peaks into the valley, while further beyond a rounded mountain stood, the valley side of which looked as though it had been sliced with a knife as one would slice a loaf of bread and which Reamer and I called the Rock of Ages."

As many times as I have seen this view while approaching the Valley on Big Oak Flat Road, Wawona Road, or Highway 140 (the three roads that converge at the Valley mouth), I still have cause for wonder at the stupendous cliffs — 3,000-foot-tall El Capitan rises on the left, the white wisp of Bridalveil Fall sways beside the three jagged forms of Cathedral Rocks on the right, and there in the distance is Half Dome, which indeed looks as though it has been sliced with a knife.

Since Abrams's day we have learned how this U-shaped valley was sculpted around 10,000 years ago, during the ice ages. The retreating glacier that tore away half of Half Dome also tore away at the beds of creeks that now fall from "hanging valleys," such as the one from which **Bridalveil Fall** spills in a swaying 620-foot-long spray. Bridalveil Fall sits near the mouth of the Valley, and so for many visitors, it is the first stop on a Valley tour.

Note: Four different roads provide entry into Yosemite National Park; each is described later in this chapter and in the "Practical Matters" at the end of the chapter.

Continue east into the Valley, and you will find that you are passing through a series of grassy meadows. These were once a chain of lakes that formed behind the huge terminal moraine that dammed the Merced River as the ice age glaciers retreated. At that time, the Merced was flowing in a canyon 2,000 feet lower than the present valley floor.

In his book *The Yosemite*, the Scotsman John Muir describes Yosemite Valley as

> situated in the basin of the Merced River at an elevation of 4000 feet above the level of the sea. It is about seven miles long, half a mile to a mile wide, and nearly a mile deep in the solid granite flank of the range. The walls are made up of rocks, mountains in size, partly separated from each other by side cañons, and they are so sheer in front, and so compactly and harmoniously arranged on

Bridalveil Fall spills from its hanging valley. Photo by Erlda Parker

a level floor, that this Valley, comprehensively seen, looks like an immense hall or temple lighted from above.

Though not a scientist by training, Muir was one by virtue of his penetrating observance of nature. He was one of the first to propose that the Valley had been given its particular features through the action of glaciers cutting into the solid granitic core of the mountain range. In *Studies in the Sierra,* he wrote:

> In the beginning of the long glacial winter, the lofty Sierra seems to have consisted of one vast undulating wave, in which a thousand separate mountains, with their domes and spires, their innumerable canyons and lake basins, lay concealed. In the development of these, the Master Builder chose for a tool, not the earthquake or lightning to rend asunder, not the stormy torrent or eroding rain, but the tender snow-flowers, noiselessly falling through unnumbered seasons, the offspring of the sun and the sea.

A Sierra juniper keeps company with an erratic boulder on one of Yosemites granitic domes. Photo by Erlda Parker

As you drive into the Valley, you will notice many signs indicating parking areas for both day and overnight use. Please consider leaving your car in one of these areas while you continue your tour on foot. If you don't want to walk, you can ride the free shuttle bus, which makes stops at every major sight in the Valley.

The main center of human activity in the Valley is about five miles in at **Yosemite Village.** The village is situated at the spot where the Ahwahneechee band of Southern Sierra Miwoks were living when William Penn Abrams (see above) first poked his head in at the Ahwahnee (the Miwok name for the Valley, which means "place like a gaping mouth"). The Ahwahneechee (dwellers in the Ahwahnee) favored the valley for its moderate climate and for the abundance of acorns and game it provided. Today, if you speak the Miwok name for this place, most folks will assume you are referring to the large and luxurious **Ahwahnee** Hotel built in Yosemite Village in 1927.

The inevitable and tragic clashes between the new population of gold era settlers with the native populations resulted in much bloodshed and an extensive change in the way of life for the Ahwahneechee. The initial clashes are given lengthy account in *Discovery of the Yosemite, and the Indian War of 1851 Which Led to That Discovery,* by Lafayette H. Bunnell (Abrams' compatriot in the Mariposa Battalion), and also by Yosemite entrepreneur James M. Hutchings in his article "In the Heart of the Sierras," published in 1888. Both works detail how Governor McDougal proclaimed the formation of militias, such as the Mariposa Battalion, to hunt out the Mariposa region's "recalcitrant Indians" who did not willingly go to the established reservations, or *rancherías,* in the Central Valley marshland. It was during one of these hunts for the fugitives that Abrams, Bunnell, and the Mariposa Battalion first saw Yosemite Valley. Bunnell, especially, fell in love with it and he went on to christen many of Yosemite's features with the names we know them by today.

To learn about life in Yosemite before 1851, visit the **Indian Village,** which is in Yosemite Village behind the Yosemite Museum. Exhibits at the Indian Village, Yosemite Museum, and the **Valley Visitor Center** provide an excellent orientation for your visit. Many sights are within an easy hike from the village.

ON INDIAN BASKETRY

The basket was an all-important tool in the daily life of the California Indians. Baskets were used for gathering and storage of most foods and materials, and for carrying babies. They were used as serving platters and communal dinner plates, and even for cooking and carrying water. The baskets were carefully and tightly woven, and could be waterproofed with pine pitch or soap root as necessary. They were also very beautiful, and it was this quality that ensured the craft's survival through the general cultural destruction. Increasingly, the baskets were made to appeal to collectors rather than for daily use.

In the recent revival of basket making among California Indians, the traditional materials, such as sedge, bracken fern, redbud, and willow, are gathered from locations that hold spiritual significance to the basket makers. As a result, organizations like the California Indian Basketweavers Association have focused their efforts on restoration and environmental reform at those sites. Basket-making demonstrations and workshops are held at various locations around the state. Look for workshops led by Julia Parker, a Kashaya Pomo who works as a cultural specialist at the Yosemite Museum, a position formerly held by her husband's grandmother, Lucy Telles, a Mono Lake Paiute. Along with her daughter Lucy, Julia Parker works to preserve the games, tools, and foods of California Indians, as well as the basketry.

EAST FROM YOSEMITE VILLAGE

It's an easy hike up the footpaths heading east from the Ahwahnee Hotel to **Tenaya Creek,** and only a short distance further to **Mirror Lake.** On a warm November day, I stood on the lakeshore trying, with some difficulty, to imagine what this wilderness spot would have been like in the 1860s when horses and wagons rumbled up the path to drop handsomely clad vacationers at a newly built hotel, boathouse, and dance pavilion, now long gone. My attention was drawn to some backpackers ambling down from Tioga Road (Highway 120) along **Snow Creek.** Up the canyon to the east, I could see the first snow of the season blanketing **Clouds Rest,** at 9,926 feet. But more compelling was the image of massive **Half Dome** (el. 8,842 feet) reflected in the ice-rimmed, wind-riffled mirror of the lake, a vision that must have entranced Bunnell and his friends when they first happened by.

The southeast end of the Valley is where **Curry Village** and most of the campgrounds are located. Paths lead south and east up stone stairways along the Merced River to the thundering **Vernal Fall** and **Nevada Fall** where rainbows arc through the misty spray on a summer's day. Along the way, trail-splits provide many choices of route. Hikers who want a close up view of the falls choose the Mist Trail, where they run the chance of being baptized in the mist. Other splits lead to such destinations as **Illilouette Fall** and a string of south rim overlooks, or Little Yosemite Valley, and up to the rounded half of Half Dome, where cables have been installed to keep hikers from careening off the slick surface. Backpackers seen along here might be beginning or ending a long trek on the **John Muir Trail** (see chapter 7).

WEST FROM YOSEMITE VILLAGE

Return to Yosemite Village to begin your exploration of the sights to its west, but before you head too far toward Yosemite Falls and El Capitan, stop in to visit the shady cemetery. It's a good place to escape the crowds in midsummer while learning a bit about Yosemite's pioneer tourists. One was James Hutchings, who arrived in the Valley the summer of 1855 in the company of artist Thomas A. Ayers. Hutchings' account of the visit, published in the *Mariposa Gazette* along with Ayers' drawings, prompted two more parties of visitors that summer. By the following summer, Hutchings had begun publication of his *Illustrated California Magazine,* and the first crude hotel appeared in the valley. Within a few years, Yosemite had wagon roads, dwellings, and amenities to support visits from hundreds of tourists.

Also in the cemetery, you will find the grave of Galen Clark, who first came to Yosemite in August 1855 and returned the following year to settle at Wawona. Clark came hoping that the mountain air would improve his health. It did. He stayed in Yosemite for 54 years until his death at the age of 96, by which time he had gained the informal title "Guardian of Yosemite."

Yosemite Creek tumbles down 2,425 feet into the Valley over the upper, middle, and lower steps of **Yosemite Falls.** In early summer, when the sun beats on the south-facing cliff and the creek is swollen with snowmelt, the trail along the upper fall is teeming with ecstatic day hikers who stop to cool themselves in the spray. In winter, the trail is closed, but many fantastic ice sculptures can be seen from the bridge below the lower fall. A favorite time to visit the bridge is at the full moon, when the bright beams cast moonbows through the mist.

Near the Yosemite Falls trailhead is the famous **Camp 4,** unofficial headquarters for the hordes of technical climbers who come to Yosemite each year to try out their skills on **El Capitan.** The climbers attract

A Yosemite resident once described how coyotes often trail him when he walks his dog through the Valley. Photo by Erlda Parker

huge audiences at each point near the road affording a view of the sheer 3,000-foot cliff. Tourists who used to come to the Valley with binoculars to watch wildlife now stand for hours trying to pick out the tiny Lycra-clad worms inching their way up the cliff along well-mapped routes. The most skilled and daring climbers seek virgin routes up the sheer face, and some continue all the way to the top in a journey of several days, sleeping in cocoons and carrying all their supplies in dangling sacks. At the top, friends who have hiked in on an easy (by comparison) eight-mile trail from **Tamarack Flat,** off Tioga Road, will be awaiting the climbers with celebratory beers kept cool in thermal sacks.

I would love to tell you about the view from El Capitan's summit, but I'd go stark raving mad if I had to sleep dangling from a rope, and our hiking trip to the summit from Tamarack Flat had to be rerouted, because of activity by the local northern goshawks. It seems we had chosen the week when the feisty gray raptors were nesting west of the summit in **Ribbon Meadow.** They were showing off their handsome striped under-portions in brilliant dive-bombing raids on any hiker who dared to pass through. I make it a habit to yield the right-of-way to wildlife.

Tioga Road

The portion of Highway 120 known as Tioga Road is an appealing trans-Sierra route during the snow-free seasons, but anyone using it for that purpose must ante up the park entrance fee, and so most of the traffic on the road consists of Yosemite sightseers. The western half of the route, from the park entrance to the May Lake turnoff, is relatively uneventful, as it is thickly forested, with only a few dramatic granitic outcroppings here and there. Keep an eye open for wildlife while you're driving it, however. On one trip, I spotted a handsome red fox crossing the road with a squirrel in its mouth. As so often happens with the curious canids, the fox stopped before disappearing into the forest, turned, and gave me a hard look.

Campgrounds along the stretch are well situated for launching day hikes or backpacking trips to the valley rim or north to the Grand Can-

(opposite) El Capitan. Photo by Erlda Parker

JOHN MUIR AND THE TRANSCENDENTALISTS

When John Muir first arrived in California in 1868, he left directly from the docks in San Francisco to walk to Yosemite, where he would spend the better part of the next decade, looking deeply into the soul of the mountains he called the "Range of Light." Muir seemed to be wholly unencumbered by thoughts of danger, cold, or hunger as he wandered through the high country for weeks on end with only an overcoat and some crusts of bread as provisions. He slept on beds of pine boughs and allowed his inquisitive mind and poet's soul to unwind the workings of nature. He looked into the ways of her smallest birds and flowers, and into the origins of her grandest glaciers and stone monuments.

Muir's way of looking at nature resonated with the concurrent rise of American Transcendentalism, a complex philosophical and artistic movement that placed Man in a spiritual relationship with Nature. In New England, the movement was just reaching its most notable fruition in the work of writers Henry David Thoreau and Ralph Waldo Emerson; painters Thomas Cole and Albert Bierstadt; landscape architect and public space advocate Frederick Law Olmsted; and the preacher, writer, and lecturer, Rev. Thomas Starr King, who was called from Boston to serve in San Francisco in 1860. After Starr King's visits to Lake Tahoe, Yosemite, and the sequoia groves, he was moved to write on his observations for the *Boston Transcript,* whose audience of powerful easterners was already deeply under his sway. Further evidence of the Sierra splendors came about as practitioners of the quickly developing art of photography joined the painters in Yosemite. Carleton E. Watkins' stereographic and mammoth plate views of Yosemite appeared before the same eyes that were reading the *Boston Transcript* and marvelling at Bierstadt's extravagant oil renderings of Yosemite. The result was an act of Congress passed in 1864 granting Yosemite Valley and the Mariposa Grove of Big Trees to the state of California for all time as a public recreation area. (The concept of a national park was yet to be envisioned.) With this seed firmly planted, the wilderness conservation movement began to grow, especially as it fell under the visionary leadership of John Muir.

Muir's presence in Yosemite drew a formidable gathering of like-minded spirits who would eventually unite to form the **Sierra Club.** The club's original tenet was that the public should become intimate with the wilderness, so that people would recognize and forever honor the role of wild nature in the collective psyche. It remains to be seen if humanity is capable of this evolution, and many recent warriors in the environmental movement have come to advocate a more distant relationship between humankind and wilderness.

yon of the Tuolumne River, Hetch Hetchy, and points beyond. At **White Wolf** there are concessions and lodging.

The eastern portion of Tioga Road offers up a string of startling vistas with dramatic granitic domes that slope right down to the road. Resist the urge to pull over to investigate every dramatic sight. There are many well-designed vista points that allow curious folks to stop safely without causing an accident.

Exfoliating granitic domes on Tioga Road in Yosemite National Park. Photo by Erlda Parker

OLMSTED POINT (el. 8,420 feet)

The quintessential views in the eastern Yosemite high country are from Olmsted Point. Half Dome is the most distinctive feature to the southwest; turn 180 degrees and the view is of Tenaya Lake shimmering in front of the Cathedral Range. Gleaming granitic domes are everywhere, their surfaces made slick by the polishing action of Pleistocene-era glaciers. As the domes weather, they fracture in layers that gradually come loose in massive blocks and slide off the domes in a process called *exfoliation*.

Olmsted Point is named for the "father of American landscape architecture," Frederick Law Olmsted, and also for his son, Frederick Law Olmsted Jr. Both played a role in the development of Yosemite National Park. The senior Olmsted was instrumental in the establishment of the Yosemite Grant, the legislation signed by Abraham Lincoln in 1864 to give official protection to Yosemite Valley and the Mariposa Grove. From 1928 to 1957, Olmsted Jr. served as an advisor on plans and policies relating to the park.

TENAYA LAKE (el. 8,149 feet)

The Ahwahneechee name for Tenaya Lake and Tenaya Creek was Pywiack, or glistening rocks. A dome to the northeast of the lake along Tenaya

Looking west toward Half Dome from Olmsted Point. Photo by Erlda Parker

Creek and a nearly inaccessible cascade further down the creek retain the name **Pywiack,** a small acknowledgement to the lost world of the Miwok. The lakeshore beckons with picnic areas, a campground, and a beach that makes a good, but chilly place to swim. Those who want to hike might head south on the trail from the campground for a seven-mile round-trip jaunt to **Sunrise Lakes.** Be sure to obtain a trail map and pack proper gear before setting out on such a journey.

TUOLUMNE MEADOWS (el. 8,592 feet)

Tioga Road continues eastward through a stretch of lodgepole pine and enters a long, peaceful meadow where massive, glittering glacier-scraped domes rise up from the grasses. In 1889, there were great herds of sheep wreaking havoc in this meadow, as homesteading and mining were rampant in the high country surrounding the valley. Rather than simply grieve over the destruction, John Muir brought *Century Magazine* editor Robert Underwood Johnson here on a camping trip. He explained to Johnson, who had substantial influence in Washington, how the sheep in this meadow were destroying the watershed of the creeks that cascade into the valley. As the two sat around the campfire, they conceived of the idea of a larger Yosemite National Park that would encompass and protect the watersheds of the Tuolumne and the Merced rivers. The idea became a reality in the Yosemite Act of 1890.

Two years later, the Sierra Club was incorporated, and its members elected Muir as their first president. On the club's first official outing, or High Trip, 96 participants spent an idyllic month at **Soda Springs** in Tuolumne Meadows, the same spot where Muir and Johnson first chiseled out their plan. The outing, like many thereafter, educated and challenged participants (men and women alike) with guided climbs of 13,053-foot **Mount Dana** and 13,114-foot **Mount Lyell,** the highest Yosemite peaks. Meals were prepared using an extensive mobile kitchen, and the evenings were filled with musical performances and presentations by renowned mountaineers and scientists.

In 1915, the Sierra Club built the beautiful **Parsons Lodge** at Soda Springs to honor Edward T. Parsons, whose mountaineering expertise had been such an asset on the first outings. The design is thought to be the work of Bernard Maybeck. With its thick walls of undressed local

Looking east at Tenaya Lake from Olmsted Point. Photo by Erlda Parker

The Cathedral Range makes an intriguing skyline at Tuolumne Meadows. Photo by Erlda Parker

rubble stone, the design embodied the "expressive use of simple natural materials," a hallmark of the Arts and Crafts movement. The lodge is now a park nature center, open in summer only.

The **Tuolumne River** runs by the front of the lodge, rushing under a stone footbridge on its way toward the magnificent **Grand Canyon of the Tuolumne River,** a remote wonder of the park, which is best visited as a multi-day backpacking adventure. At the end of this 15-mile canyon is O'Shaughnessy Dam, which holds back the Tuolumne's waters in the notorious Hetch Hetchy Reservoir (see later in this chapter). After the dam, the river flows unencumbered in its protected Wild and Scenic run to Groveland.

A trail of braided ruts meanders southwest from the bridge at Soda Springs, heading through the meadow in the direction of a group of whimsical granitic spires — part of the Cathedral Range. The 10,911-foot-high mountain that looks like it has a little medieval chapel perched on its top is appropriately named **Cathedral Peak.** To its east are the finger-like projections of **Echo Peaks** and **Cockscomb** (el. 11,065 feet), and the big gray horn of **Unicorn Peak** (el. 10,823 feet).

A visitor center, ranger station, campground, and the Tuolumne Meadows Lodge are all located on the south side of the road. The "lodge" is the centerpiece of the six **High Sierra Camps,** a circuit of camps set at six- to nine-mile intervals. Hikers who are lucky enough to win the reservations (divvied out by lottery each winter) speak dreamily of a week spent hiking the circuit, or riding it on horseback, with only a daypack full of clothing, water, snacks, and maybe a book. At each camp, they get a shower, two meals, and a night on a real bed in a canvas tent.

TIOGA PASS (el. 9,945 feet)

Tioga Road crosses the Sierra crest in a saddle between 11,004-foot **Gaylor Peak** and 13,057-foot **Mount Dana.** Here at the park's eastern boundary, the granitic Sierra Nevada batholith butts up against the older, metamorphic host rocks. The latter look startlingly varied in color by comparison. Mount Dana, to the south, is a remnant of a violent volcanic eruption that took place roughly 220 million years ago. A most appealing place in which to investigate the volcanic landscape is the 20 Lakes Basin northwest of Saddlebag Lake.

SADDLEBAG LAKE (el. 10,087 feet)

Just outside the park are campgrounds and services at **Tioga and Ellery lakes.** About two miles east of the **Tioga Road Entrance,** watch for Saddlebag Lake Road. Take this northwest for 2.5 miles to reach Saddlebag Lake Campground, which is set in a grove of stubby whitebark pine beside the lake. At just above 10,087 feet, this is the highest drive-to campground in the Sierra. You might simply sit beside the lake to watch the ospreys and bald eagles swooping in for their breakfast, but it is well worth the effort to lace up your boots and hike to the **20 Lakes Basin.** A water taxi service, offered in summer by the Saddlebag Lake Resort, allows hikers to skip the long haul through scree on either side of the lake. The hike continues on into the splendid terraced gardens of water and colorful metamorphic rocks on the flanks of 12,590-foot **Mount Conness,** 12,242-foot **North Peak,** and the **Shepherd Crest.**

Highway 120 — Big Oak Flat Entrance

Frequent Yosemite visitors who use the Big Oak Flat Entrance on Highway 120 don't look forward to the long and winding stretch called Priest

Grade Road that lies west of Groveland. An alternate route, the old Priest Grade Road on the south side of the canyon, is faster, but very steep. Both can leave riders feeling queasy, and there's the unsettling sight of crosses and plastic bouquets all along the way. Beginning or ending this ordeal, some travelers are inclined to stop at historic Groveland for food and lodging.

HETCH HETCHY RESERVOIR (el. 3,800 feet)

Just outside Yosemite National Park, about a mile west of the entrance station, is Evergreen Road, the route to Hetch Hetchy, a side trip that should be made by anyone who truly wants to know Yosemite and its history. From Highway 120, take Evergreen Road north for about seven miles to Evergreen Lodge (a comfortable base of operations, in the seasons when it is in business) and continue another nine miles to the parking lot at O'Shaughnessy Dam.

Engineers for the city of San Francisco began building O'Shaughnessy Dam at the mouth of Hetch Hetchy Valley in 1913, and by 1938, they had completed a dam rising 430 feet. Other components of the project, which supplies water to more than 2.5 million residents of the San Francisco Bay Area, can be visited at sites further west. (See chapter 9.)

When John Muir died of pneumonia in 1914, many believed it was from heartbreak over the loss of the long fight he had waged to save the Tuolumne River's Hetch Hetchy Valley from San Francisco's plans to make it into a reservoir. He called Hetch Hetchy the "Tuolumne Yosemite," and Yosemite Valley, the "Merced Yosemite." In *The Yosemite*, he describes a scene that is now partly lost beneath 360,360 acre-feet of water:

> Imagine yourself in Hetch Hetchy on a sunny day in June, standing waist-deep in grass and flowers (as I have often stood), while the great pines sway dreamily with scarcely perceptible motion. Looking northward across the Valley you see a plain, gray granite cliff rising abruptly out of the gardens and groves to a height of 1800 feet, and in front of it Tueeulala's silvery scarf burning with irised sun-fire. In the first white outburst at the head there is abundance

(preceding spread) The Mono Craters seen from Tioga Pass. Photo by Erlda Parker of visible energy, but it is speedily hushed and concealed in divine repose . . . changing to varied forms of cloud-like drapery. Near the bottom the width of the fall has increased from about twenty-five feet to a hundred feet. Here it is composed of yet finer tissues, and is still without a trace of disorder — air, water and sunlight woven into stuff that spirits might wear.

Some say that what is lost under the water in Hetch Hetchy is, perhaps, gained back in solitude, since few people come to this forgotten corner of Yosemite National Park. Today's visitors can follow a trail across O'Shaughnessy Dam for a hike above the reservoir along the valley's north cliffs. The trail continues on to cross paths with Tueeulala and Wapama falls, both awesome sights during spring runoff. The views across the water to tall Kolana Rock give a sense of the former majesty of Muir's Hetch Hetchy Yosemite. Backpackers continue beyond the reservoir and on into the Grand Canyon of the Tuolumne, or they climb one of several trails up the north side of the canyon to begin an exploration of the northern Yosemite backcountry.

Highway 140 — Arch Rock Entrance

Two giant blocks of fallen granitic rock form the striking stone archway at Yosemite's Arch Rock entry station. As you exit the park on this route, you will be following the Merced River down through its canyon. Flood and landslide have often closed this roadway, and the resulting isolation adds to the mystical quality that hovers over the river. Heightening the feeling is the presence of a stretch of distorted rocks noted to be the oldest of the old metamorphics in the Yosemite region, and the abandoned bed of a railroad that once followed the river along its north bank. From 1907 to 1945, Yosemite visitors could ride the **Yosemite Valley Railroad** up the Merced to **El Portal**. Today, as part of the Yosemite Plan to relieve overuse of Yosemite Valley by visitors and park services, some of the national park's infrastructure is being moved to El Portal, a development that also gives some hope to the idea of reviving the rail line.

About eight miles west of El Portal, Highway 140 crosses a bridge over the South Fork Merced River at its confluence with the main Middle Fork coming out of Yosemite Valley. For the next 10 miles along this stretch of National Wild and Scenic River, it is possible to pick out a faint trail that contours high along the steep northern bank above the old rail bed. The path is now abandoned, but in earlier times, it was a busy route for Indian traders on long treks between coastal, mountain, and Great Basin regions. In places, the handiwork of ancient stonemasons can be seen in brief retaining walls, but in others, the gradual effects of time and water have pulled the hillside toward the river, erasing portions of the trail. If you were to ford the river and climb up to walk along the trail, you might find no other recent human footprints, only those of prowling bobcats and coyotes. This I learned from Lettie Barry, proprietress of the Redbud Lodge, a quaint inn located at the river junction. The lodge occupies the former site of prospector James D. Savage's trading post, burned down by the Ahwahneechee, an act that led to the formation of the Mariposa Battalion. Near the Redbud Lodge, along the northeast bank of the South Fork Merced, the Miwok trail continues to the old mine at **Hite's Cove.** This upper portion of the trail is still very much in service (and badly overused). The high, steep riverbank here bursts out with a stunning profusion of wildflowers in the spring.

Wawona Road to the South Entrance

Highway 41 from Yosemite Valley to Wawona dates back to the first days of Yosemite tourism when it was a footpath often used by early resident Galen Clark. Clark chose a high meadow well to the south of the valley for his home, a place that came to be called Wawona. The Wawona Road was built in 1875, but the tunnel did not go in until 1933. The parking area just before the tunnel affords a good last view of the valley. Hikers can start out from here on a strenuous trek to **Inspiration Point** and a string of great valley overlooks.

Seven miles south of the tunnel, **Glacier Point Road** heads off to the east from Highway 41. It leads 16 miles to, surprise, **Glacier Point.** The road is open during snow-free months, offering motorists a unique view of Vernal and Nevada falls, Half Dome, Mirror Lake, and the valley floor more than 3,000 feet below. The Glacier Point Lodge is a comfortable place to linger, especially after a long hike on one of the many trails to the valley or the backcountry that can be accessed from this route.

WINTER ON GLACIER POINT ROAD

In winter, Glacier Point Road is kept plowed as far as **Badger Pass** (el. 7,300 feet). Skiers started coming here shortly after 1927, when the opening of the All-Year Highway and the swank new Ahwahnee Hotel made Yosemite Valley into an appealing winter destination. Activities at first were essentially flatland sports — skating and hockey, with ski jumping and sledding taking place on constructed terrain. But with the formation of the Yosemite Winter Club's Western Ski School, skiers began making cross-country excursions into the high country.

As the 1929 Winter Olympics approached, the newly formed Curry Company (which was to run the Yosemite concessions until 1990) decided to put in a bid to host the games. But the Olympic Committee thought the Sierra Nevada was too wild and unknown a place, and decided to hold the games in Lake Placid, New York, instead. In 1929, there was no

The back of Half Dome from Horizon Ridge. Mount Hoffmann is the high point on the horizon.
Photo by Mark Middlebrook

snow at Lake Placid and the games had to be held on hay bales. It was a record winter for Sierra snowfall.

In the early 1930s, a new high country lodge equipped with the Upski, a newfangled contraption of two counterbalanced sleds, made Badger Pass into the nation's first true ski resort. Today, the little resort has modern chairlifts and a legendary ski school that is over 70 years old. Badger Pass remains a favorite ski destination for families, novices, and those who want to experience Yosemite in the relative solitude of the winter season. This is also a take-off point for some great cross-country skiing.

Adventurous skiers carry their packs out into the backcountry, perhaps spending the night in a snow cave or simply stretched out on the snow. Others prefer to make the 10-mile glide on groomed track to Glacier Point and spend the night at Glacier Point Lodge. For a day trip, it is hard to beat the experience of the three-mile backcountry trail to

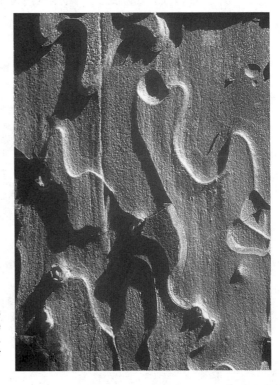

Ponderosa pine bark flakes into forms shaped like pieces from a jigsaw puzzle. Photo by Erlda Parker

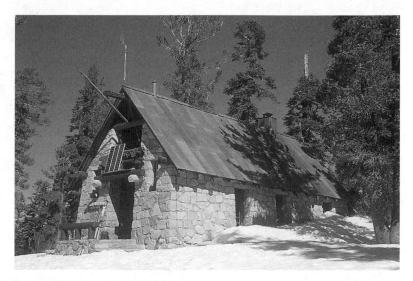

Ostrander Hut. Photo by Mark Middlebrook

Dewey Point, where a rocky promontory affords superb views down into Yosemite Valley. Along the way is a majestic ponderosa pine. I once stopped here to rest on the apron of bare ground around the tree's massive, fissured trunk. The wider ring of snow beneath the reach of the tree's massive limbs displayed a scattered tapestry of twigs, bundles of needles, curled seed pods, bark flakes shaped like pieces from a jigsaw puzzle, and clumps of the iridescent green wolf lichen that clings to tree trunks all through the forest. A pair of glossy black ravens put on a low soaring display — the air flowed over their powerful wings with a rattling whistle that broke the prevailing silence.

One year in March my husband joined me on an overnight excursion that tested the limits of my interest in skiing with a backpack. Our packs contained all the gear we might need if we were to become stranded by a snowstorm somewhere along the 10-mile route to **Ostrander Hut.** As we set out southeast over 8,000-foot **Horizon Ridge,** we looked to the north to see the rounded back of Half Dome, still wearing its white winter cap. To the east stood the long, snow-draped ridge of the **Clark Range.** Ahead, to the south, lay the ice-covered **Ostrander Lake** and beside it,

BACKPACKER'S WILD MUSHROOM STEW WITH POLENTA

Backpackers often note that the simplest meal prepared out on the trail can seem like a gourmet feast, but my feeling is that there is no reason not to have a gourmet feast while out in the wilderness. The ingredients and tools needed for this dish are all lightweight and durable enough to carry in a backpack, and the presentation makes a great impression on fellow campers. Serves 4 (or maybe only 2, if they are extremely hungry).

1 ounce dried wild mushrooms, soaked in 1-½ cups hot water for 30 minutes
1 pound fresh mushrooms, any variety, but a mixture is nice
  (substitute an additional 2 ounces of dried mushrooms—soaked in 3 more
  cups hot water—if you don't want to pack in the fresh ones)
3 tablespoons of olive oil (or duck fat, if you happen to have some)
3 ounces of prosciutto or dry ham (such as Westphalian), chopped
2 shallots, minced
1 clove garlic, minced
5 sun-dried tomatoes, chopped
¾ cup of a soft fruity white wine (and just think, you get to drink the rest of
  the bottle with dinner!)
salt and pepper, to taste
2–4 tablespoons chopped fresh parsley (dried is not a substitute)
1 lemon
½ cup stone-ground cornmeal or polenta (you might want to use the
  quick-cooking variety)
2 cups water

Drain the soaked mushrooms, setting aside the soaking liquid after straining it through a coffee filter to remove the grit. Heat the olive oil in a large saucepan, and sauté the dried mushrooms briefly before adding the soaking liquid. Simmer over medium heat until most of the liquid has evaporated. Stir in the ham, shallots, garlic, and sun-dried tomatoes, and let simmer for 1 minute. Add the fresh mushrooms and simmer, stirring occasionally, until the fresh mushrooms have given off their moisture. Add the wine, salt and pepper to taste, and simmer for 20 minutes.

While the stew simmers, bring the 2 cups of water to a boil in another saucepan and slowly whisk in the polenta or cornmeal. Bring to a boil again, and then adjust the heat so the polenta can bubble without becoming explosive as it thickens. Cornmeal or standard polenta should be cooked for at least 20 minutes. (Quick-cooking polenta only takes a few minutes, so you could start it cooking shortly before the mushroom stew is done simmering).

the beautiful hut, constructed of granite and logs by the Civilian Conservation Corps in 1940. As it turned out, we did not get caught in a blizzard, and we enjoyed our wild mushroom stew with polenta at the hut's long wooden table. For company, there was hut-keeper, photographer, and ski-mountaineer, Howard Weamer; Bill Bowie, a former Yosemite Valley physician and expert backcountry skier; Kristen Kusic, a naturalist who had catalogued all the birds of Yosemite the summer before; and Walter Heady, another birder, who performed a perfect imitation of a mockingbird imitating a car alarm.

Making our way home though the sun-cupped snow, we recognized the odd thumping sound that Kristen had described as that of the ground-nesting blue grouse. Over in a nearby stand of fir we caught a lucky glimpse of a marten in pursuit of a tasty rodent.

WAWONA (el. 4,012 feet)

First-time guests who make overnight reservations in Yosemite are sometimes disappointed when they find they've booked themselves in at Wawona without realizing how long it takes to drive between the hotel and the valley. And then to add insult to injury, there are no TVs at the Wawona Hotel. For some of us, that's all the better. The Wawona Hotel is a gracious Victorian mansion set on a sprawling lawn, with a quaint, old golf course running off into the adjacent meadow. If I ever find myself becoming a lady of leisure, I will don an elegant Victorian gown and spend a few days reading steamy novels in one of the Adirondack chairs on the Wawona lawn. I'll take my dinner in the dining room and then retire to the parlor where baritone Tom Bopp accompanies himself on the grand piano. Within Bopp's repertoire are songs by Stephen Foster and Robert Burns, along with lesser-known works — paeans to Yosemite from old sheet music printed with woodcuts of Yosemite's waterfalls on the covers. Bopp's performances turn into illustrated history lessons that wander back to the days when Galen Clark, the "Guardian of Yosemite," lived at Wawona. Some evenings, Bopp even includes a show of slides from his Wawona archives. He says his favorite quote about Wawona comes from *Yosemite Trails,* a travel book published in 1911 by J. Smeaton Chase: "I for one always feel that if Yosemite has the greater glory, Wawona has the deeper charm."

At the far end of Wawona Road, near the park's south entrance, is the **Mariposa Grove,** a magnificent stand of giant sequoias. The regal trees seem to stand aloof from the multitudes of visitors, most of whom

Through the magic of software, Tom Bopp, pianist and devoted historian of all things Wawona, imagines himself in earlier times at the Wawona Hotel. The brochure is from 1920. The portrait is by photographer/historian Leroy Radanovich.

don't venture beyond the fire-scarred Grizzly Giant located a short walk from the parking lot. The giant's estimated age of 2,700 years makes it one of the world's oldest living sequoias. There is nothing to compare to the sublime experience of climbing through the grove on skis or snowshoes in winter; this is when I find the trees to be in their most eloquent disposition.

Practical Matters

Visit Yosemite Valley in any season. Winter closure of Tioga Road into the high country begins with the first significant snow accumulation (usually in November) and lasts often until May. For more on Sierra weather, including climate statistics for Yosemite National Park, see the introduction.

ROADS

Automobiles enter Yosemite National Park through three gateways on the west side of the range and one on the east side. At each entrance, there is a per-car-fee charge, which covers a stay of up to a week. From the San Francisco, Sacramento, and other Northern California areas, the **Big Oak Flat Entrance** on Big Oak Flat Road (Highway 120) is most convenient. (Allow a four-hour drive from San Francisco.) The **Arch Rock Entrance,** 75 miles northeast of Merced on El Portal Road (Highway 140), is best for those coming from the Central Coast and San Joaquin Valley areas. (Seasonal traffic restrictions may apply to Highway 140.) Drivers coming from Southern California often use the **South Entrance,** which is 64 miles north of Fresno via Wawona Road (Highway 41). (Allow a six-hour drive from Los Angeles.) The **Tioga Pass Entrance** (open in snow-free months only) lies 12 miles west of Lee Vining via Tioga Road (Highway 120). This entrance is most convenient for visitors coming from Lake Tahoe and points in Nevada, and it is an alternative to the South Entrance for visitors coming from Southern California. Anyone visiting the Sierra Nevada in winter should carry tire chains and be prepared for snow, cold, and icy conditions that may cause delays and road closures.

OTHER MEANS

Because of overcrowding, the park administration encourages *alternate modes of transportation* to the park. **By air,** Fresno-Yosemite International is the nearest major airport, located 90 miles from Yosemite's southern entrance. Merced Airport is 73 miles from the Arch Rock Entrance. **By bus,** Yosemite Area Regional Transportation System (YARTS) provides transit service from communities near Yosemite National Park in the Mariposa, Merced, and Mono county regions. A variety of shuttle bus and guided-tour options are available within Yosemite Valley and to major high country sights. **By train,** Amtrak provides train service from the San Francisco and Sacramento areas to Merced, with bus connection directly into Yosemite Valley.

WHERE TO STAY AND EAT

Inside-the-park accommodations are plush at the Ahwahnee Hotel, middle-class at Yosemite Lodge, and basic at Curry Village. There are also lodges at White Wolf and Tuolumne Meadows on Tioga Road (Highway 120) and at Wawona (on Highway 41).

Outside the park, services can be found at Groveland (near the Big Oak Flat Entrance on Highway 120), El Portal (near the Arch Rock Entrance on Highway 140), Oakhurst (near the South Entrance on Highway 41), and Lee Vining (near the Tioga Pass Entrance on Highway 120).

CAMPING

There are 13 campgrounds inside the park boundaries. You can make reservations for them through the National Park Reservation System. Near the park's borders, there are campgrounds in the Stanislaus (west side) and Inyo (east side) national forests. Wilderness permits for backcountry camping inside the national park are available at the Wilderness Center in Yosemite Valley and at the Tuolumne Meadows Visitor Center.

U.S. FOREST SERVICE

Stanislaus National Forest (www.fs.fed.us/r5/stanislaus/): **Groveland Ranger District,** 24545 Highway 120, Groveland, 209–962–7825. **Inyo National Forest** (www.fs.fed.us/r5/inyo/index.shtml): **Mono Basin National Forest Scenic Area Visitor Center,** Lee Vining, 760–647–3044.

NATIONAL PARK SERVICE

Yosemite/Sierra Visitors Bureau (www.nps.gov/yose/): 41969 Highway 41, Oakhurst, 559–658–7588.

REGIONAL GUIDES

Wolf, Kurt, Amy Marr, David Lukas, and Cheryl Koehler. *Yosemite National Park.* Victoria, Australia: Lonely Planet Publications, 2003.
Krist, John. *50 Best Short Hikes in Yosemite and Sequoia/Kings Canyon.* Berkeley, Calif.: Wilderness Press, 1993.

9

Gold Country: A Tour on Highway 49

For 326 miles, from near Yosemite National Park's south entrance to the stream-threaded wetlands of the Sierra Valley in the north, Highway 49 runs a wandering course, navigating a rugged terrain of ridges and river canyons. The experience along this route is not one of visiting a great mountain wilderness. Rather, it becomes a vast recollection of an astonishing moment that lasted barely three years in recent human history, the period known as the California Gold Rush.

At nearly every mile along Highway 49, and along many of this region's back roads, the Gold Rush story presents itself, interpreted by green-suited rangers at history parks, by actors in period garb at reconstructed mining villages, by history buffs watching over artifacts in old schoolhouse museums, and, yes, by vendors of souvenir bric-a-brac at far too many gift shops. But even in places where there is no one on hand to testify, the story is still being told, by silent stone ruins sitting at odd turns in the highway, by rusted machinery abandoned deep in the forest, or by bronze plaques placed by innumerable local history societies.

But there are other stories here as well. Tales of the Ancients are revealed in secluded forest parks and tribal museums, and all along the way there are colorful examples of the Western ranching tradition. Of late, tourists are flocking to the foothills to experience the revival of the fruit growing and winemaking that began here during the gold rush.

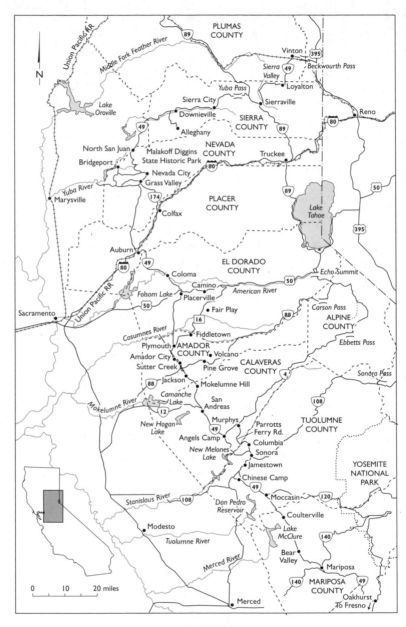

HIGHWAY 49

The California Gold Rush: A Brief History

From the discovery of gold in California in 1848 until the passage of the Sawyer Act in 1884, the economy, geography, and landscape of California went through a profound and rapid change, the likes of which has rarely been seen in human history. The land was tunneled through and blasted open. It was tromped over by the feet of thousands of men and domesticated creatures, and entire sections of virgin forest were leveled to build flumes and mine shafts, and to feed the furnaces that drove the stamp mills. The sound of machinery pounding quartz to dust became deafening. Rivers were rerouted to expose gold deposits in their beds and to harness the phenomenal Sierra waterpower that could blast away any piece of earth that stood between the miner and a suspected deposit. Entire towns sprang up wherever a glimmer of gold caught a prospector's eye, only to be burned down by wildfire or torn down months later as the miners moved to richer diggings.

The summer of 1848 has been described as a time of enchantment for the roughly 5,000 men who came in the first year of the Gold Rush to sift the Sierra riverbeds for golden flakes and nuggets. There was enough for all in the makeshift society that sprang up at the river bars; the gold dust could be simply picked out of the gravel from behind rocks and boulders, or panned, dredged, and sluiced with long toms and rockers. These methods of mining were referred to as placer mining.

Among those in at the beginning of the Gold Rush were a great many Californios (Spanish-speaking inhabitants of California who had been living there before its annexation by the United States, first under Spanish, then Mexican rule), as well as new arrivals from the Mexican state of Sonora. Although this population was largely disdained by arriving Yankee miners, the Spanish speakers contributed much to the methodology and terminology of gold rush. They christened the richest veins *la Veta Madre,* or the Mother Lode, a name that would endure even as the Foreign Miners Taxes of 1850 and 1852 pushed many Spanish-speaking miners out of the workforce.

By the end of 1849, an estimated 42,000 gold seekers (often called Argonauts) had arrived by land and another 39,000 had arrived by sea, coming from every part of the world. The crowded camps became tem-

pestuous places where fortunes were made and lost in a day's work or a night's indulgence. Those selling goods or services to the miners often came away with the most enduring fortunes.

For shelter, the miners built crude brush shacks, simple wooden cabins, or canvas tents, all of which were vulnerable to fire. What fire did not destroy, the miners themselves would tear down to cart off for reassembly at the newest gold strike. Even the more tenacious supply centers were constantly gutted by fire, and so the merchants began to rebuild with brick and native stone, outfitting doors and windows with iron shutters.

As prospectors swarmed through the Sierra, they became both cartographers and geologists as they mapped the rivers and followed the gold underground into fossil riverbeds from the Tertiary period. Miners also became engineers as they redirected the current-day rivers to filter the earth from these dry diggings using ever-more ingenious systems

(above) On Highway 49 in Bear Valley.
(opposite) Gold Country foothills in spring. Photo by Erlda Parker

of flumes. When gold was found trapped in deep veins of quartz, hard rock mining commenced, bringing a new wave of immigrants, including the renowned Cornishmen, whose hard rock skills had been developed through centuries of mining for tin and copper in Cornwall, England.

Hydraulic mining took a leap forward in 1853, when a miner named Edward E. Mattson used a metal nozzle at the end of a hose to wash down a gravel bank near Nevada City. This concept was then developed to become a powerful water canon, called a "monitor," capable of harnessing the power of the rivers and aiming it directly at the gold-rich earth.

It was not long before the ecological cost of hydraulic mining became apparent in clogged navigation routes downstream. The floods created "slickins" of silt and sand downstream, ruining the rich farmlands of the Sacramento Valley, and prompting a series of local and then federal lawsuits. Debates in the California Legislature ended with the injunction issued in 1884 by Federal Circuit Judge Lorenzo Sawyer, prohibiting the mining industry from discharging its debris into the rivers. With this new directive, hydraulic mining became too costly to pursue. However, the diversion of water in California would continue, and would become the lifeline of a very different industry, that of Central Valley agribusiness.

Mariposa County

The county at the southern end of the Mother Lode bears a poetic Spanish name left by the military wayfarer Lieutenant Gabriel Moraga, who explored the Central Valley with his men in 1806. As they climbed into the foothills near Yosemite, the party encountered a swarm of *mariposas* (Spanish for butterflies), and they gave that name to the region. The beautiful name came to represent both a town and an entire county. The Moraga party also christened three of the rivers that flow from the Sierra into the Central Valley: *el Río de los Santos Reyes, el Río de San Joaquin,* and *el Río de Nuestra Señora de la Merced,* now shortened to the less poetic Kings, San Joaquin, and Merced.

In 1846, the intrepid explorer John C. Frémont (who we met in chapters 3 and 6) put down roots in this southern end of the Mother Lode country, becoming a landowner and entrepreneur as he acquired the

44,000-acre Mariposa Grant, previously held by Juan Bautista Alvarado, the last Mexican governor of California.

The Mariposa Grant was a "floating grant," in that the deed specified its size but not its exact boundaries. As gold strikes were made on the Mother Lode, Frémont reinterpreted his claim to include land considerably uphill from his Rancho de las Mariposas. The ensuing question of boundaries resulted in much litigation with considerable influence on subsequent mining-era law. One might fault Frémont for using his power and influence to deprive miners making worthy claims, but his enterprises were an economic asset to the area, and became a basis for the orderly development of communities in Mariposa County.

MARIPOSA (el. 1,950 feet)

Start your tour in the Mariposa civic center, at the unpretentious **Mariposa County Courthouse,** located on Bullion Street between 9th and 10th. When it was built in 1854, the courthouse served a much larger geographical area than it does today. At that time Mariposa County comprised a full fifth of the state of California. A series of charts in the courthouse hallways show how the "Mother of California Counties" gradually became apportioned into 11 different counties. The resulting diminution of the county's importance has perhaps saved the Greek Revival–woodframe building from obsolescence, to the enrichment of us all. The clock in the tower is still wound by hand. The handcrafted benches, lamps, and cast-iron stove in the working courtroom still serve their original functions. It's fun to climb the old wooden staircase to admire the old courtroom, but visitors should be respectful of those here on official business.

On a stroll past the renovated gold era structures of the bustling business district, pay a visit to the **Mariposa County Arts Council** art gallery at 5009 5th Street. The gallery features works by locally based, nationally known artists, most of which pay homage to the extraordinary Yosemite and Sierra scenery and the rich local history and culture.

For a crash course on the science behind Sierra mining, head southeast of town to the Mariposa County Fairgrounds, where the **California State Mining and Mineral Museum** can be found on the northeast side of Highway 49. The museum's exhibits are especially helpful in identification of the native rocks and minerals, such as a locally occurring mineral mariposite. This sparkling green mica is often found mingled into milky-white Mother Lode quartz. Together they make a striking appearance as a building material used all around the town of Mariposa in paving stones, building foundations, and retaining walls. Look for the stone on the Highway 140 bridge over Mariposa Creek on the south side of town.

On the northwest side of town is Jesse Street, named for Jesse Benton Frémont, wife of John C. Frémont and daughter of the powerful Missouri senator, Thomas Hart Benton. At 5116 Jesse Street you will find the **Mariposa Museum and History Center,** a large museum offering a fanciful interpretation of local history, with fun exhibits for kids and many compelling photographs from the archives of local historian, rancher, and artist Leroy Radanovich.

MOUNT OPHIR RUINS

Leaving Mariposa and heading northwest on Highway 49, watch for Mount Ophir Road, which comes up on the left shortly after you pass through the town of Mount Bullion, and parallels the highway's southwest flank. Mount Ophir Road is little more than a short frontage road, and the few vehicles you will see in its makeshift parking slips will likely belong to fishermen.

Park beside the monument marking the site of a once-thriving mining district, and consult the plaque mounted on it for the main features of the story. Then go around to the back of the monument to see the vein of white Mother Lode quartz set in a jagged line down the back. It seems to symbolize the white quartz outcroppings that appear again and again all along the foothill gold region. In places along the road ahead you might see the quartz rising out of the ground like rows of great white teeth.

At the Mount Ophir site, the shade of a few scraggly trees and the creek trickling through Norwegian Gulch provide some respite from the summer heat, but at the height of the mining excitement, any tree growing in the once-flourishing mining district was destined for building materials or firewood.

Grassy hummocks now hide the crumbled foundations of several buildings, and one should take care not to stumble into a grown-over mining tunnel or piece of rusted machinery. The most prominent of the ruins consists of some high but tumbling stone walls, once part of a thriving trading post run by Louis Trabucco, who is known to have set up shop around 1854. The Trabucco name can be found on an old sign in Mariposa and on a store in Bear Valley, just ahead, where Louis' descendents were still in business the last time I checked.

BEAR VALLEY (el. 2,050 feet)
Bear Valley is a tiny town on Highway 49, 11 miles northwest of Mariposa. It was on this spot that John C. Frémont built the headquarters for his mining operations in 1858. His elegant home and a wooden hotel both succumbed to fire, but a few exemplary stone and brick buildings, along with some ramshackle ruins, still stand beside the town's more recently constructed edifices.

(Note: There are several places known as Bear Valley in the Sierra Nevada.)

Northwest of Bear Valley, Highway 49 descends toward the Merced River on the path of a former rail line that was built to bring ore up from Frémont's Josephine and Pine Tree mines. A sign on a pullout marks the site of a fort that Frémont built to defend his claim during the controversies. It is quite clear why Frémont chose this particular location. It commands an astonishing view down toward the mine ruins and far out into the steep and sinuous canyon of the Merced River. The area is called **Hell's Hollow.** Such sublime scenery seems too nice for the denizens of the underworld, although when I drove through in 2001, a recent forest fire had given the chasm a distinctly sinister cast.

COULTERVILLE (el. 1,740 feet)
Seventeen miles beyond Bear Valley, in Coulterville, the handsome wisteria-draped **Hotel Jeffery** beckons visitors to stop for the night, as early Yosemite-bound travelers often did. The hotel's first manifestation was a two-story adobe, built in 1851, at that time called the Mexican Hotel. It included a saloon (still operating) and *fandango* hall. (In Spain, the fandango was a popular dance form, a lively arrangement of steps set to a 3/8 or 6/8 meter. In Mexico and in gold era California, *fandango* came to mean simply a ball or gathering where people danced.) In its time, the Mexican Hotel had to compete with the Coulter Hotel across the high-

Highway 49 crosses the Merced River at Hell's Hollow.

way, but that now-reconstructed 1860s-vintage stone structure no longer takes overnight guests. Instead it houses the **Northern Mariposa County History Center.**

The most compelling structure in town is located several blocks up Main Street on a short tangential street signed Chinatown Main Street. The **Sun Sun Wo Store** is all that is left of Coulterville's once-thriving gold era Chinatown. The humble brown adobe store is attached to another adobe by a series of cheerful yellow wooden lean-tos. The restoration is exceptional and enhanced by colorful free-roaming chickens that stalk the yard for insects. A family of goats lives across the street.

The Sun Sun Wo store in Coulterville.

Tuolumne County

At the junction of Highway 49 with Highway 120 (the Northern Yosemite Highway), 14 miles northwest of Coulterville, massive pipes and concrete blocks dominate the landscape, but there is a quiet elegance about the salmon-pink **Moccasin Powerhouse** on the east side of Highway 49 at Moccasin (el. 950 feet). This graceful, Mediterranean Classical structure is a public works gem from 1925. In spite of its beauty, the powerhouse is likely to bring to mind the controversies to which it is tied. The retired powerhouse is a former component of the San Francisco Public Utilities Commission (SFPUC) complex on the Tuolumne River, a chain of water and power projects of which Hetch Hetchy Reservoir in Yosemite National Park is a part (see chapter 8). Barely a mile ahead on Highway 49 is the huge **Don Pedro Reservoir.** Advocates for restoring Hetch Hetchy Valley argue that Don Pedro Reservoir could easily hold all the water currently impounded behind Hetch Hetchy's O'Shaugnessy Dam.

Between Hetch Hetchy and Don Pedro reservoirs, the Tuolumne River is free to unleash its fury over being so rudely confined. My friend John Kramer, a Calaveras County resident who is both a geologist and river

The Don Pedro Reservoir below Moccasin. Photo by Erlda Parker

guide, calls this 18-mile, class iv–v Wild and Scenic stretch "the champagne of whitewater rafting."

Rafters who frequently sip this champagne are well acquainted with an old Tuolumne River ferry crossing, which they often use to come out of the Tuolumne's deep canyon at the end of a run. The single-lane paved **Wards Ferry Road** runs to the crossing, roughly paralleling Highway 49 between the Groveland (Highway 120) and Sonora (Highway 108) areas. The drive down the switchbacks on the northwest side of the river requires nerves of steel and a trustworthy vehicle, but as I made my way, the only traffic I encountered (much to my relief) was a group of hikers out to take in the glorious April display of wildflowers that was unfurling provocatively on the steep cliffs. Bold yellow mule ears mingled with purple-petaled *brodiaea* and pale Mariposa lilies; poppies and buttercups spread like showers of gold dust through the tenacious greenery. The hikers had driven down the easier-to-negotiate southeast side, parked at the rafters' access and hiked up the northwest side.

CHINESE CAMP (el. 1,261 feet)

Highways 49 and 120 proceed together from Moccasin to Chinese Camp, where the most visible enterprise is a huge logging depot with mountain-

UNDER TABLE MOUNTAIN

Argonauts tunneling under Table Mountain found little to satisfy their gold lust, but a few emerged with Tertiary fossils instead, igniting a controversy of interpretation that involved none other than Josiah D. Whitney, head of the California Geological Survey. Author Bret Harte makes a small error of 300 million or so years in pegging the alleged fossils as Paleozoic, but as an artifact of the gold era society at Table Mountain, this poem is priceless.

I reside at Table Mountain, and my name is Truthful James;
I am not up to small deceit or any sinful games;
And I'll tell in simple language what I know about the row
That broke up our Society upon the Stanislow.

But first I would remark, that it is not a proper plan
For any scientific gent to whale his fellowman,
And, if a member don't agree with his peculiar whim,
To lay for that same member for to "put a head" on him.

Now nothing could be finer or more beautiful to see
Than the first six months' proceedings of that same Society,
Till Brown of Calaveras brought a lot of fossil bones
That he found within a tunnel near the tenement of Jones.

Then Brown he read a paper, and he reconstructed there,
From those same bones, an animal that was extremely rare;
And Jones then asked the chair for a suspension of the rules,
Till he could prove that those same bones was one of his lost mules.

Then Brown he smiled a bitter smile, and said he was at fault,
It seemed he had been trespassing on Jones's family vault;
He was a most sarcastic man, this quiet Mr. Brown,
And on several occasions he had cleaned out the town.

Now I hold it is not decent for a scientific gent
To say another is an ass, — at least, to all intent;
Nor should the individual who happens to be meant
Reply by heaving rocks at him, to any great extent.

Then Abner Dean of Angel's raised a point of order, when
A chunk of old red sandstone took him in the abdomen,
And he smiled a kind of sickly smile, and curled up on the floor,
And the subsequent proceedings interested him no more.

For, in less time than I write it, every member did engage
In a warfare with the remnants of a palæozoic age;
And the way they heaved those fossils in their anger was a sin,
Till the skull of an old mammoth caved the head of Thompson in.

And this is all I have to say of these improper games,
For I live at Table Mountain, and my name is Truthful James;
And I've told in simple language what I know about the row
That broke up our Society upon the Stanislow.

— "The Society upon the Stanislaus," Francis Bret Harte (1839–1902)

ous stacks of Sierra timber. The gargantuan skyhorse and gantry crane look especially macabre at night when the big dangling claw is dramatically lit as if ready to perform in a film about our crashing ecosystems. After recovering from the sight of this startling structure, visitors often look around expecting to find a Chinese restaurant. In fact, the town is named for the Cantonese miners who worked the dry diggings here in 1856, when the population numbered 1,000 and the camp served as a vital transportation center. Today, only a few gold era structures and ruins can be found in the town, which is tucked away to the southwest of the highway.

TABLE MOUNTAIN

At Chinese Camp, Highway 49 turns northward to join Highway 108 (which heads northeastward toward Sonora Pass) and Highway 120 swings westward to join Highway 108 into the Central Valley. Travelers using this corridor often take note of a flat-topped gray-brown landform that winds sinuously down from the mountains like the Great Wall of China. Table Mountain seems to parallel the course of the **Stanislaus Riv-**

This locomotive, built in 1910 for the Sugar Pine Railroad, has spent its whole life in Tuolumne County. It's now stranded on a piece of track near Jamestown. Photo by Beth Burleson

er, and in fact it is, or at one time it was, the Stanislaus River. Table Mountain is a casting in latite lava of the Stanislaus's former bed. During the Sierra Nevada's volcanic activity of the Tertiary period (30 million to 3 million years ago), a volcanic eruption upstream poured lava into the river's channel, filling it as far west as Knights Ferry. Lighter and more erodible volcanic ash settled all around to form a broad layer of tuff (the rock that many gold era buildings are constructed of). The river, thus evicted from its bed, established a new course while the forces of erosion began washing away the lighter tuff, eventually leaving the more resistant latite lava standing as an image in negative of the old riverbed.

One of the best places to get a close-up view of Table Mountain is on Rawhide Road (E5), which provides a Highway 49 bypass just west of the traffic-clogged but picturesque town of Sonora. South of the Rawhide Road junction is the charming village of Jamestown, affectionately known as Jimtown.

JAMESTOWN (el. 1,406 feet)

Jamestown is one of several spots in the Gold Country where families might spend a few days of quality amusement all in one place. From the historic replica hotels on Main Street, visitors can stroll out onto the balcony-shaded plank sidewalks to poke into bustling boutique shops and restaurants. Kids will be struck dumb by the stores full of toys, dolls, and books, and the mesmerizing displays of sugar-spangled cookies and pies at coffee shop counters. Visitors can relive the gold era past by panning for gold or watching the occasional staged gunfight, saloon brawl, or quick-draw competition. But it is just as easy to navigate through the New Age at shops offering crystals, beads, dragons, yoga classes, and even politically enlightened coffee.

The ornate wood-frame **Emporium,** built in 1897, will no doubt catch your eye. On one visit I found it crammed with antiques from every era — spinning wheels, old slot machines, wood-and-gut snowshoes, scary-looking early electrical appliances, old license plates and traffic signals, and antique toys galore.

However, the most exciting antique toys on display in Jamestown are the real trains at **Railtown 1897,** a California State Railroad Museum situated on a large spread just uphill from Main Street. This popular park preserves the roundhouse, depot, and some of the rolling stock of the historic Sierra Railroad. From 1897 until its demise in the Great Depression, the extensive rail system served mining camps, logging operations, and even the builders of Hetch Hetchy Dam. The park owes much of its present-day glamour to its role as a film and video location. Engine #3, an 1891 steam locomotive, is perhaps the most famous movie star (and certainly the oldest) to be found on the site. Anyone who watched *Petticoat Junction* will remember #3 from that show's memorable opening credits sequence. In *The Wild Wild West,* #3 served as James West's rolling headquarters train.

SONORA (el. 1,826 feet)

From Jamestown to Sonora, Highway 49 follows Woods Creek through an area where prospectors made many extraordinarily rich surface gold strikes in 1849. One of the first groups to set up camp on the creek was a contingent of miners from the Mexican state of Sonora. By the following year, the Sonorans' camp had become a very lively place with a population of 5,000. The phenomenal pocket mine named Big Bonanza, located on Piety Hill in the center of town, began operating the following year.

Sonora eventually became the Tuolumne County seat, and its commercial viability was later enhanced by the arrival of the Sierra Railroad. The wealth of the 19th-century town still can be perceived in the long and attractive row of gold era structures on Washington Street (Highway 49). Traffic on this main thoroughfare is notorious, so it is better to park and stroll the town. The walker is ineluctably drawn toward the north end, to the little red Gothic revival structure of **St. James Episcopal Church,** which has beamed its beneficence onto the population since 1859. Sonora was in need of the calming influence in 1851 when Enos Christman, editor of the *Sonora Herald,* described the town and its populace in that paper:

> Sonora is a fast place and no mistake. Such a motley collection as we have here can be found nowhere in California. Sonora has a population hailing from every hole and corner of the globe — Kanakas, Peruvians, Negroes, Spaniards, Mexicans, Chileans, Chinese, British convicts from New South Wales . . . Englishmen, Frenchmen,

St. James Episcopal Church is the highlight of a drive through Sonora. Photo by Erlda Parker

Papeete's home at Columbia State Historic Park.

Dutch, Paddies, and not a small sprinkling of Yankees. We have more gamblers, more drunkards, more ugly, bad women, and larger lumps of gold, and more of them, than any other place of similar dimensions within Uncle Sam's dominions. The Sabbath is regarded as a holiday, granting men and women a more extensive license to practice vice than any other day of the week.

COLUMBIA STATE HISTORIC PARK (el. 2,143 feet)

A few miles northwest of Sonora on Highway 49, signs point the way north on Parrots Ferry Road (E18) through a landscape of strange marbleized limestone to Columbia State Historic Park. An especially eerie outcropping forms a maze of sculptural corridors on the southeast edge of the park, very near the parking lot. Not so long ago, this limestone lay underground. It was brought into view during a spate of hydraulic mining in the 1850s, as miners sought to extract the placer deposits from the site. At that time, the burgeoning town had no water source of its own, and so streams were rerouted and cisterns were installed beneath the town's streets.

Now highly restored and inhabited, but with cars banned from its streets, this "living history" park is one of the most enjoyable stops on a Gold Country history tour. Those who want to step back in time for the night can stay in the elegantly restored and period-furnished City and Fallon hotels. The Fallon has a theater offering top-notch live productions, and the City's restaurant is unmatched in the region.

Columbia can also work its charms in even a brief stay, as I found out when I arrived on the day of its annual firemen's muster. By the end of the event I was utterly smitten — although I'm not really sure if it was because of the firemen or the equipment. Among the fire engines brought out to compete was Papeete, a little 22-man hand-pumper that generally lives in the Tuolumne Engine Company No. 1 Firehouse. Papeete is red, black, and gold, with brass and copper fittings, and its sides are hand-painted with seductive murals of Neptune, water nymphs, and a reclining nude. The engine was manufactured in Boston in 1852 for King George of Tahiti, but it got waylaid in its journey when the ship that was transporting it dropped anchor in San Francisco in 1857. All the sailors jumped ship to head to the diggings, taking the sails to make tents. The little fire engine sat on the docks for two years until some wily "businessman" got the idea of selling it to Columbia.

It was also in Columbia that I began sorting out the stories of the region's infamous bandits, Joaquin Murieta and Black Bart. As I was checking out the collection of books for sale in the Columbia Gazette Printing Office at 11185 Washington Street (a replica of the original building), I got caught up listening to the *Gazette*'s editor and proprietor, Floyd Øydegaard, who was showing off the working letterpress while regaling visitors with local lore. Øydegaard is a big burly fellow with flashing eyes who used to do Black Bart impersonations. He explained that Black Bart was a real person (one Charles Bolton, who signed his rhyming notes as "Black Bart the PO 8"), whereas Joaquin Murieta was a fictional composite derived by miners intent on driving out the *Californios*. (Joaquín was a common given name among them.) After putting those accounts in order, Øydegaard moved on to the subject of local geology, debating the origins of the local limestone with another resident authority, who happened to have dropped in, on all-things-gold-country.

As I toured the town, I found that Columbia's residents and shopkeepers all have ready answers to questions on local lore, and when no one has a question, they will effortlessly break into soliloquy. If the chatter gets too tiring, take a hike to the northeast side of town, where a two-story red brick schoolhouse sits on top of a big hill. The schoolhouse is still furnished as it was in 1860, its opening year, when more than 300 children attended classes. Just down the hill from the front door is a three-seater outhouse; the holes were cut to varying sizes to accommodate a variety of bottoms. To the west of the schoolhouse is the town's old cemetery, and to the east is a signed nature trail that leads through mountain lion habitat. It is best to avoid hiking there at dusk, when the big cats are looking for dinner.

From Columbia, you can retrace your steps back to Highway 49 or continue north on Parrots Ferry Road for a more scenic approach to the gold towns on the southeast border of Calaveras County. The well-graded pavement of Parrots Ferry Road makes for an easy descent of 1,300 feet into the canyon of the Stanislaus River, where raptors hover in the updrafts and swallows swoop and dive near the water. In spring the canyon is filled with lavender spikes of lupine, great red paintbrushes, intricate white and purple Chinese houses, and the demure purplish-pink spray of the blossoming redbud trees. Mossy caves of marbleized limestone hide in the folds of the northwest slope. Park at the Natural Bridges trailhead, well marked on the road of the northwest slope, for an easy hike down to some beautiful limestone formations, or continue up the road to the **Moaning Caves** for more stylized and extensive tours.

Calaveras County

Parrots Ferry Road comes out of the Stanislaus River canyon at Highway 4 just beyond the little town of Vallecito. Five miles to the west, where Highway 4 meets Highway 49, is **Angels Camp,** the town Mark Twain made famous in "The Celebrated Jumping Frog of Calaveras County." Twain's endearing tale of a gold miner's gambling shenanigan gave rise to the institution of the Frog Jump, held annually in May at the Calaveras County Fair. (The fairgrounds are southeast of town off Highway 49.) Each year's slimy green long-jump champion is immortalized by having its name and winning distance etched in bronze plaques on Angels Camp's sidewalks.

It would be utterly foolhardy to leave this region without visiting Murphys, about 10 miles up Highway 4 from Angels Camp. Along the way, you will pass through the little hamlet of **Douglas Flat** (el. 1,965 feet), which is noted for its 1850s-era schoolhouse, on Main Street, north of the highway. This simple wood-frame structure is said to be the oldest

Each year's Frog Jump winner is immortalized on the Angels Camp sidewalk.

standing schoolhouse in Calaveras County, which would seem to conflict with a similar claim made about the Altaville Grammar School (see later in this chapter). Perhaps more important is the fact that the schoolhouse has never gone out of use as a public gathering place. Many of the folks who assemble here for community events are descendants of original gold rush settlers. A lecture series in the spring of 2003, held as a schoolhouse renovation fundraiser, drew substantial crowds of local folks eager to hear their scholarly (or simply loquacious) neighbors expound on local lore. Quite a few speakers were members of the old ranching families, and one even admitted to having attended classes in the schoolhouse. Many claimed to be descendants of either Manny or John Airola, brothers who came from Genoa, Italy, in the 1870s. Manny was described as "a man who could ride anything," and Manny's friend, Bud Reister, was remembered for allowing himself to be hanged every year in front of the Angels Camp hotel during the Frog Jump. They said Bud would shake his boots to signal that he was ready to be cut down, after which he would go into the bar for a drink.

MURPHYS (el. 2,711 feet)

Placer mining in Calaveras County was quite lucrative, but operating a trading post was generally a better investment, or at least it was so for John and George Murphy, who came to California with the Stephens immigrant party of 1844. In 1848, the brothers set up a trading post at an Indian encampment on Angels Creek, 10 miles upstream from Angels Camp, and convinced the Indians to go out and dig up lumps of gold in exchange for meat and blankets. They left camp a year later, but by then, the location had acquired their name. At various times, it was called Murphy's New Diggings, Murphy's Rich Diggings, Murphy's Flat, or Murphy's Camp, but in the end, it became simply Murphys. There are no plans to drop the "s" or put back the apostrophe.

Today, Murphys' gold era buildings are nearly lost in the allure of the commercial renaissance along the attractive, tree-lined Main Street, located to the west of Highway 4. Here the Mother Lode hoi polloi and visitors can dine at trendy restaurants and shop at an upscale market for truffles and artisanal cheeses. The Murphys Historic Hotel offers the most authentic gold era experience in town, and boasts a long-running and

On the ECV Wall of Commemorative Ovations in Murphys, the Clampers add another level of myth to the story of Snowshoe Thompson, claiming that the "Mailman of the Sierra" relied on a "wonderful stimulating drink known as 'ECV Foot Tonic.'"

venerable guest list, including U. S. Grant, John Bidwell (see chapters 1 and 10), Horatio Alger, Henry Ward Beecher, J. P. Morgan, Sir Thomas Lipton, Mark Twain, and Charles Bolton, a.k.a. Black Bart the PO 8). Across from the hotel, on the corner of Main Street and Sheep Ranch Road, is the historic Peter L. Traver Building, the oldest store building in Murphys and the location of the **E Clampus Vitus Wall of Comparative Ovations,** a fun and attractive gallery of plaques depicting figures from Sierra history. (For more on E Clampus Vitus, see chapter 4.)

Well-marked side roads from the center of Murphys lead to several appealing destinations. Turn south onto South Algiers Street, next to the Murphys Hotel, continue to the stop sign at Six Mile Road, turn right, and a mile later you will arrive at **Ironstone Vineyards,** a large, handsome complex designed to lure in and efficiently process busloads of tourists. Wine is but one draw here. Many come to ogle a 44-pound chunk of crystalline gold on display at the Ironstone Heritage Museum and Gallery. The astounding piece of precious metal was unearthed in Jamestown in 1992, reminding local landowners that they might quite literally be sitting on a gold mine. Besides the museum and tasting room, Ironstone offers restaurants, gift shops, and acres of pleasantly landscaped gardens, including a lake and an outdoor amphitheater that hosts a summer concert series featuring prominent performers.

For a rather different wine-related experience, return to Main Street in Murphys, go one block west and turn north on Sheep Ranch Road. After a winding, picturesque three-mile drive, you will arrive at **Mercer Caverns,** known for its formations of rare aragonite flos ferri ("flowers of iron"). Situated in an alluring setting of blue-hued limestone in the steep terrain below the caverns is the **Stevenot Winery,** established by fifth-generation Calaveras County resident Barton Stevenot in 1973 on the old Shaw Ranch. The intimate tasting room occupies the Shaw family home, which was built in 1870. Summer entertainment at Stevenot is likely to be a full-length Shakespearean play enacted by local performers.

From Murphys, retrace your path down Highway 4 to Angels Camp or go west on Main Street and bear left with the traffic onto Murphys Grade Road, an alternate route back to Highway 49. At several points along the north side of Murphys Grade Road, you might catch sight of the gold era flume that, amazingly, is still a functioning part of the local water system. It connects into more modern equipment, visible on the left as Murphys Grade Road approaches Altaville.

At Altaville, turn right onto Highway 49 and watch the southwest side of the road for the little red **Altaville Grammar School,** built in 1858 and reputed by some sources to be the oldest grammar school in California. This is at odds with the claim made for Douglas Flat's schoolhouse (see earlier in this chapter). Putting aside the superlatives, it would be more useful to point out that the tiny structure has been beautifully restored and maintained, with old maps and desks set up as if the children were just about to arrive for their geography lesson.

In his 1889 short story "Cressy," set in Tuolumne County, Bret Harte describes a scene much like those that Altaville's school must have witnessed many times:

They came in their usual desultory fashion — the fashion of country school-children the world over — irregularly, spasmodically, and always as if accidentally; a few hand-in-hand, others driven ahead of or dropped behind their elders; some in straggling groups more or less coherent and at times only connected by far-off intermediate voices scattered on a space of half a mile, but never quite alone; always preoccupied by something else than the actual business on hand; appearing suddenly from ditches, behind trunks, and between fence-rails; cropping up in unexpected places along the road after vague and purposeless detours — seemingly going anywhere and everywhere but to school!

SAN ANDREAS (el. 1,008 feet)

San Andreas, the Calaveras County seat, is on Highway 49, 10 miles northwest of Angels Camp. Its beautifully preserved historic and civic enclave sits a block off the highway on a narrow one-way street. Especially appealing is the Hall of Records, a sparkling orange and white Romanesque revival structure that now houses the Calaveras County Historical Museum. A few businesses trumpet the fact that Black Bart slept in San Andreas as he was awaiting trial at the courthouse, which is located directly behind the Hall of Records.

MOKELUMNE HILL (el. 1,474 feet)

A mile northwest out of San Andreas, Highway 49 makes a northward turn at the junction with Highway 12. Nine miles beyond, the town of Mokelumne Hill sits tucked away east of the highway on the narrow divide between the North Fork Calaveras River and the mighty Mokelumne River. The idyllic and timeless ambience along the few dusty streets of Mokelumne Hill belies a rough and rowdy past. A bad combination of incredibly rich placer deposits and large, ethnically divided gangs of miners led to a series of "wars" here that fill the local annals.

The Hotel Leger, built circa 1851 of gray rhyolite, makes an inexpensive and appealing base of operations in the vicinity. While in town, be sure to visit the saloon beside the old I.O.O.F. Hall. The wall inside is hung with every imaginable type of stringed instrument, the collection of propri-

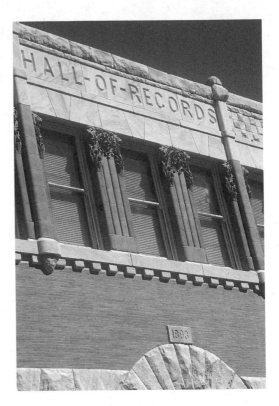

The Calaveras County Hall of Records sits on a very narrow, one-way street in the San Andreas historic district.

etor Randy Sparks of the old New Christy Minstrels. Make friends with the bartender, and you might be invited to travel through the old Coke machine to the back room, where two stuffed buffalo slumber beside the billiard table and seating is derived from various derelict transportation devices.

Amador County

Toward the end of the 20th century, Amador County rediscovered itself as a wine region, but the county still has more than its share of fascinating gold towns, many of which still contain a rich diversity of immigrant cultures. Of special note is **Jackson** (el. 1,240 feet), five miles north of Mokelumne Hill. The impressive graveyard district, located along Jackson Gate Road, reads like a history book of America's melting pot. At St. Sava Serbian Orthodox Church, inscriptions on the oldest stones in the cemetery are lettered in Cyrillic. Look for the memorial and gravesite of the Serbian victims of the devastating Argonaut Mine Disaster of 1922. The Catholic cemetery is nearby, as is the site of the Mother Lode's first synagogue.

Jackson is notable as a Gold Country destination because of its two very deep and rich mines, the Argonaut and the Kennedy. Tours of the Kennedy Mine ground-level features are offered on some weekends, but even if you do not get in on a tour, make sure to stop at the vista point on the west side of Highway 49 north of Jackson, where there is a good view of the mine's tall metal headframe looming up on the far ridge. Even more striking is the view from an opposing angle at quiet and shady **Kennedy Tailing Wheels Park** on Jackson Gate Road. Trails leading through the city-run park up the steep, oak-covered hillside (or up the steep treeless slope on the opposite side of the road) bring you among the mine's four giant tailing wheels. These were constructed in 1914, when the mine was under orders to shut down or handle its waste, which was polluting the agricultural lands downhill. For almost 30 years, the wheels conveyed

Kennedy Tailing Wheel #4.

a slurry of mine debris up and over the two hills to a gulch where it was impounded. When the mine closed in 1942, the metal shacks protecting the wheels were removed and the wooden wheels were suddenly exposed to view, creating a great delight for visitors. In their unprotected state, the four gigantic wheels are in a state of decay. The last time I visited, two of the wheels were lying like piles of bones on the ground, reminding me of the dinosaurs dropping dead in the *Rite of Spring* section of Walt Disney's *Fantasia*.

CHAW SE' INDIAN GRINDING ROCK STATE HISTORIC PARK

At the town of Jackson (el. 1,200 ft.), Highway 49 intersects with Highway 88, which leads northeast to Carson Pass. Nine miles up this highway is the little town of Pine Grove (el. 2,500 feet), entryway to Indian Grinding Rock State Park and the quirky town of Volcano, both a short drive to the north. Turn left onto the Pine Grove–Volcano Road, drive past the sign for the Chaw se' campground, and turn left at the main entrance to Chaw se' Indian Grinding Rock State Historic Park.

Chaw se' was once a favored home of the Mountain Miwok, and it remains an important gathering place for Native Americans. The centerpiece of the park is a large, flat slab of marbleized limestone bedrock, which emerges from the grass beneath a grove of ancient black oak trees in the main meadow. This *chaw se'* (which means "grinding rock" in Miwok), is pocked with hundreds of mortar holes and marked with faintly etched designs, an indication that many generations of Miwoks lived, worked, and celebrated in this meadow.

The Chaw se'
(grinding rock).

A Miwok home at Chaw se.'

Such grinding rocks are found throughout California's extensive oak forests, where the native peoples could gather an abundant harvest of nutritious acorns each autumn. They stored the acorns in wickerwork granaries, and extracted them for use throughout the year. Preparing acorn for consumption is a complex task, because the meat contains a large quantity of bitter tannins, which are toxic to humans in such high concentrations. First, the acorn has to be shelled of its outer and inner husks. Then it is crushed into flour, a task the Indian women performed in the mortar holes of these grinding rocks. When they were done grinding, the women placed the flour in a bed of sand, using ash-water to leach out the tannin, after which the flour was dried. The classic preparation was to mix the flour with cold water in a watertight basket. The resulting mush was then cooked by placing heated rocks in the basket. Service was communal style, with everyone eating from the same basket in which the acorn was cooked. According to Julia Parker (see chapter 8), the daily work of preparing acorn was made lighter by lively conversation.

Like most California tribes, the Miwok remained nomadic through the changing seasons, following wildlife migrations and supplementing their diet with a cornucopia of wild plant foods: nuts and seeds, mushrooms, honey, wild onions, greens, herbs, manzanita and juniper berries, elderberries, blackberries, roots, and wild grapes. There was little incentive to develop agriculture, especially in a climate characterized by persistent summer drought.

Today, Chaw se' is a vibrant gathering place for intertribal basketmakers' conventions and traditional celebrations with dancing, drumming, and singing. But even if one comes by on a quiet day between celebrations, or when few other visitors are about, mule deer, ground squirrels, and rabbits might be doing a foraging dance while Western tanagers and Bullock's orioles decorate the meadow with their bright plumage. Accompaniment is by the local ensemble—hermit thrush on melody and acorn woodpecker on percussion. Regardless of what might be happening here (or not happening), please pay the parking fee at Chaw se', even if the museum is closed, both to avoid a ticket and to support this worthy park.

VOLCANO (el. 2,053 feet)

Another mile and a half north of Chaw se' is the town of Volcano, where the eminent eruptions have been cultural and scientific rather than volcanic in nature. The stone outcroppings here are marbleized limestone, and if the spot could be called a hotbed in any way, it would be for the stage activity, which had been going 30 years strong, last I checked. The thespians perform both in the Cobblestone Theatre (built in 1856 as Adolf Meyer's Tobacco & Cigar Emporium, and later serving as Lavezzo's Wine Shop) and in an outdoor amphitheater created out of a stone ruin across the street. The stately, three-story, balconied St. George Hotel has offered lodging and dining in high style since 1863, and simpler fare is available at the soda fountain in the old general store. There are three stools at the soda fountain, all likely to be occupied by the pack of locals that finds daily entertainment in their own company here or on the benches outside. Strike up a conversation with one of these folks, and you might hear a long and rambling history that goes back to the gold rush days.

You can reach Sutter Creek, the next stop on our tour, by retracing your path back to Highway 49 and heading north, or by taking Sutter Creek Road west.

Knight Foundry at
Sutter Creek.

SUTTER CREEK (el. 1,198 feet)

John A. Sutter of the eponymous mill and fort (see chapter 1) briefly tried
his hand at gold mining in this vicinity. Today, people look for treasure
in the antique and gift shops, and a few come to visit the original **Three
Dog Bakery,** which occupies a little house on Eureka Street. Many people think the perfectly decorated cookies and cakes are too pretty to be
wasted on dogs. Dog lovers disagree, as do their canine companions.
Humans will find adequate opportunities to tie on the feedbag among
Sutter Creek's copious eateries.

The assemblage of corrugated metal barns and sheds toward the end
of Eureka Street is the quarters of **Knight Foundry,** a large operation
that once cast and machined a large portion of the mining equipment
now rusting in the Gold Country landscape. The machine shop, which
is notable for being powered entirely by water, is still in operation. If the
volunteers are available, there might be a tour available.

AMADOR CITY (el. 954 feet)

Shopping opportunities continue in Amador City, a tiny borough huddled into a tight curve two miles up Highway 49 from Sutter Creek. If
the doors are open at the Imperial Hotel, step inside to see the interior
design, which artistically blends brick, crumbling plaster, and art of the
hotel's 1879 vintage with whimsical, mock-Victorian paintings by local
artist John Johannsen. Outside the hotel, Amador Creek trickles brightly

This burned-out house is located alongside the Little Amador Railroad, a garden railway in Amador City.

The Chew Kee Store in Fiddletown has been described as a time capsule or snapshot of the gold era Chinese community. Courtesy of the Fiddletown Preservation Society

alongside Water Street over a washboard-like bed of stratified metamorphic rocks flooded in summer with a tangle of blackberry canes, wild mint, and rushes. After crossing under the road, the creek wanders past the magical world of the Little Amador Railroad, a privately constructed garden railroad designed to mimic a rail trip through the Gold Country.

Three miles northwest of Amador City is **Drytown** (el. 620 feet), where visitors can't help but wonder if spirits are available. At the height of the Gold Rush the town was hardly dry; 26 saloons once poured liquor to satisfy miners working the diggings at Dry Creek. A mile north of Drytown, Highway 49 makes a right turn and arrives shortly at Plymouth (el. 1,086 feet), the gateway to Amador County wine country. Turn right onto Fiddletown Road and continue six miles to Fiddletown.

FIDDLETOWN (el. 1,687 feet)
An anonymous local scribe noted that little is known about Fiddletown's gold era settlers except that whiskey flowed like water and lice were prev-

alent. When water ran in the creeks, the people mined. When the rains stopped they fiddled.

I did not find any fiddlers at play on any of my visits, but I did have the luck to come by on an afternoon when anthropologist Jane Russell was minding the **Chew Kee Store,** a rammed earth cottage and former Chinese apothecary that is often described as a time capsule. When it was unsealed in 1985 after 20 years as mothballed state property, the artifacts inside were carefully catalogued and replaced just as they were found. The collection is unique, because it survived the period in the early 20th century when artifacts in so many similar sites were being carted off by bottle-collectors. During those years, the store's contents remained under the stewardship of the adopted son of the merchant Chew Kee, Jimmy Chow, who by the time of his death in 1965 was the sole survivor of Fiddletown's once-flourishing Chinese community.

Today, the only patent medicines available here are the fine, locally produced wines that make Fiddletown a good place to warm up for this book's winery tour of the Sierra foothills.

Wine Country Tour

The gold era hordes may have been whiskey swillers, but they were enthusiastic imbibers of wine as well. Thus winemaking started in earnest in the Sierra foothills in the 1850s, and by the late 19th century, this region could boast of some 10,000 acres of vineyards and over 100 wineries, with production far surpassing that of Sonoma and Napa counties combined. In 1919, Prohibition effectively destroyed the wine industry here as elsewhere in California.

A new generation of enterprising winemakers got things going again in Amador and El Dorado counties in the 1970s. They inherited high-elevation, cool-climate growing areas and, in some cases, historic vineyards containing some of the oldest Zinfandel vines in the state. Indeed, this is the place to come for Zinfandel, but what's unique about tasting in the Sierra (as opposed to in Sonoma or Napa) is that here it is often the winemaker who is pouring the tastes. The following tour focuses on smaller operations making excellent wines (or places with special character), but there are dozens of places to try the big Zins. For a comparative

Big Zins at Dobra Zemlja Winery.

tasting all in one spot, come to the town of Plymouth in June, when the Amador County Wine Grape Growers' Association hosts its Wine Festival at the county fairgrounds.

From Plymouth, set out east into the California Shenandoah Valley AVA (American Viticultural Area) by heading up Fiddletown Road and turning left shortly onto Shenandoah Road. Three and a half miles up Shenandoah Road, turn left onto Dickson Road, and then right into the unadorned tasting room for **Domaine de la Terre Rouge.** Here Bill Easton coaxes Rhône varietal wines and some impressive Zinfandels out of the red earth of the Gold Country. One unbiased wine expert I know considers these to be benchmark wines for the area.

Back on Shenandoah Road, watch for Bell Road and turn left, climbing for two miles to 10505 Bell Road, the home of **Story Winery,** where the woodpecker-pocked tasting room shack is as rustic and picturesque as the ancient oak and walnut groves that surround it. Story makes wine from the fruits of their gnarled, 90-year-old Mission grapevines, but their best wines are chocolaty, unctuous Zinfandels from vines that are nearly as old as the Mission vines. From this hilltop perch there is a great view down into the Cosumnes River valley.

Back on Shenandoah Road, drive another mile northeast and turn left onto the Steiner Road loop, where there are many opportunities for tasting. Be sure to stop at 12505 Steiner Road, the last winery on the loop, where veteran grape farmer Milan Matulich dug a cave out of the steep hillside for his **Dobra Zemlja** winery, taking a name from his native

Croatian—Dobra Zemlja means "good earth." Matulich, who turned to winemaking in 1995, is an artist and a real personality. Among his offerings is an interesting Sangiovese-Mourvèdre blend and a series of Zinfandels that Matulich claims to be the biggest wines in Amador County. It would be hard to argue with him.

Steiner Road ends at a T-junction with Shenandoah Road. Turn left and then watch on the right for 14430 Shenandoah Road, which comes up shortly. Swiss immigrant Adam Uhlinger settled at this location in the 1860s. He built a three-story residence of oak and native stone, and established the ground floor as a winery. Wine has been produced at this site ever since, even during Prohibition. Italian immigrant Enrico D'Agostino bought the property in the early 20th century, and his family made wine there into the 1960s. Today, it is the home of **Sobon Estate,** a family operation that produces some of the area's more sophisticated (and more expensive) wines. Sobon's Zinfandels are excellent models of the classic Amador style—rich, chewy, old-vine, high-alcohol Zinfandel that is almost a meal in itself. Sobon Estate is also the site of the **Shenandoah Valley Museum,** where the fascinating (and free) exhibits depict winegrowing, winemaking, and the sundry farming and home crafts practiced in this valley since 1850.

The Fair Play AVA of El Dorado County is easily accessible from this end of Shenandoah Road. Continue up E16 (Shenandoah Road) to Mount Aukum. Turn east on Omo Ranch Road and north on Fair Play Road.

El Dorado County Gold and Wine

The **Fair Play AVA** spreads out on a large, mountainous knoll with good views of the Sierra ridge. The high elevations and relatively remote location seem to nurture outsized personalities. Turn in at **Van der Vijver Estate,** the sign of the giant wooden shoe at 7451 Fair Play Road, and you will meet Robert van der Vijver, a congenial winemaker who wears a ponytail and wooden clogs, and speaks in a lilting Dutch accent. A stone's throw away at 7740 Fair Play Road is **Fitzpatrick Winery & Lodge,** where Brian Fitzpatrick offers up an impressive Irish bed and breakfast inn, which he built himself out of whole logs, putting in a wood-fired oven

There's plenty of character
behind the wines of Fair Play.

where he makes pizza. Somehow, he still finds time to grow and make
organic wine as well as apple cider.

Fair Play Road loops back onto E16. Now called Mount Aukum Road,
E-16 continues toward Pleasant Valley. Turn left on Pleasant Valley Road
and watch the signs for **Sierra Vista Winery,** located at the top of Caber-
net Way. It is perched at nearly 2,900 feet on a ridge affording an excellent
view of the Sierra's Crystal Range, 30 miles to the east. The best time to
visit is at sunset. Taste the winery's excellent Syrahs, and then go outside
to watch the snowy peaks turn golden orange, then fiery magenta, then
magnificent purple as they disappear into the velvety night sky.

As Pleasant Valley Road rambles off to the west turn north on Snows
Road. The road passes under U.S. 50 before it ends at Carson Road in
the middle of Camino. (See chapter 3 for more on this area.) Turn left
on Carson Road and drive a little over two miles to High Hill Road.
Turn right and follow the signs to **Madroña Vineyards.** Here you can
taste, among other wines, some beguilingly crisp and vivid Rieslings and

Used for many years as a tasting room, the original wine-making cellar at Boeger Winery now serves as a small museum. Ancient grapevines and fig trees surround the building.

Gewürztraminers. The eponymous madrone tree is a 300-year-old beauty that watches over the vineyards, a zone that is off-limits to visitors. The younger madrones guarding the tasting room door give an artist ideas as they show off the delicate curls of their thin red and amber bark peeling away to reveal a luscious contrasting green.

Continue west on Carson Road and turn right on Union Ridge Road. Turn right again onto Hassler Road, and left a mile later on Fruitridge Road to reach **Lava Cap Winery.** Here the complex mélange of volcanic soils gives the wines a particular aromatic appeal. The view from this 2,800-foot vantage point includes acres and acres of vineyards with the hazy Sacramento Valley in the distance.

A last wine stop is at 1709 Carson Road, the home of **Boeger Winery,** which is set in a dramatic, creek-threaded hollow with ancient pear, apple, and fig trees. A grapevine planted in the 1870s arches over the driveway and twines around the wooden rafters and second-story porch of a picturesque building that was constructed post–Gold Rush and pre-Prohibition as a winery. It served through the end of the 20th century as

Boeger's funky, atmospheric tasting room, but was replaced with a bright, new tasting room, where a bevy of cheerful employees serve up familiar varietals wines and a few that are more obscure, such as Charbono and Refosco.

Continue west on Carson Road into Placerville.

PLACERVILLE (el. 1,866 feet)

A rich placer deposit discovered at dry Weber Creek lured the gold rush here in the summer of 1848. Dry Diggings was the first name of the settlement, but after three miners were "launched into eternity" from ropes strung on the limb of a big white oak tree in January of 1849, the place came to be known as Hangtown. The name of Hangtown was changed to Placerville in 1854, and, at some point, the oak tree was replaced by a saloon, a good one, by saloon standards, but alas, they don't serve a Hangtown Fry, the omelet of eggs, oysters, and bacon that became a popular repast with miners who wanted the best breakfast gold could buy. It has been years since I've had any luck locating a specimen of the elusive omelet on Placerville's bustling Main Street. However, there is plenty

A mural inside the J. Pearson Building by local artists D. Kiggins and G. Guisso depicts the exterior of the Placerville Soda Works.

more to enjoy in town, such as **Placerville Hardware,** which has been in continuous operation at 441 Main Street since 1852. This real, old-fashioned hardware store has creaky wood floors, wooden bins full of nails, and merchandise stacked to the rafters.

Be sure to head down to the old stone **Soda Works** at 594 Main Street. The building sits against a very steep hill where an early proprietor dug tunnels to store ice and soda. Current proprietors still use the cave to chill drinks. Along Main Street and up into surrounding neighborhoods there are plenty of vintage buildings housing shops, inns, and eateries. Some of my favorite finds have been belly dance costumes, early-20th-century travel literature, Persian rugs, and live jazz performed by authentic Big Band era musicians.

A mile north of town on Bedford Avenue are the old "neighborhood mines" of the Poverty Hill district. These were worked mostly during the Depression, but now sit as interesting exhibits along the pleasant hiking trails through the 61-acre **Gold Bug Park.** Two of the main sights are wheelchair accessible, as is the museum and visitor center. One of the outdoor exhibits provides Gold Country visitors one of their only opportunities to look into an actual mine shaft. The park has a picnic area set beside a gurgling creek, where on one occasion I found a tree almost entirely covered with golden-orange ladybugs.

After Placerville, Highway 49 winds north for seven miles through ranchlands and orchards as it approaches Coloma.

SUTTER'S MILL (el. 784 feet)

The South Fork American River dances raucously in its broad, pebbly bed, reflecting golden shards of summer sunlight as it rambles past the site of Sutter's Mill at **Coloma.** Brewer's blackbirds bathe in the dusty paths, and Western fence lizards dart, pose, and pant on the rounded river stones along the trail, while on the far riverbank, the tawny grasses spread out in wave upon velvety wave into the surrounding foothills. A thick forest of oak, pine, cottonwood, sycamore, and cedar once covered this landscape, but the trees were brought down in the gold rush frenzy. The new growth appears almost an intrusion on the sea of grass.

On a hot weekday afternoon, there is little motion by the river, save that of the water, the birds and lizards, and a slight wavering of the dry

People still pan for gold on the South Fork American River at the site of Sutter's Mill.

grass under the relentless blue sky. A few visitors wander from the parking lot to the rugged trails at the **Marshall Gold Discovery State Historic Park** or through the outdoor museum with its rusting mining equipment, ruins, and replica structures — the mill, some Chinese stores, the jail, shops, and churches. A few people hover at the picnic tables under the trees, and a few more pan for gold on the quiet riverbank, the same spot where hundreds and then thousands of men came, as if on pilgrimage, at the start of the California Gold Rush.

Much of the Gold Country now exudes the lonely, forgotten quality that one senses by the river at Coloma, and so a visit to the mining era past is essentially an exercise in imagination. The gold one sees today is more likely to be the gold of the dry summer grasses.

Placer County

Highway 49 crosses the divide between the American River's south and north forks near the early-day travelers' landmark of Pilot Hill (el. 1,869 feet). Descending toward the north fork, the highway passes through **Cool,** from which mountain bikers and equestrians stage excursions into

Knickerbocker Creek Canyon on the Olmsted Loop Trail. Between Cool and Auburn, the highway enters the **Auburn State Recreation Area,** negotiating the impressive canyon where the American River's middle fork converges on the north fork. Here, the river swirls in frothy green pools as it makes its way over diagonal ridges of ancient green serpentine bedrock. In winter, notch-cut brown leaves fallen from oak trees litter the moist and mossy dirt on the steep cliff-side trails, and the prickly-leafed toyon is hung gaily with red berries.

The high, graceful bridge seen overhead spanning the North Fork American River is an interesting artifact of the notorious Auburn Dam, which was destined to become the largest concrete arched dam in the world until the project was halted in 1975 due to growing concern about its seismic vulnerability. The Foresthill Bridge, highest bridge crossing in California, third highest in the United States, and ninth highest in the world, was constructed in anticipation of the completion of the Auburn Dam, which would have submerged the road from Auburn to Foresthill beneath the Auburn Reservoir.

Highway 49 enters **Auburn** (el. 1,236 feet) from the east, arriving in the vibrant upper town. An attraction here is the former Auburn Hotel, a handsome California Mission–style structure constructed in 1914 and now in use as an office complex. To reach Old Town Auburn, continue downhill and go straight ahead on Lincoln Way as Highway 49 makes a right turn to head out the other side of town.

Old Town is well marked and easy to find, because the imposing domed and columned **Placer County Courthouse** is at its center. The courthouse holds an historical museum. All around it, stuffed into historic buildings, are cute shops and eateries, some of which try to emulate the businesses present in the era when Auburn was a transportation hub for the mining activity. The old brick Chinese section is especially intriguing, as is the unbelievably quaint **Auburn Hook & Ladder Company Firehouse,** built in 1893. The volunteer fire department here predates the structure and is one of the oldest in the state. Claude Chana, the man who first struck gold here in Auburn in 1848, looms larger than life

(opposite) This firehouse in Auburn, built in 1893, is younger than the all-volunteer Auburn Hook and Ladder Company.

in a little park on the edge of a ravine on the northwest side of the historic district. The remains of his mining camp are located down in the ravine.

FROM AUBURN TO GRASS VALLEY

The stretch of Highway 49 from Auburn to Grass Valley is fraught with slowdowns from traffic lights and shopping malls. Fortunately, there's a scenic detour that is well worth the extra miles it adds to the trip. From Auburn, go east on I-80 for 13 miles to **Colfax**. Exit and follow the signs into historic Colfax, a small village that was once an important rail-shipping point for the local fruit growers. Amtrak travelers can disembark at the original station house, now beautifully restored, and walk up to the Colfax Chamber of Commerce, which is housed in a retired Pullman car parked in front of the old Colfax Hotel. The historic California Fruit Exchange complex is a short walk south on South Railroad Avenue, and when last I checked, it was housing a small restaurant. More shops and eateries are located on North Main Street across the tracks.

Continue north on North Main, to pick up Highway 174 for the 10-mile drive to Grass Valley. On leaving Colfax, watch to the right for the plaque marking the **Colfax Cape Horn Promontory** overlook. The overlook is dedicated to the Chinese workers who built this historic bend on the Central Pacific Railroad. (For more on the history of the railroad, see chapter 1.) For the rest of the way to Grass Valley, Highway 174 threads through a bucolic corridor of horse ranches, orchards, and cafes offering fresh-baked fruit pies.

Western Nevada County

As tolerance is often a touchstone of progressivism, Nevada City liberals are apt to note with great pride a list of the county's diversities. These are not ethnic diversities, however, as the county is overwhelmingly white. In western Nevada County, folks will tell you, descendants of aristocratic mine owners live in harmony alongside the great-grandchildren of downtrodden miners, all of whom manage to get along with a huge population of exurbanites from the San Francisco Bay Area. The latter migration started in the 1960s as environmentalists, artists, and intellectuals followed the call to "get back to the land." On their heels came New

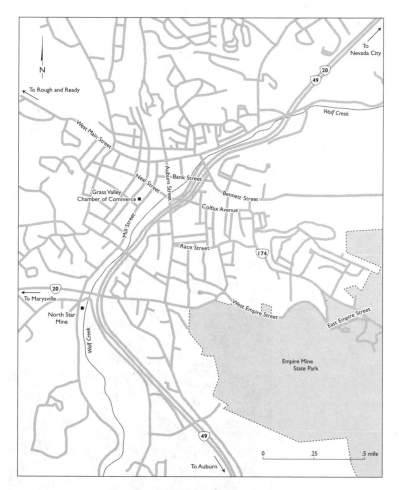

GRASS VALLEY

Age proponents seeking fertile ground on which to "grow" their spiritual communities. By the 1990s, the new wave was made up of telecom-
muters, retirees, and a large contingent of young anarchists armed with
mountain bikes.

This population ensures a lively year-round roster of activities, including lectures, symposia, workshops, and exhibits in the area encompass-

ing Nevada City, Grass Valley, and the San Juan Ridge. Here, too, you will find an astounding number of independent bookstores and coffee shops.

EMPIRE MINE STATE PARK

As you approach Grass Valley on Highway 174, watch to the left for East Empire Street and the sign for the Empire Mine State Park. The park is a must-see on any Gold Country history tour. (Visitors arriving via Highway 49 will exit onto West Empire Street to head east into the park.)

At the park's main entrance on East Empire Street, the handsome old administration building gives an immediate sense of the stability that distinguished this gold era mining operation from so many others. This building, like many on the park's attractive grounds, was constructed of rough-hewn greenstone brought out of the mine's 367 miles of excavated

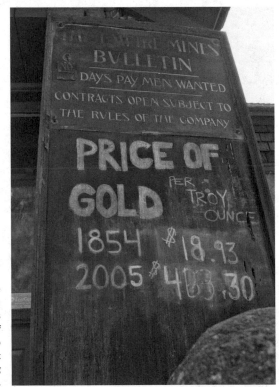

A sign on the Empire Mine's administration building shows the effects of inflation on the value of gold. But even at $463.30 per troy ounce, the cost of mining and processing gold exceeds its value.

shafts. The shafts run almost a vertical mile down into the quartz-laden rock that gave up 5.8 million ounces of gold to the miners who worked there from 1850 until the mine was closed in 1956. The shafts are now filled with groundwater, but there is still much more gold that might be taken out if the value were ever to exceed the cost of extracting it.

Outdoor tours of the extensive mine yards begin at the visitors' center, but you won't want to bypass the exhibits inside. Of special interest is a three-dimensional map of the mine. Built in secret by the company's chief engineer in 1938, this map provides today's visitors with a sense of the vast complex of underground corridors. Also inside the museum are a splendid display of gems, rocks, and minerals, and numerous storyboards that explain the workings of the mine and describe the lives of the miners from Cornwall, England, who brought their hard rock mining expertise and their traditions to Grass Valley. Make sure to look for the Cornish lunchpail, an item that will be discussed in the next section of this chapter.

The park entrance fee allows you to wander at will through the mine yard and out into the impeccable gardens that surround the luxurious clubhouse and the Bourn Cottage, a beautiful English-manor home designed by Willis Polk in 1897. Stately ponderosa pines rise up out of the manicured lawn as if to remind us of the Sierra wilderness not far beyond the gate. Ancient rose varieties in the garden behind the cottage claim ancestry to Medieval Europe.

Local hikers, bikers, and equestrians prefer the park's northern entrance. From there they can set out onto 12 miles of trail through 845 acres of woodlands thick with ponderosa pine, manzanita, and madrone. The trails cross back and forth over Wolf Creek, winding through piles of tailings and the ruins of a stamp mill and a cyanide plant. Grasses, vines, and wildflowers climb through the ruins.

More mining exhibits can be found at the remnants of the North Star Mine on Mill Street in Grass Valley, just south of the junction of Highway 20 and Highway 49. Among the exhibits in the North Star Mine powerhouse is North America's largest Pelton wheel, a remarkable invention that very effectively harnesses water power in a way that revolutionized not only mining, but milling as well. It was invented in the late 1880s by Lester Pelton, a carpenter who was working in nearby Camptonville.

GRASS VALLEY (el. 2,411 feet)

Prospectors following Wolf Creek through this area found it an attractive place to graze livestock, and in 1850, when George Knight discovered gold-bearing quartz in his field, several mining companies immediately got to work.

The bustling town of Grass Valley, which spreads out to the northwest of Empire Mine State Park, is now the commercial center of western Nevada County. Mill Street, once the main trail through the area, is a good place to begin a walking tour.

Turn north onto Mill Street from Highway 20, west of the Highway 49 junction, and park near 248 Mill Street. This is the former address of the popular gold era entertainer Lola Montez, and now the location of the **Grass Valley Chamber of Commerce.** An impressive array of pamphlets and maps greets the visitor, but one will look in vain for any sign of the flamboyant performer or the black bear she once kept here as a pet, because the house is only a replica of the Montez home. In her day, Montez had affairs with Franz Lizst and Alexandre Dumas (*père*), was the mistress of King Ludwig I of Bavaria (he made her a countess but was forced to abdicate in part because of having done so, while she had to flee Bavaria), and danced for miners in Australia as well as California (with no undies on). Like so many other free spirits throughout history, she died indigent.

A Montez protégé named Lotta Crabtree once lived nearby at 238 Mill Street. Described as a precocious girl, Crabtree followed her mentor into a similar career of performance tours through the rough-and-tumble mining camps. Unlike Montez's exhibitions, Lotta's shows were of the G-rated variety. Her phenomenal success allowed her to retire early and live on as a grand dame of the town.

Northeast along Mill Street, the town shows off a trove of lusciously painted early-20th-century masonry structures, such as the red brick **Public Library** at 207 Mill Street, built in 1916 with funding from the Carnegie Foundation, and the **Nevada County Bank** at 131 Mill Street, built in 1917 with a handsome ribbed-dome-and-ornate cornice. The striking Art Deco spire of the **Del Oro Theater** pierces the sky at 165 Mill Street. It was built in 1942, five years after the Masons built their sleek Art Deco temple around the block on South Auburn Street. The temple is

(top) Grass Valley's Public Library. (bottom) Nevada County Bank in Grass Valley.

across the street from the old post office, another Classical Revival design that echoes the themes of the library and bank.

If an overnight stay is called for, check in to the pleasingly painted and upholstered **Holbrooke Hotel,** at 212 West Main Street. The 1862-vintage hotel still has its cage elevator. The adjoining Golden Gate Saloon has remained in operation since it opened in 1851. The saloon's ornate bar traveled to California around the Horn, and is often well appointed by authentic old-timers stationed on its stools.

CORNISH TREATS

Come to Grass Valley at holiday time or in late August for the Miner's Picnic, and everyone will be celebrating in the Cornish style with food, games, and music. During the rest of the year, visitors settle for the delicious Cornish pasties served at Cousin Jack's (101 South Auburn Street) and Marshall's (203 Mill Street). At Marshall's, the cooks wear period costume, and the pasties can be carried up a cramped wooden stairway to a little old-fashioned lunchroom.

There is a simple beauty to both the pasty (pronounced *pass-tee*) and the Cornish miners' traditional three-tiered lunchpail. The pasty, a handheld pie filled with a thick stew of meat and vegetables, is easy to eat while hunkered down in a dark mineshaft. Each morning, the miner's wife would place one of these pastries into the middle chamber of her husband's lunchpail. In the bottom chamber she put some tea, and in the top, a saffron bun. At lunchtime, the miner would heat the tea with a candle held beneath the pail. The rising steam would heat the pasty and bun in the upper chambers.

Grass Valley's Del
Oro theater and
Marshall's Pasties.

OUT THE ROUGH AND READY HIGHWAY

A miner is buried in Rough and Ready. As shovels move, gold appears in his grave.
Service continues while miners stake claims. So goes the story, from dust to dust.

— from *Assembling California,* John McPhee

Take Main Street northwest out of Grass Valley and you will be headed to **Rough and Ready** (el. 1,880 feet), where in April of 1850, the citizens protested a newly imposed miners' tax by declaring their town to be an independent republic. The Republic of Rough and Ready lasted only until a little before the Fourth of July when the citizens realized they would be left out of the national Independence Day celebration if they did not immediately rejoin the union. Today, there is not much to see in Rough and Ready, but many visitors stop at the old post office in order to have their cards to home postmarked from the "republic."

From Rough and Ready, head back east a few miles and pick up Newtown Road. Head north over Deer Creek and up onto Kentucky Ridge, then turn west onto Bitney Springs Road. Here abandoned orchards alternate with wetland pools in a landscape made rugged by the hydraulic mining operations (see the upcoming section on Malakoff Diggins). In winter the wetlands are aflutter with waterfowl. Listen for the hoot of a barn owl and watch overhead for hawks and turkey vultures riding the air currents above the ridge.

At Pleasant Valley Road, turn north to descend into the gentle canyon of the South Yuba River, where the road crosses the river beside an old covered bridge, the longest single span arch-truss covered bridge in the United States. Remnants of an old settlement called Bridgeport serve as the visitor center for the **South Yuba River State Park,** a 20-mile-long patchwork of parcels that extends upstream to near Malakoff Diggins. In the hot summer months, swimmers flock to the sandy riverbank, but on a cool autumn day, the only footprints might be those of a thirsty raccoon. Cross the road and the river to the trailhead for the **Buttermilk Bend Trail.** This wheelchair-accessible trail is noted for its April display of wildflowers, which might include larkspur, delicate fairy lanterns, Sierra iris, and fields full of golden California poppies. (More information on hiking trails in the Yuba River watershed will be easy to find in Nevada

City—ahead—or at the Tahoe National Forest Yuba District office in Camptonville. Also, see the list of resources at the end of this chapter.)

To return to Highway 49, you can either retrace your steps or continue north on Pleasant Valley Road, which will place you on Highway 49 south of North San Juan and north of Nevada City.

CALIFORNIA'S CUP OF GOLD

The golden poppy is God's gold,
The gold that lifts, nor weighs us down,
The gold that knows no miser's hold
The gold that banks not in the town,
But singing, laughing, freely spills
Its hoard far up the happy hills;
Far up, far down, at every turn, —
What beggar has not gold to burn!

—Joaquin Miller, 1837–1913

NEVADA CITY (el. 2,500 feet)

For a stretch of about six miles from Grass Valley to Nevada City, Highway 49 becomes a divided highway. Exit at Broad Street and cross over the highway to enter Nevada City's historic district. As the reader interested in names will remember, "nevada" is Spanish for "snowy." Snow occasionally falls here in winter, but this picturesque Victorian hamlet clinging to the steep ravine of Deer Creek hardly appears to be a "city." The original name of the hamlet was Deer Creek Dry Diggings, but in 1850, the residents renamed it Nevada. In 1864, when a portion of the Utah Territory to the east became the state of Nevada, "City" was added to the town's name to avoid confusion.

The entire downtown of Nevada City is on the National Register of Historic Places. This designation gives the town leave to operate its old gas streetlights and deny infiltration by chain stores. Entrepreneurs have made the most of the situation, pouring on the historic charm and enhancing the area with upscale lodging, shopping, and dining pleasures.

The best way to get to know Nevada City is to stay for at least a day and wander around on foot. The streets can be a daunting maze at first, but the historic center is quite small, and there are interesting things to

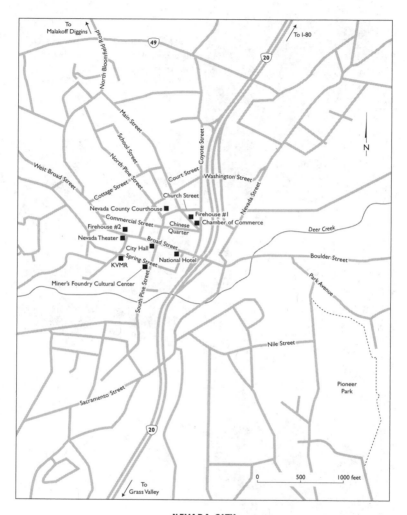

NEVADA CITY

discover, even while one is lost. If walking seems too ambitious, hire one of the horse-drawn buggies for an orientation tour.

Start by picking up brochures and maps at the Chamber of Commerce, 132 Main Street, in the old offices of the South Yuba Canal Company. At the height of the hydraulic mining era, the canal company oversaw a huge

(left) Nevada City's old gaslights and hitching posts still function for modern-day use.
(below left) Nevada City Firehouse #1.
(below right) Nevada City's award-winning City Hall.

network of flumes and ditches. It eventually merged with several other utilities to form the powerful conglomerate, Pacific Gas & Electric. Next door is **Ott's Assay Office** where, in 1859, the first samples of Utah Territory silver were weighed, setting the stage for the rush to the Comstock Lode east of Tahoe.

The skinny gingerbread and brick building at 214 Main Street is Firehouse #1, now home of the **Nevada County Historical Society.** Among the exhibits in its little museum are relics from the Donner Party, Maidu artifacts, and a shrine from a Chinese joss house. (A joss house is a Taoist temple).

Take a left turn at Church Street to walk up toward the **Nevada County Courthouse.** The original 1855 courthouse burned in 1856, was rebuilt in 1864, and got its current look in 1937 as an undertaking of the Works Projects Administration. The tall, sleek Art Deco building looks down the hill toward 317 Broad Street, the location of a showier Art Deco public building, Nevada City's **City Hall.** An award-winning restoration of the city hall maintained the original 1937 façade, gold-leaf lettering, and lighting fixtures.

On the way down South Pine Street toward City Hall, turn right on to Commercial Street to peruse the old **Chinese Quarter.** Gradual renovation is turning the strip into a monument to the Chinese merchants and residents who lived and worked here during the gold era. Many of the Chinese left after the passage of the Chinese Exclusion Act of 1882, legislation that prohibited naturalization of the Chinese labor force, and by the early 1940s, most of this little Chinatown had become vacant. Current development of the quarter has encouraged the establishment of businesses that in some way acknowledge the former residents, although the interpretation is pretty loose, with pan-Asian themes prevailing over anything Chinese of the Victorian Era. I found the old Chinese grocery at 313 Commercial Street in business as the Golden Flower Trading Company & Museum (also known as the Quan Yin Store in honor the Goddess of Compassion). Quan Yin was sitting in a ceiling alcove watching over (among other things) a 200-year-old silk scripture banner from the 13th Dalai Lama, an altar cloth from the Joss House in Grass Valley, Tibetan and Nepalese jewelry, blue moonstones, silk feng shui paintings, and an apothecary case original to the street.

From Commercial Street, head south on any cross street to reach Broad Street for a stroll down this bustling commercial strip. At 401 Broad Street, you'll find an odd barn-like brown brick structure keeping company with the Victorians. This is the **Nevada Theater.** Established in 1865, it's the oldest theater building in California. At the time of this writing the Foothill Theatre Company, a professional thespian troupe, was presenting a full season of performances. Across the street from the theater is the tall and skinny brick and balconied **Firehouse #2,** which once housed the volunteer fire department.

From Broad Street, head the short block down Bridge Street to Spring Street for a look at the **Miner's Foundry Cultural Center.** Built in 1856, the foundry was important for its role in creating new technologies for the mining industry, and later the skiing industry. Now it serves as a hotspot for cultural activities. Just a block away is the revered local radio station KVMR, located at 89.5 on the FM dial or number 401 on Spring Street. The volunteer-based, listener-supported community station dedicates itself to social change through diverse programming. Shows have had names like Dangerous Rhythm of Life, Voices of Resistance, Realm of the Muses, The Tibetan Radio Hour, Legends of the Lounge, and Space Age Bachelor Pad. The best-known program (due to its syndication) might be Loafers' Glory: A Hobo Jungle of the Mind, hosted by the inimitable U. Utah Phillips, a Nevada City–area resident. Anyone who has ever heard his "Moose Turd Pie" story will never forget the punch line.

If you choose to spend a few days in Nevada City (which I highly recommend you do), you can select from an appealing array of historic accommodations, including many B&Bs housed in Victorian mansions. At 211 Broad Street, you will find the 43-room **National Hotel,** where the balconies offer the best perch on parade days. Established in 1852, the hotel bills itself as the oldest continuously operating hotel west of the Rockies. The Clampers have dedicated the hotel to the Ladies of the Night. My favorite Nevada City quarters during the years of research for this book were at 575 East Broad Street, where a renovated 1940s era motor court was doing business as the Outside Inn. Hopefully, this unique establishment will endure, and you will find its lobby still jammed with up-to-date information on area hiking, biking, and rafting.

Nevada City fare is often of a higher caliber than what you will find in much of the Sierra. Beer lovers will find a good local brew called Nevada City Gold, and wine lovers can visit the downtown tasting rooms for **Indian Springs Vineyards** and **Nevada City Winery.** The actual vineyards are well to the west of the city at elevations of almost 2,000 feet. Much of the soil consists of iron-rich clay, which gives a distinctive tannic twang to the red wines and provides good aging potential.

Wine fanatics might want to make the long haul west across the Yuba River to visit **Renaissance Vineyard and Winery** near the tiny town of **Oregon House,** where the red clay soil is worked by the Fellowship of Friends, a spiritual community founded here in the 1970s based on ideas from the metaphysical philosophers George Gurdjieff and P. D. Ouspensky. (The winery is now a separate corporation, but Fellowship members continue to play a major role in it, from grape harvesting to staffing the tasting room.) Call ahead to arrange a visit, and allow time to stroll around the serene classical statuary and lovingly tended roses in the Fellowship sculpture garden.

SAN JUAN RIDGE

On leaving Nevada City, it is possible to head north on North Bloomfield Road, a fairly direct route to Malakoff Diggins (see below). Otherwise, follow Highway 49 as it makes a northwesterly exit from Nevada City and continues toward the South Yuba River. Look out for a trailhead on the east side of the road. The well-marked **Independence Trail** is one of a growing number of wilderness trails designed to accommodate wheelchairs.

Leaving the South Yuba canyon, the highway ascends a pine- and cedar-covered ridge, where the smooth red branches of mature manzanita twisting through the understory make a handsome filigree against the green conifers. After the highway crosses Shady Creek, it arrives at the well-marked turnoff for Tyler Foote Crossing Road. Head right for a fascinating ride over the mythical San Juan Ridge into the eerie world of the Malakoff Diggins.

"The Ridge," as it is locally known, is home to a loose band of artists and intellectuals who migrated here in the early 1970s. Since 1980, the community has kept a full schedule of cultural events going at the **North Columbia Schoolhouse Cultural Center,** which lies at 17894 Tyler Foote

Manzanita on San Juan Ridge.

Road in the hamlet of North Columbia. This simple, white Colonial-style schoolhouse was built in 1875 and now hosts such events as art shows, storytelling festivals, readings and screenings of books and films on Sierra or conservation topics, nature programs by the Yuba Watershed Institute, and unique events like "Ridgestock," a music and sustainability expo. Many of the well-known artists and speakers on the programs live in the neighborhood.

MALAKOFF DIGGINS STATE HISTORIC PARK
From North Columbia, there are two ways to get to Malakoff Diggins. One is to continue on Tyler Foote Crossing Road, which changes its name to Cruzon Grade Road, and then to Backbone Road. When the

road becomes gravel, make a right turn onto Derbec Road and drive into the park. Alternately, just around the corner past the North Columbia schoolhouse turn right off of Tyler Foote onto the unpaved Lake City Road and then left on the North Bloomfield–Graniteville Road. Either route you take, the diggings will start to appear along the way as mounds and trenches of pink gravelly soil. The central destination is the tidy little "living history" town of North Bloomfield, which serves as headquarters for the park. The town was very quiet on my late October visit. A fox moved off silently into the trees, and it was obvious from the big piles of scat that bears had recently feasted at the pear tree in the center of town, to which some fruit still clung.

North Bloomfield was first settled in 1851. The population had grown to around 800 when the hydraulic mining activity peaked in 1876. Around that time, the Central Valley farmers were beginning to make headway in their suits against the hydraulic mining companies, voicing their extreme displeasure over the severe flooding of their towns and fields due to the ruinous flow of mining debris out of sites like Malakoff Diggins. It took another decade before the historic Sawyer Decision of 1884 would

Malakoff Diggins State Historic Park is an outdoor museum where you can see the extreme erosion caused by hydraulic mining.

bring about a permanent injunction against the dumping of mine tailings into the Yuba River, effectively shutting down the hydraulic mining operations.

Cross over the little tributary to Humbug Creek west of town and follow the Church Trail to the old church and cemetery. From the church, there is a 2.7-mile loop into the diggings, and a shorter, but steeper hike of 0.6 mile up the Slaughterhouse Trail to the Rim Overlook on the edge of the park's campground. From either vantage point, the diggings emerge — sand castle–like formations of eroded rock and soil in cliffs, spires, and fluted buttresses banded in tan, orange, and white. During dry periods, hikers with boots and flashlights can take the Hiller Tunnel Trail out of the diggings, passing through the 556-foot-long drain tunnel that once funneled the water and gravel slurry through the miners' sluices and down to the river via Humbug Creek.

FOOTE CROSSING SIDE TRIP

Leaving Malakoff Diggins State Park, most drivers will want to head back through North Columbia and take Tyler Foote Crossing Road west for several miles, then turn north (right) onto Oak Tree Road, which hits Highway 49 at North San Juan (el. 2,105 feet). However, the very adventurous might want to head down Cruzon Grade and, where it transitions into Tyler Foote Crossing Road, turn right (north) on Tyler Foote instead of continuing straight on it to North Columbia. Following the road north and east, you will experience the spectacular unpaved descent to Foote's Crossing, which spans the Middle Yuba River. The road, designed as a toll road by A. D. Foote, was built just as the first automobiles appeared on the scene at the beginning of the 20th century, and it is only wide enough to accommodate one Model T at a time. The challenge of building in the steep terrain was significant, but the road was so beautifully engineered that it has gained some renown, appearing in several different historic and architectural registers. Gnarled oaks, splintered metamorphic outcroppings, and mossy, dripping seeps give it a wild garden-like appearance. My mother-in-law, who made this crossing with me, wondered if I should put this side trip in this book at all. But here it is. In retrospect, I'd recommend hiking it, as it might be a better way to enjoy the scenery.

Sierra County

Visitors who have taken the more cautious option of returning to Highway 49 should proceed north and then east to **Goodyears Bar,** where the old Helm's St. Charles Inn might be open for business. The old schoolhouse in Goodyears Bar is still used for community events and church services.

Those who have continued to Foote Crossing on Tyler Foote Crossing Road will climb out of the Middle Fork Yuba to arrive at the remote, untouristed semi–ghost town of **Alleghany** (el. 4,419 feet), site of the still-functioning Sixteen-to-One Mine. The mine has a little museum that offers tours by special arrangement. From Alleghany, proceed over Pliocene Ridge, heading north on Mountain House Road through the quiet borough of **Forest City** (or Forest, as it is sometimes called), noted to have been a lively camp in the mid-1850s, but one that depopulated suddenly when the diggings at Alleghany proved more fruitful. Visitors can sometimes find a map for a walking tour of the town at the Forest City Dance Hall.

Continue north, across Henness Pass Road, once a significant trans-Sierra thoroughfare, but now just a rugged dirt road popular with 4WD enthusiasts. (For more on Henness Pass Road, see chapter 1.) Keep following Mountain House Road north and you will emerge onto Highway 49 near Goodyears Bar.

DOWNIEVILLE (el. 2,899 feet)
The spot where the Downie River meets the North Yuba River was simply called The Forks in the mining era. Eventually, it was given the name of its first citizen, Scotsman Major William Downie, who arrived in November 1848, setting up camp on nearby Jersey Flat, not too far from The Forks. His party included 10 black sailors, an Indian, an Irish boy named Michael Deverney, and a Hawaiian named Jim Crow, who had the luck of catching a trout that had swallowed some gold flakes, which were found at the bottom of the kettle in which it was cooked. The men stayed through the winter to work the local placers and almost starved to death when they were snowed in. However, it was not too long after the

snows melted that miners poured in at The Forks, bringing bars and eating establishments with them. Downieville became the supply center for a ring of nearby camps, and by 1852 it was designated as the seat of the newly formed Sierra County.

The fork where Downie Creek meets the North Yuba is still an impressive geographical feature, and a good place to sit and nibble a sandwich while contemplating a river trip through the Yuba's renowned rapids. White-water outfitters are easy to find in town, as are shops to serve the scads of mountain bikers that frequent the town. Many of them come here to catch a shuttle up the Sierra Buttes for a hair-raising ride down 6,500 feet of mountain trail back to Downieville, where they nosh on the ubiquitous pizza and burgers.

Before you leave town, look for the publishing office of the *Mountain Messenger,* or just pick up a copy of this historic weekly for later reading. The *Messenger* began reporting the news in 1853, and has never ceased in this endeavor. The current editor (as of this writing) has an irreverent Clamperesque style.

From Downieville, Highway 49 climbs for 11 miles past many appealing river- and creek-side campgrounds to the picturesque town of **Sierra City** (el. 4,187 feet). The town's many 1860–1880-era structures have the jagged Sierra Buttes (el. 8,591 feet) as a most impressive backdrop. (See chapter 10 for the Sierra Buttes.) Sierra City claims to be the gold era birthplace of the satirical fraternal society E Clampus Vitus.

Past Sierra City, watch to the left for the entrance road to the **Kentucky Mine.** Docents at the museum give enthusiastic tours of the mine's fully operational stamp mill, describing how the ore was ground into fine particles in a deafening pounding action of the machinery. At a subsequent stage of the tour, you learn how the gold was extracted through the use of mercury, which poisoned the workers. Docents will also give a loving description of the treasured colony of endangered Townsend's long-eared bats that have taken up residence in the stamp mill. Needless to say, the stamp mill is kept quiet to protect the bats, and the once-popular summer concert music series, formerly held in the outdoor amphitheatre above the museum, no longer occurs, since the music was upsetting the bats. The park's shady outdoor tables are perfect for a summer picnic.

Ahead on Highway 49 is Bassetts Station, which is the turnoff for Gold

(above) Clamper headquarters in North Bloomfield. Photo by Erlda Parker
(below) The Kentucky Mine stamp mill. Photo by Erlda Parker

Lake Road, the southern entrance to the beautiful Lakes Basin (see chapter 10). Thirteen miles further is **Yuba Pass** (el. 6,701 feet), an unremarkable spot in the dense forest of red fir. As Highway 49 descends from the pass by twists and turns, watch for a well-designed pullout on the right. A map and display at this overlook describe the extraordinary scene below — the expansive Sierra Valley. One midsummer day, I took the opportunity to linger here while a dramatic afternoon thundershower sent jagged bursts of lightning between heaven and earth, and curtains of rain swept through the spacious valley.

As Highway 49 drops into the Sierra Valley, it comes to a T-junction with Highway 89 and then joins this route for a five-mile jaunt southeast through Sattley (el. 4,935 feet) to Sierraville (el. 4,950 feet). At Sierraville, visitors headed toward the Lake Tahoe region, Reno, or Interstate 80 can continue south on Highway 89. A sight along this portion of Highway 89 is included in a side trip in chapter 1.

Sierra Valley (el. 5,000 feet)

This vast sub-alpine valley is a noted refuge for wildlife, especially for birds that drop in from the Pacific Flyway, but it has also been a place of pilgrimage for humans since prehistoric times. Five thousand years ago, the hot springs on the southernmost point of the valley were recognized for their healing powers by a migrating tribe of ancient Washoe people. These days, the springs sometimes host New Age tribesmen on pilgrimage to the Burning Man festival in Nevada. The **Sierra Hot Springs** resort is operated by the nonprofit New Age Church of Being. You can join the church for a day to participate in the bathing rituals, but most folks come for longer stays, enjoying workshops or one-on-one sessions in rebirthing, yoga, and therapeutic massage. Some people even fly in by private plane, landing at the Sierra Dearwater Airport north of the resort. I opted for a soothing soak in one of the outdoor pools where I found myself in the company of a pretty yellow American goldfinch. That evening I enjoyed a scrumptious vegetarian dinner in the basement of the main lodge, followed by a few quiet hours of reading on a richly upholstered couch in the living room. I finally retired to a comfortable cot in the dormitory upstairs, but was kept up all night as a family of barn owls carried on outside the window, apparently mindless of the establishment's some-what restrictive code of conduct.

To reach Sierra Hot Springs from Sierraville, go a half-mile east on Highway 49 and turn right on Lemon Canyon Road. Turn right again on Campbell Hot Springs Road and proceed to the main lodge where everyone must check in and pay the daily dues. The bathing facilities are clothing optional.

SIERRA VALLEY BIRD-WATCHING

East of Sierraville, Highway 49 makes a sharp turn north as it skirts along the Sierra Valley's Antelope Valley Wildlife Area, a strip of marshy land threaded with some of the myriad channels that form the headwaters of the Middle Fork Feather River. As the highway turns east, watch for Heriot Lane, which leads north into a network of farm roads that are popular perches for bird-watchers. One September morning, I was on Marble Hot Springs Road (A24) in the middle of the valley wishing I had a canoe so I could paddle behind a couple of mallards that were swim-ming silently among the tule and cattails. A great blue heron came in for a landing, folding its gangly wings, while a fussy little Savannah sparrow hopped onto a barbed-wire fence, perhaps unaware that it was being eyed as a possible morning snack by an American kestrel perched high atop a telephone pole. Steam hovered over geothermal spots in the meadow and raucous flocks of Brewer's blackbirds rose up from their favored spots among the cow pies, arcing over the grassy pastures in loose and shifting formations.

East of Heriot Lane, Highway 49 passes through **Loyalton** (el. 4,936 feet), which has a museum dedicated to the history of the Sierra Val-ley's farming and logging industries. Leaving Loyalton, Highway 49 turns north to traverse the east side of the valley, completing the 11-mile stretch to its terminus at Vinton on Highway 70.

From Vinton, one looks east toward **Beckwourth Pass,** which at 5,228 feet appears as little more than a gentle depression in the high desert. However, in 1850, when explorer James P. Beckwourth gazed from a dis-tance at this ridge, he saw it as a hopeful new route through the daunt-ing Sierra barrier. Beckwourth had arrived here via a long and adventur-ous route from Frederick County, Virginia, where he was born in 1798

Sierra Valley in summer. Photo by Wayde Carroll

to an African slave woman and a knighted Englishman. For nearly 30 years before Beckwourth established his trans-Sierra route, he traveled the continent along with many of the century's most noted mountain men. Historians suggest that Beckwourth was prone to exaggeration of his own accomplishments, but few can refute that he played a significant role in the opening of the western frontier. As a guide, he directed or led many wagon trains through the pass and on to a trans-Sierra trail he laid out all the way to Marysville, 80 miles to the southwest (as the crow flies). A traveler in one of these trains was Ina Coolbrith, who in 1915 would become California's poet laureate. She was only 10 when her family came

Sierra Valley in winter. Photo by Carl Piesch

through the Sierra Valley in 1851. On the way to the pass, Beckwourth asked Ina's mother if the girl would like to ride through it with him. In *Ina Coolbrith: Librarian and Laureate of California,* biographer Josephine DeWitt Rhodehamel describes the scene.

> At the pass, Beckwourth dismounted and helped the girl off the horse. An autumn wind had come up, stinging their faces, whipping their clothes. Storm clouds were gathering, darkening all the landscape except the valley lying to the west below them. The sun lighted it as if on purpose for this moment. Jim pointed to the glowing valley lying against a range of blue. "There, little girl," he said, "there is California! There is your kingdom!"

Practical Matters

A tour of the Gold Country can be enjoyable at any time of year, but summer is when tourist sights and services are in full swing. In spring, the wildflowers, luscious green hills, and rampaging rivers are a true highlight. In autumn, the changing leaves and golden grasses are a delight as well, but check for reports of wildfires. The fires can close off certain routes and cause widespread problems of reduced visibility and poor air quality. Winter can be a very peaceful time to visit the Gold Country, but rain and tule fog in the lower elevations and snow in the upper can make driving hazardous. (For more on Sierra weather, including climate statistics for Sonora and Nevada City, see the introduction.)

ROADS

Highway 49 is well maintained but very curvy. Alternate routes on back roads look enticing on the map, but some can turn into twisting, white-knuckle, single-lane rides into deep and remote canyon areas. Mariposa, the beginning point of this south-to-north tour, is 30 miles southwest of Yosemite National Park, 37 miles north of the Central Valley city of Merced, and 76 miles north-northwest of Fresno. The end point is in the Sierra Valley north of Lake Tahoe, 32 miles from Reno, Nevada. Reno and Fresno both have airports.

WHERE TO STAY AND EAT

Inns, hotels, motels, B&Bs, and dining options are plentiful along Highway 49, especially near the main Gold Country attractions: Mariposa, Jamestown, Sonora, Columbia, Murphys (on Highway 4), Jackson, Sutter Creek, Placerville, Auburn, Nevada City/Grass Valley, and Downieville. In the Sierra Valley, look for food and lodging in Calpine, Sierraville, and Loyalton. The Tahoe National Forest, Sierraville Ranger District offers lodging in an old lookout tower in Calpine.

CAMPING

Until you get north of Nevada City, there are very few campgrounds along Highway 49, although there are plenty to choose from around the reservoirs or uphill in the national forests. North of Nevada City, Highway 49 heads directly through the Tahoe National Forest, where camping options improve immensely.

U.S. FOREST SERVICE

Tahoe National Forest (http://www.fs.fed.us/r5/tahoe/): **Headquarters,** 631 Coyote Street, Nevada City, 530–265–4531; **North Yuba Ranger District,** 15924 Highway 49,Camptonville, 530–288–3231; **Sierraville Ranger District,** 317 South Lincoln Street, Sierraville, 530–994–3401.

VISITORS BUREAUS

Amador County Chamber of Commerce, www.amadorcountychamber. com, 125 Peek Street, Jackson, 209–223–0350.

Calaveras Visitors Bureau, www.visitcalaveras.org, 1192 S. Main Street, Angels Camp, 209–736–0049, 800–225–3764.

Mariposa County Chamber of Commerce, www.mariposa.org, 5158 Highway 140, Mariposa, 209–966–2456.

Placer County Visitors Council, www.placer.ca.gov/visit/, 13411 Lincoln Way, Auburn, 530–887–2111.

Sierra County Chamber of Commerce, www.sierracounty.org, Sierra City; 800–200–4949.

Tuolumne County Visitors Bureau, www.thegreatunfenced.com, 800–446–1333, 209–533–4420.

REGIONAL GUIDES

Koeppel, Elliot H. *The California Gold Country — Highway 49 Revisited.* La Habra, Calif.: Malakoff & Co., 1995.

Meals, Hank. *Yuba Trails 2: A Selection of Historic Hiking Trails in the Yuba River and Neighboring Watersheds.* Self-published, 2001.

Fauver, Toni. *Wildflower Walks and Roads of the Sierra Gold Country.* Grass Valley, Calif.: Comstock Bonanza Press, 1998.

10

The Lost Sierra

In the far north, the Sierra's granitic backbone slopes down to a trifling 5,000 feet as it disappears under the young lava rock of the Pacific Northwest's Cascade Range. No precipices mark the eastern escarpment, and only modest peaks press their stony tops out of a dense cloak of conifers along the crest.

While the mountains do not tower, there is plenty of wild beauty here; tiny lakes sparkle in glacier-scraped basins, and grassy valleys — once ice age lakes, now threaded with a myriad of marshy channels — teem with wildlife. These fertile valleys were the favored dwelling places and hunting camps of the Mountain Maidu, the northern Sierra's native people. As settlers came into the northern Sierra looking for gold and timber, they found that these valleys were ideal for ranching.

The Sierra's northern region has remained sparsely settled in modern times. Rarely have the developers looked northward from Tahoe, and so strip malls and condominiums are few and far between. Instead, the traveler finds authenticity and hospitality from the heart. History reveals itself in surprising nooks and crannies. There are no national parks and few designated wilderness areas, but nature is always near at hand.

Portola (el. 4,860 feet)

This tour begins on the Feather River Scenic Byway (Highway 70) in the headwaters of the Middle Fork Feather River, a region popular with

LOST SIERRA

Rolling stock at the Portola Railroad Museum. Photo by Tom Rath

bird-watchers, boaters, and fishermen. The braided water channels of the Sierra Valley and the recreational opportunities at Lake Davis and Frenchman Lake to the north are the draw. But it is the little town 24 miles west of Hallelujah Junction that garners all the fame.

For international railroad enthusiasts, Portola is a virtual shrine. The **Portola Railroad Museum** is likely to be the start or the finish of a pilgrimage along Highway 70 between Portola and Pulga. Train buffs follow the route of the **Western Pacific Railroad** through the Sierra, expecting to witness the passage of a train through each of several world-renowned railroad wonders.

The laying of the rails from San Francisco to Salt Lake City was the dream of surveyor Arthur W. Keddie. Keddie saw the Western Pacific Railroad through its entire design and construction, and he watched it carry its first freight and travelers through Quincy in 1910. The stretch over the Sierra Nevada, with its soaring trestles, artful rock-hewn tunnels, and graceful bridges, is regarded as an engineering masterpiece. The wonders will be seen on the tour ahead, but here at the Portola Railroad Museum, exhibits are almost wholly limited to the huge rolling stock of vintage steam and diesel engines, cars, and cabooses presented in haphazard display out in the yard. While clambering over tracks to admire the meticulously maintained machinery, you might hear a whistle and notice that a diesel engine is backing down the track to disappear around a bend. Chances are that the engine is being driven by another visitor — one who has arranged ahead, paid for the privilege, and is receiving instruction from museum staff.

A few blocks away from the museum, at 256 Commercial Street in Portola, the comfortable Pullman House Inn serves as an informal outpost of the museum. It's jammed ceiling to floor with railroad memorabilia including many of the vivid, naïve-style paintings of steam engines by the museum's colorful resident gandy dancer, Kenneth Roller.

GOLD MOUNTAIN SIDE TRIP

Highway 70 continues west for nine miles to reach the Mohawk Valley. This tour, however, takes an alternate route, leaving from Portola's 3rd Street (southwest of Commercial Street) on the Portola McClears Road (A-15) and following a southwest-trending ridge above the Middle Fork Feather River. The point of this detour is to pay a visit to a unique community. The upscale development at **Gold Mountain** has been assembled following unused drawings found in the portfolio of the esteemed, early-20th-century architect Frank Lloyd Wright. The centerpiece of the development is **Nakoma,** a clubhouse made up of linked octagonal and hexagonal "wigwams" of intricate wood and stone construction. In Nakoma's clerestory are Wright's signature stained-glass windows, and classic Wright-designed furnishings are placed meticulously in each room. The public is welcome at Nakoma's restaurants and at the trendy underground spa where massage rooms are lit with glowing crystals. The resort's state-of-the-art golf course, The Dragon, is known as one of the country's most challenging.

The Portola McClears Road (A-15) meets Highway 89 in the southeastern corner of the serene **Mohawk Valley.** Northeast of the junction is the little borough of Clio. The Clio business strip is limited to a post office and an old general store, but I found a delicious sandwich and a comfortable bed here on a visit in 2001.

Lakes Basin Recreation Area

Head northwest on Highway 89 for a mile beyond Clio to find Gold Lake Road, a route that connects through to Highway 49 at Bassetts Station (see chapter 9) in snow-free months. This is the main access into the Lakes Basin Recreation Area, one of the northern Sierra's most splendid destinations for camping, hiking, and general lakeside enjoyment. The pristine little tarns and lakes number more than 20. They were created when ice age glaciers scraped into the ancient meta-volcanic seafloor rocks. (These predate the formation of the Sierra's granitic batholith.) **Gold Lake** (el. 6,409 feet) is the largest, at two miles across. **Long Lake** is a far second in size. **Jamison Lake, Bear Lake, Round Lake, Goose Lake,** and the **Salmon Lakes** all make pleasing hiking destinations, and several can be visited in a single hike. Some are directly accessible by car.

Nestled between the lakes are several old resort lodges, mostly crafted of knotty pine. They are open in summer only and rooms are always fully booked by the first of the year, so don't expect to snag one on the fly. I had heard that one might squeeze in for dinner, so I tried at the Sardine Lake Lodge, however, it took five minutes of pleading and a big crocodile tear to get the hostess to let me sit alone at the edge of the bar for dinner. The evening started with drinks in the lakeside gazebo. Moonlight filled the enchanted Sierra sky, and the massive Sierra Buttes cast dark purple shadows over the water.

The Sardine Lakes are at the southernmost end of the Lakes Basin Recreation Area. Turn west at Sardine Lakes Road, which is also the northside approach to the Sierra Buttes.

SIERRA BUTTES (el. 8,591 feet)

The dark and ragged prominence of the Sierra Buttes holds dominion in this landscape of gentle, tree-lined ridges. Hikers with stamina and nerves of steel will want to climb to the top of the ancient quartz porphyry buttes where a high fire lookout affords an even better view. Although footpaths lead up directly from the Sardine Lakes, the more practical route begins from the top of Packer Lake Road (a right fork off of Sardine Lake Road). The steep but wide trail to the top of the buttes passes through mats of manzanita and regal stands of red fir. Look for the feathery branches of the mountain hemlock, and the western white pine, identified by its checkered bark. Along the way, spectacular views from the lower buttes . open out toward the east. Young America Lake sparkles in a steep-sided cirque below, and the Sardine Lakes form a perfect paternoster chain pointing toward distant Haskell Peak (el. 8,107 feet) and beyond to the Sierra Valley. The view south reaches to the peaks around Donner Pass. To the north are more lakes, and to the west is the deep and green canyon of the North Yuba River.

MOHAWK VALLEY TOWNS

Return north on Gold Lake Road to Highway 89, turn left, and continue northwest past the Graeagle Meadows Golf Course into the old sawmill town of **Graeagle.** The row of neat little red-and-white cabins in Graeagle once provided sawmill company housing, but now serve as antique shops and snack bars.

Barely a mile north of Graeagle is **Blairsden,** a community offering some of the better dining options in the area. Just before Blairsden, turn left onto County Road A-14, passing by the Plumas Pines Golf Course (unless you choose to visit it). The county road continues through the little community of Mohawk and then climbs to the old mining town of **Johnsville** (el. 5,160 feet). Little plaques affixed to the handsomely weathered-brown buildings in Johnsville allow for a self-guided walking tour, but the homes are private dwellings. I did, however, find one open to the public. Behind the sign for The Iron Door was an upscale restaurant decked out with so many local artifacts that it appeared to be a museum.

Plumas-Eureka State Park

Continue up A14 into Plumas-Eureka State Park. Here stony-headed Eureka Peak rises up to 7,447 feet, and the towering ruins of the Eureka stamp mill lean up against the mountain's eastern flank. The stamp mill is one of several outdoor exhibits of the park's museum. Indoor exhibits illustrate the history of Johnsville. The museum also serves as the resource center for the park's hiking trails, which are part of a network into the Lakes Basin Recreation Area to the southeast (see earlier in this chapter).

One of the best hikes in the basin starts at the ruins of the Jamison Mine, located a short distance from the museum on Jamison Mine Road. The trail follows Little Jamison Creek past a waterfall in a secluded woodland glade, and past bushes thick in summer with juicy grape-like clumps of elderberries. (Note: Always make a positive identification before you eat any wild foods, as some berries are poisonous.) The trail continues on between mounts Washington and Elwell to a series of little lakes. Here the handiwork of miner-stonemasons can be seen in the finely wrought stone dams built to direct the water into flumes, which still channel water in places alongside the trail.

LONGBOARD SKIING

Plumas-Eureka State Park is very popular with cross-country skiers. Trails follow old mining roads, and some zigzag right up the high flanks of Eureka Peak. For many years, the Plumas Ski Club maintained a poma lift on the mountain, and although the little ski area has had its ups and downs (so to speak), it continues to be the focal point for the revival of a noteworthy local tradition.

It was here in the Lost Sierra that downhill ski racing was invented. Norwegian gold miners, using their savvy on how to get around in winter, fashioned long flat boards into contraptions that their non-Scandinavian associates called snowshoes or skates. Other miners followed suit, and for good reason — even a pair of barrel staves strapped to the feet could allow someone to travel over the snow when food, medicine, and other vital supplies were needed at the mining camps up in the snow belt. But the stir-crazy miners also started seeing a great new form of entertainment. They found they could ride their ore buckets up the mountain and then blast down through the snow on their makeshift skis. With gambling being such an integral part of the Argonaut culture, the placing of wagers on races was not long behind. By 1856, ski racing was a popular activity in the mining camps of Sierra and Plumas counties, and a circuit of races was established between the camps of La Porte, Johnsville, Jamison City, Poker Flat, Sierra City, Monte Cristo, and a few smaller camps, with a $500–$1000 purse to be won at each camp.

In Norway and Sweden, the idea of skiing for sport was only just emerging. The first touring race from Telemark to Christiana (now Oslo) took place in 1867, and the first European downhill competition was held in Sweden in 1879. But the world's first official downhill ski race, sponsored by the newly formed Alturas Snow-shoe Club, took place in 1867 at Lexington Hill near La Porte (see later in this chapter). The winner was a miner known as Cornish Bob. It must have been a blow to the Norwegian miners to be beaten out by a man from the relative tropics of Cornwall, but it was duly noted that Bob reached a speed of 88 miles per hour riding 12-foot-long skis.

Called longboards, for obvious reasons, the racing skis were hand-carved, usually from Douglas fir, and strapped to the miners' boots with a simple laced-up leather binding. A single stout pole with a knob-like tip served to push off and to stop. Stopping was achieved by sitting on the pole, like a witch on a broom, so that the tip would drag deeply, sending an impressive rooster tail of snow out behind the skier. Longboarders soon learned the value of the "tuck" position (now well known to ski racers), but the real secret of success was in the concoction applied to the bottom of the skis and known as "dope" or "Sierra lightning" (wax, in modern parlance). Each racer would contract with a dopemaker to develop a unique recipe for his dope. The winning recipes were a closely

A longboard ski racer coming to a stop. Photo by Mark Middlebrook

guarded secret, but would always include spermaceti, a waxy substance from a cavity in the head of the sperm whale (now an endangered species). Other ingredients might be oil of cedar, turpentine, oil of tar, wintergreen, soapstone, balsam of fir, pine pitch, or any odd substance that the maker thought might give his racer the edge. By tradition, a winning racer would split the purse with his dopemaker.

The races ran strong for a good 10 years at the camps and continued at some mining towns until about 1911, when gold mining itself had nearly dwindled away. By the late 1930s, a small number of old longboarders still could be found in Plumas County. With some encouragement, a few of them were set up to challenge the champions who were racing on modern equipment at the new resorts in Donner Pass (see chapter 1). To the utter astonishment of all, the longboarders took the laurels in every race. The most famous upset was at Sugar Bowl in 1941 when longboarder Johnny Redstreake beat Austrian and U.S. downhill champion Hannes Schroll.

From time to time longboard races have been resurrected, and I found a thriving series going when I first visited the Lost Sierra in 2001. Since 1992, the Plumas Ski Club has been summoning all willing and able riders to compete in the Historic Longboard Revival Series at the old Plumas Eureka Ski Bowl on Eureka Peak. Anybody 18 or older is welcome to participate, as long as they ante up the nominal entry fee, make an attempt at period garb, and strap on the longboards (their own or a pair borrowed from the club). Additionally, contestants must be ready to hoof it to the top of the ski run carrying their longboards, which typically weigh 20 pounds or more. The latter requirement makes for a slow pace to the event, but food, music, and good spirits (of varying sorts) create a festive mood. The races are officiated by the local chapter of E Clampus Vitus. Each heat starts with a clang on an old-circular sawblade, sometimes manned by a one-armed Clamper affectionately known as Slot Machine. Another colorful fixture of the Johnsville races is Scott J. Lawson, a Mohawk Valley resident, Clamper, and director of the Plumas County Museum in Quincy. Lawson carries on the colorful tradition of dopemaker at the races while simultaneously educating racers, spectators, and reporters, giving a thorough historical account of the races and their customs. For more information on the races, contact the Plumas County Visitors Bureau (see Practical Matters at the end of this chapter).

Scott Lawson, dopemaker and master of ceremonies for the Historic Longboard Races at Plumas-Eureka State Park. Photo by Mark Middlebrook

Blairsden to Quincy

From Blairsden, Highway 70/89 leaves the Mohawk Valley, heading northwest past the old Feather River Inn and Golf Course, which is now owned by the University of the Pacific and used as a conference center. For a stretch of about 10 miles, the Middle Fork Feather River flows languidly beside the highway. Road and river diverge just before Cromberg, the highway continuing northwest to make the gentle climb to 4,431-foot Lee Summit, while the river bends westward to begin its wild rampage

On the Middle Fork Feather River. Photo by Rick Stock

down the western slope through the heart of the Lost Sierra. This was one of the first rivers to be given the captivating designation of Wild and Scenic River, which protects it from agricultural and hydropower interests. Rafting and canoeing are feasible in the spring in the English Bar Scenic Zone and Recreation Zone, which begins at Clio (see the Gold Mountain Side Trip, earlier in this chapter) and continues to Red Bridge, accessed from the Quincy La Porte Road out of Quincy. By early July, even a complete novice on an air mattress can float safely through this zone.

Expert river runners put in at Red Bridge for a wild ride with class V+ rapids, large boulders, steep canyon walls, and impassable waterfalls in the Upper Canyon Wild River Zone. Once in the water at Red Bridge, there is little opportunity for a change of heart, as the next road access is 32 miles away. Rick Stock, director of the Outdoor Recreation Leadership program at Feather River College in Quincy, described the run to me as the "best paddling in the world — the Nectar!" However, he would direct novices toward the easier rides in the Milsap Bar Scenic River Zone, accessed from the Oroville-Quincy Highway out of Lake Oroville (see the Lake Oroville section, later in this chapter).

WILLIAMS LOOP (el. 4,000 feet)

As Highway 89/70 descends from Lee Summit through the town of Spring Garden, keep your eyes on the road, but watch the railroad tracks as well, and you may catch quite a show. The phenomenon only occurs when a train of sufficient length passes through; observed from the highway, the train will appear to be going in one direction and then turning around to go the other. If the train is long enough, it will pass over itself. The Williams Loop, a mile of track that runs in a 360-degree loop, was designed to achieve surveyor Arthur Keddie's goal of maintaining a gradient of less than 1.33 percent while crossing over the river divide between the American and Mohawk valleys.

Quincy and Surrounds

Stretched out on the southern rim of the lush American Valley is Quincy (el. 3,423 feet), which at fewer than 2,000 people is the largest community in Plumas County and also the county seat. A wise first stop would be at the **Plumas County Visitors Bureau,** on Highway 70 near the airport, just west of town. This is, hands down, the most helpful visitors' bureau in the Sierra, offering a treasure trove of all kinds of advice. Ask about a good place to stay right in town, and enjoy the ease of getting around on foot.

The centerpiece here is the **Plumas County Courthouse,** built in 1921 in the "Sierra Classical Revival style," as historian Scott Lawson calls it. It has a three-story atrium adorned with marble veneer, stately Ionic columns, a coffered ceiling, and a 2,000-pound bronze and glass chandelier. The **Plumas County Museum,** at 500 Jackson Street, is also well worth a visit. A substantial corner is devoted to the Mountain Maidu, with several beautiful examples of finely wrought baskets, woven from materials the Maidu gathered here in their valley home. The museum complex also includes an "industrial history wing" and a restored 1878 Victorian home, furnished with items from the museum's collection.

Before leaving the museum, pick up a Heritage Walk brochure. Many structures in town date back as far as 1854 when Quincy was an important stop on the Beckwourth Trail, but my favorite on Main Street dates only to 1908. An American Valley rancher constructed the **Clinch Build-**

A SACRED SONG OF THE KONKOW MAIDU

Hu´-tim yo´-kïm koi-o-di´,
  (The acorns come down from heaven,)
Wi´-hi yan´-ning koi-o-di´,
  (I plant the short acorns in the valley,)
Lo´-whi yan´-ning koi-o-di´,
  (I plant the long acorns in the valley,)
Yo-ho´ nai-ni´, hal-u´-dom yo nai, yo-ho´ nai-nim´.
  (I sprout, I, the Black-oak-acorn, I sprout, I sprout.)
— transliterated from the Maidu by Stephen Powers, 1877

ing to serve as a meat market, but gave the façade a fanciful treatment with a set of brick niches that hold samples of local rocks, colorful ores, glittering minerals, and even a mortared-in metate that the Maidu might have used for grinding acorns or grain.

The vibrancy of Quincy area culture bursts out everywhere, at cafés where locals might be putting on music or poetry performances, and the **Plumas Art Gallery** where works by regional artists are displayed. The nearby **Feather River College** draws on local expertise to offer such unique courses as stream surveying and watershed revegetation, Sierra wildlife and winter ecology, recreation leadership, horse training and ranch operations, telemark skiing, and even longboard ski-making (the skis are used in the historic longboard races). There is also notable involvement with environmental issues in Quincy, and it's easy to track down a member of the **Quincy Library Group**. This group of citizens first met in the Quincy Library in 1992 and went on to draft statewide legislation for forest restoration and protection of wildlife habitat. The group outgrew the library and now is housed in the same facility as the Plumas County Visitors Bureau on Highway 70, just west of town.

BUCKS LAKE ROAD

If you stop at the excellent Visitors Bureau in Quincy and express an interest in wilderness scenery, there's a good chance you will be sent up Bucks Lake Road with a handful of trail maps. About 10 miles up the road, just past the community of Meadow Valley, Forest Road 24N29 takes off to the right toward Silver Lake Campground. This is one of several trail-heads for **Spanish Peak,** a mountain of 7,000 feet that stands above any other feature in this part of the northernmost Sierra. Its bare, craggy face looms out from the forest cover of the **Bucks Lake Wilderness,** beckon-ing Pacific Crest Trail trekkers hungry for a view. According to the hik-ers' register that sits in a metal box on the summit, most of the folks who climb up here are from the neighborhood, and they mostly approach via the splendid trail from Silver Lake, which rambles over manzanita-covered moraines and across a huge sloping granitic slab.

Bucks Lake (el. 5,027 feet) is such an easy drive from Quincy (a mere 17 miles on Bucks Lake Road) that it attracts many families to its camp-grounds and lodges during the summer season. Fishermen come on a quest for the huge Mackinaw trout that are hauled out of this well-stocked reservoir on a regular basis. On the northwest shore, silvery mounds of sage adorn the lake's beaches of granular decomposing granite, and grace-ful Jeffrey and sugar pines stretch their long branches out across the blue sky. Visiting the south shore one autumn, I found golden aspens shim-mering at sunset while a flock of common mergansers herded a school of fish down Haskins Creek.

The lake is snowed in from November to Mother's Day, but not the lodges. Their proprietors gladly send snowmobile escorts to Bucks Sum-mit to carry in gear for cross-country skiers and snowmobilers who want to spend a few days exploring the trails.

KEDDIE WYE

About 8 miles north of Quincy on Highway 70/89, watch for the signs for Keddie and the Keddie Wye. Rail fans wait for hours at this awkward spot, hoping to get a photograph of a train riding the soaring trestles through the "wye," a split between the railroad's main line and its "high line," a spur that heads north beside Highway 89 to Indian Valley. Finding a safe place to park can be difficult.

A couple of miles beyond the Wye, Highway 89 turns north toward Indian Valley as Highway 70 (the Feather River Scenic Byway) continues west. The junction comes at a somewhat dangerous curve in the road, made even more dangerous by exasperated train buffs making U-turns after looking in vain for any decent place to park near the Keddie Wye.

Coming through the Keddie Wye. Photo by Bill Gilbert

Indian Valley (el. 3,500 feet)

Drive six miles north from Highway 70 on Highway 89, and you will arrive at Indian Valley. This gentle, grassy, creek-threaded valley sits within the embrace of Keddie Ridge, Mount Jura (el. 6,275 feet), and Mount Hough (el. 7,232 feet). The grasses provide forage for cattle (among which there are quite a few buffalo), and sandhill cranes nest in the marshes. Overhead, majestic golden eagles soar in serene loops while bold northern goshawks plan their ambush attacks from the valley's perimeter. In fall, when the valley's countless apple trees are groaning with their loads of sweet fruit, the Sierra's ubiquitous black bears come in for a picnic.

On one visit I found a creative and elegant meal incorporating local organic produce and locally raised buffalo at the Crescent Hotel in **Crescent Mills** (el. 3,515 feet), a lumbermill town on the railroad's high line. The rooms upstairs at the hotel were simple and comfortable, as it seemed they might have been when they served as millworkers' quarters. Downstairs at the bar, some local musicians had come to their favorite haunt for an impromptu jam session. I was told that this is where the newer

**Sandhill cranes
(*Grus canadensis*).
Photo by Carl Piesch**

residents hang out and that the long-time residents prefer the tavern in **Taylorsville** (el. 3,545 feet), in the southeastern corner of the valley. Taylorsville is home to the Indian Valley Museum, where I found the local history presented in a freewheeling and delightful style. Among the items that caught my eye were: a late-nineteenth-century map of Plumas County by surveyor Arthur Keddie; a photo essay on a favorite member of the community, the late Seymore Smith, a Maidu born here in 1891 who became a prizefighter and racer; and a "ukelin," which looks like a cross between an autoharp and a cheese cutter. The sign says that it is unplayable — a scam sold by catalog in 1932. Another fascinating exhibit was a photo essay on the arborglyphs from aspen trees in nearby Squaw Queen Valley (and an actual arborglyph-bearing log cut from the aspen in the years before people understood the value of leaving artifacts in their setting). One photographed glyph, dated 1871 and signed "Mejor

Pistolero Jesus Mallea," shows a hand and a pistol. (See chapters 3 and 4 for more on arborglyphs.)

Here at the museum, I also learned about the popular Solar Cook-off, held at the Taylorsville Campground every year since 1991 on the weekend after the Fourth of July. Entrants come from all over the state. According to museum curator Ann Ruffner, "It always rains," and a local music aficionado, "It's just an excuse for all the musicians to get together."

Wanting to get a taste of an even more remote part of the far northern Sierra, I took a side trip up Genesee Road, which runs southeast from Taylorsville into narrow **Genesee Valley** (el. 3,680 feet). Out in the meadow below avalanche-torn Grizzly Peak, a spirited white horse shook its wild mane and trotted through the grass toward the old Hosselkus ranch. Across the road at the remarkable Genesee Store, I sidled up next to the Standard Computing Scale that sits on the old wooden counter and ordered a sandwich, then settled in on the sun-drenched front porch. I passed the time watching for traffic that might be heading east on the old stage road through Red Clover Valley, Beckwourth Pass, and on to Reno, but there wasn't any. The owner explained that the historic property, first settled in 1865, is held in a trust, and that he regards himself as a curator of the estate, which is the sum total of the holdings in the valley. At the time, he was just beginning renovation of the gingerbread-trimmed, brick-manor house, with its gracious lawn and many wooden outbuildings, in the hopes of creating a country inn. I felt tempted to wait there on the porch for the inn to open.

Greenville (el. 3,570 feet), the Indian Valley's largest town, is located at the valley's far northwest corner. It has several pleasing historic buildings, friendly people on the streets, antique shops to browse, a luthier's shop (of all things), and several lodging options. There are also a few places to eat and drink, but the fare is no match for the lively, local ambience.

From Greenville, Highway 89 heads to **Lake Almanor** (el. 4,519 feet), skirting the lake's southwest shore and continuing north and west into Lassen Volcanic National Park. Mount Lassen is the southern outpost of the Pacific Northwest's Cascade Range. Its obsidian fields overlay the far northern edge of the Sierra Nevada batholith, the granitic core that defines this great mountain range. Mount Lassen is also the cradle of the Sierra Nevada's northernmost river, the North Fork Feather River.

Lake Almanor. Photo by Tom Rath

North Fork Feather River

On an expedition into the northern Sierra foothills in 1821, Captain Luis Argüello found a stretch of river that appeared to be covered with waterfowl feathers. He christened the waterway "El Río de las Plumas" (the river of feathers). In all likelihood, Argüello did not travel up into the impressive water-sculpted canyon of the North Fork Feather River, where creeks cascade over darkened granitic slabs, falling into swirling green pools in the canyon bottom. Today, such a sight entertains travelers on an impressive ride down the Feather River Scenic Byway (Highway 70) to Oroville.

From Lake Almanor, return south on Highway 89 to rejoin the Byway at Paxton (el. 3,080 feet). From here the highway follows the East Branch of the North Fork Feather River to its meeting with the main fork just below **Rich Bar.** This was once a lively mining camp, where the colorful exuberance of daily life was captured in the letters that Mrs. Louise Amelia Knapp Smith Clappe wrote to her sister in Massachusetts, later published as *The Shirley Letters: From the California Mines, 1851–52.*

On September 20, 1851, Dame Shirley wrote: "Through the middle of Rich Bar runs the street, thickly planted with about forty tenements, among which figure round tents, square tents, plank hovels, log cabins, etc., the residences varying in elegance and convenience from the palatial splendor of "The Empire" down to a "local habitation" formed of pine boughs and covered with old calico shirts."

The miners' communication and supply center was **Belden Town** (el. 3,400 feet), now just a ramshackle resort serving Pacific Crest Trail hikers making their way over the highway and river. The most notable artifact at Belden Town, however, comes from the early 20th century. The **Belden Powerhouse** is one of seven steps on the Pacific Gas & Electric Company's "Stairway of Power," a gantlet of dams and powerhouses through which the North Fork Feather River must pass on its way to Lake Oroville.

The Stairway of Power is but a small part of the engineering spectacle along the Feather River Scenic Byway to Oroville. The highway and Keddie's Western Pacific Railroad masterpiece make impressive appearances here as well in a series of soaring trestles, graceful bridges, and resolute rock-hewn tunnels through the deep river gorge. Watch for the bridges at the historic Tobin fishermen's resort and the stunning spectacle of the famous **Pulga Bridges,** where the road suddenly sweeps over the river on a graceful 680-foot span 200 feet above the churning whitewater while the railroad crosses the river on another bridge 170 feet below. About five miles after the Pulga Bridges, the highway passes through Jarbo Gap (el. 2,200 feet) and spills out into the Sacramento Valley beside North Table Mountain.

Lake Oroville (el. 900 feet)

The three forks of the Feather River come together at a place once known as Bidwell Bar. General John Bidwell, a member of the first emigrant party to cross the Sierra (see chapter 1), found gold here in 1848. The discovery site is now lost below the waters of Lake Oroville, as is the original site of the Bidwell Bar Suspension Bridge, the first suspension bridge built in the western states. The materials for the bridge were shipped around the Horn to San Francisco from Troy, New York, and then upriver to Marysville and by wagon to Bidwell Bar. Originally, the bridge was 372 feet long and spanned 130 feet of riverbed. It was dismantled in 1966 to save it from being inundated by the rising waters of Lake Oroville. Relocated to Bidwell Canyon on the south end of Lake Oroville, it is no longer a suspension bridge but is preserved as an attraction along with its original tollhouse. It also serves as a crossing for the Oroville-Quincy Highway, which leads northeast toward the Bucks Lake Wilderness (see earlier in this chapter) and then on to Quincy.

Heart of the Lost Sierra

The Oroville-Quincy Highway is one of several mountain roads that lead from the Lake Oroville area back into the true heart of the miners' Lost Sierra. Even when the mining camps here were jammed with gold seekers, the trails to these remote camps were steep and rugged, with heavy rains and deep snows making the camps even less accessible. Poker Flat, Port Wine, Howland Flat, American House, Poverty Hill, Gibsonville, Onion Valley, Union Hill, and St. Louis are now ghost towns, or mere markers of towns that burned or were washed away by hydraulic mining, but the camp at **La Porte** has survived to the present. Today's population hovers around 25 souls, but the Union Hotel still serves as the social center here as it did in the 1860s when the ski-racing gold miners formed the first ski club in the United States, the Alturas Snow Shoe Club. La Porte remains a winter destination, but visitors tend to prefer snowmobiling. To reach La Porte, go east from Lake Oroville on the Forbestown Road, and then head north on the Quincy La Porte Road.

(opposite) The Pulga Bridges. Photo courtesy of Plumas National Forest

Longboard racers wearing the Alturas Snow-shoe Club logo. Photo by Mark Middlebrook

After visiting La Porte, cross the South Fork Feather River below the Little Grass Valley Reservoir to reach Lumpkin Ridge, and then follow Lumpkin Road along this ridge back toward Lake Oroville. Along the way watch north for the turnoff to the Feather Falls Scenic Area, where trails plunge down into the middle fork's canyon through blackberry brambles and poison oak. Attractions include the magnificent **Feather Falls** (at 640 feet, it's the sixth highest waterfall in the United States) and Bald Dome Rock where, according to the Mountain Maidu, the monster Uino watches over the river.

Practical Matters

The Lost Sierra is a great year-round sporting and touring region. In winter, access to more-remote areas is limited, but some resort inns provide snowmobile service for visitors. Back roads in the upper elevations are usually clear by May. Spring brings wildflowers and the excitement of watching the snowmelt rage down the Feather River. Summer sports include fishing, hiking, horseback riding, boating, and golfing. (This is a golfer's paradise.) Autumn is great for leaf peeping and hiking. (For more on Sierra weather, including climate statistics for Portola, Quincy, and Oroville, see the introduction.)

ROADS

Highways 70 and 89, the main routes described in this chapter, are kept open year round, except on an occasional day or two in winter, when snow removal can't keep up with the snowfall. Chains are required in snowy conditions. Reno, Nevada, is the closest city on the east side with a major airport. Sacramento has a major airport on the west side.

WHERE TO STAY AND EAT

On Highway 70, the greatest selection is available in Quincy. Also look in Blairsden, Graeagle, and Portola. To stay and dine in more remote areas, look in the Lakes Basin Recreation Area (summer only), Indian Valley (Crescent Mills and Greenville), and Bucks Lake. On the west side, look in Oroville and La Porte.

CAMPING

Most campgrounds in the Lost Sierra are clustered around recreation lakes, with a few scattered along or near Highway 70.

NATIONAL FORESTS

Plumas National Forest (www.fs.fed.us/r5/plumas/): **Headquarters**, 159 Lawrence Street, Quincy, 530–283–2050; **Beckwourth Ranger District,** Mohawk Road, Blairsden, 530–836–2575; **Feather River Ranger District,** 875 Mitchell Avenue, Oroville, 530–534–6500; **Mount Hough Ranger District,** 39696 State Highway 70, Quincy, 530–283–0555.

VISITORS BUREAUS

Plumas County Visitors Bureau, www.plumascounty.org, 159 Lawrence Street, Quincy, 800–326–2247 or 530–283–6345.

REGIONAL GUIDES

DeMund, Tom. *Feather River Country Adventure Trails.* Berkeley, Calif.: Wilderness Press, 2002.

11

Topics of Interest to Sierra Nevada Travelers

Throughout my years of Sierra travel, I have found that the more I know about nature, the more I am able to notice what's out there. I would always advise carrying along a natural science field guide or two from the list below, but for those who are not ready to plunge into wholesale field identification, the following essays provide a good start.

Note: The appendix of this book includes an extensive list of Sierra flora and fauna shown with their scientific names.

A Primer on Sierra Conifers

For some people, conifers all look alike — pointy trees with needles that stay green all winter. With a little basic study, however, you'll find that the character of each species can become as familiar as the face of an old friend.

Start by looking at the silhouette of the tree; a fir (genus *Abies*) will have layered, fanlike foliage, while a pine (genus *Pinus*) reaches out with tousled arms. The firs have needles sprouting singly along the branches, while a pine's needles are arranged in clumps on the ends of twigs. As a fledgling botanist, I have yet to learn how to distinguish a red fir (*Abies magnifica*) from a white fir (*Abies concolor*), but the various pines easily can be identified by the count of their clustered needles, by the shape and size of their cones, and by the distinctive patterns of their bark.

The Douglas fir, as you might determine by scrutinizing its Latin name

(*Pseudotsuga menziesii*), is not a true fir. This handsome tree with graceful, drooping limbs is found in the middle and northern reaches of the range.

Pines can be quite easy to distinguish at a glance. For instance, in the Sierra's middle elevations, you might need only to look upward to spot the regal sugar pine (*Pinus lambertiana*). Its immense cones can be up to 18 inches in length, and they dangle from the ends of the graceful, arching branches like Christmas ornaments glittering with sap. The sugar pine's needles are about four inches long and grow in bundles of five.

The tall ponderosa (or yellow) pine (*Pinus ponderosa*) is also found in the middle elevations. Its reddish-tan plated bark makes a striking appearance, and the trunk lets off a delicious butterscotch aroma. Up close, the flakes of bark look like pieces of a jigsaw puzzle. The needles are exceedingly long and clumped in puffy clusters of three. The ponderosa is closely related to the Jeffrey pine (*Pinus jeffreyi*), which is found at higher elevations. The easiest way to tell them apart is by picking up a pinecone. The ponderosa's cone is prickly and the Jeffrey's is not.

One of the most ubiquitous pines in the higher elevations is the unassuming lodgepole pine (*Pinus contorta*), the only Sierra pine with needles in clumps of two. When the lodgepole dies and the bark falls off, the distinctive spiral pattern of its growth emerges to view.

The low, rounded, shrub-like silhouette of the pinyon pine (*Pinus monophylla*) makes an extensive appearance in the lands of the eastern Sierra. This tree does not offer much shade from the desert sun, but it has been an essential resource for native people, since its nuts are very nutritious, as well as delicious. (Other pines have edible nuts, but none are as tasty as the pinyon's.)

Other conifers of note:

The mountain hemlock (*Tsuga mertensiana*) has a nodding top, drooping branch tips, and lacy foliage, making it easy to pick out from a distance.

The Sierra juniper (*Juniperus occidentalis*) is a compact tree found in mid-to-high elevations throughout the range. It can live to a great age, often growing into a spectacular sculptural form. (See photograph in the Ebbetts Pass section of chapter 3.)

(opposite) Red fir forest.

Sugar pine.

The incense cedar (*Calocedrus*) has aromatic, scale-like leaves and fibrous, cinnamon-colored bark on an elegant, tapering trunk. Incense cedar logs were often used as columns in the construction of 19th-century Sierra mansions and lodges.

There are two more conifers that are of great interest to Sierra travelers. The giant sequoia (*Sequoiadendron giganteum*), a cousin to the coast redwood (*Sequoia sempervirens*), is introduced in the Calaveras Big Trees section of chapter 3 and in the Sequoia National Park section of chapter 7. The Western bristlecone pine (*Pinus longaeva*) is described in chapter 5.

My Favorite Fauna

The highlight of every trip to the Sierra is the sighting of one of its wild creatures. It takes patience and a keen eye, along with a good knowledge of where to look, to spot the more reclusive members of the Sierra animal kingdom, but sometimes you just get lucky. I've come upon bobcats, foxes, badgers, and weasels caught momentarily off guard on the edges of meadows, and watched bighorn sheep leaping along distant slopes. I've found big paw prints of roaming mountain lions, and observed whole families of yellow-bellied marmots out sleeping on boulders. I've never run into a porcupine, but I hear tales of dogs getting a sharp and painful reprimand for tangling with them.

At every elevation there is some species of squirrel or chipmunk racing back and forth, tail aloft, stashing seeds and nuts. In the white fir forests the Douglas squirrel will announce its presence by lining its collections of cones neatly atop fallen logs. Mule deer and coyote move about with great nonchalance, and sometimes it's hard to tell which of us is more interested in watching the other. In each of my trip diaries I have noted at least one surprise fauna sighting, although sometimes it's nothing more than an amazing moth or a swarm of ladybugs.

Soaring birds of prey are a regular feature, and sometimes I've had the blessing of spotting them perched near their nests or of hearing their guarding calls. The rhythmic noises made by owls, woodpeckers, and blue grouse can create a constant backfill to the soundscape, but by standing quietly and following the sound, you have a good chance of seeing them as well as hearing them. Visitors who are up for going out at dawn might witness a veritable pageant of waterfowl in the marshes. However, there is no need to get up early or even leave the campground to meet the ubiquitous extroverts of the Sierra bird world, the Clark's nutcracker and the Steller's jay. These cocky birds are campground bandits par excellence, and at times it seems that one of them is assigned to every picnic table. The Steller's jay is quite dashing with his iridescent blue feathers and velvety black hood.

Here are some of my favorite field guides and natural history books:

Johnston, Verna R. *Sierra Nevada: the Naturalist's Companion*. Berkeley and Los Angeles: University of California Press, 1998.

Lanner, Ronald M. *Conifers of California*. Los Olivos, Calif.: Cachuma Press, 1999.

Sibley, David A. *The Sibley Guide to Birds*. New York: Alfred A. Knopf, 2000.

Smith, Genny, Ed. *Sierra East: Edge of the Great Basin*. Berkeley and Los Angeles: University of California Press, 2000.

Storer, Tracy, Robert Usinger, and David Lukas. *Sierra Nevada Natural History*. Berkeley and Los Angeles: University of California Press, 2004.

Whitney, Stephen. *A Sierra Club Naturalist's Guide — The Sierra Nevada*. San Francisco: Sierra Club Books, 1979.

Thoughts on Sierra Geology

The shape of a new mountain is roughly pyramidal, running out into long shark-finned ridges that interfere and merge into thunder-splintered sierras. You get the saw-tooth effect from a distance, but the near-by granite bulk glimmers with the terrible keen polish of old glacial ages. I say terrible; so it seems. When those glossy domes swim into the alpenglow, wet after rain, you conceive how long and imperturbable are the purposes of God.

—from *The Streets of the Mountains*, Mary Austin, 1903.

When I was young and awakening to a keen interest in geology, I remember feeling frustrated over the slow pace of geologic time. A tender human being like myself would never have the chance of witnessing the profound rearrangement of the earth's surface wrought over millions of years by plate tectonics. I longed to observe the drama of continents careening around the planet, smashing into each other and breaking apart, the horror of rocks getting sucked down into deep ocean trenches to be melted and spewed forth again as lava from chains of volcanoes, the vertigo of fault blocks dropping and rising to give birth to new basins and ranges. Given the time frame of such things, it seemed pretty clear that I'd grow old and die without ever seeing even a relatively fast-paced event like a glacier dropping off a terminal moraine.

The problem, as I discovered, was that I was reading more than I was looking. As I tucked away my books long enough to cast a gaze across the Sierra's magnificent contours, I began to observe a landscape in motion. In the cycle of every year, wind, water, fire, ice, and living organisms reshape the land in various ways, sometimes in the drama of a landslide, rock fall, or flood, but always in the subtle activity of ice crystals and sprouting seeds wedging rocks apart, or dead trees decaying into humus. In some of the Sierra's restless volcanic or fault zones, all I had to do was stay put long enough to feel the earth shake, or step into a hot spring to feel the heat of melting rock below. Truly, there is no place in the Sierra or on the planet where the earth has grown cold and silent. It moves, just as I move, and it rests no more than this devoted traveler cares to rest.

Here are the resources on Sierra Nevada geology that I have found most interesting and useful:

Alt, David D. and Donald W. Hyndman. *Roadside Geology of Northern California*. Missoula, Mont.: Mountain Press Publishing Co., 1986.

Jenkins, Olaf P. *Geologic Guidebook Along Highway 49 — Sierran Gold Belt*. State of California Department of Natural Resources, Division of Mines, 1948.

Hill, Mary. *Geology of the Sierra Nevada*. Berkeley and Los Angeles: University of California Press, 2006.

Konigsmark, Ted. *Geologic Trips: Sierra Nevada*. Gualala, Calif.: GeoPress, 2002.

McPhee, John. *Assembling California*. New York: Farrar, Straus, and Giroux, 1995.

U.S. Geological Survey Volcano Hazards Program. Website for the Long Valley Caldera: http://lvo.wr.usgs.gov/index.html

Plant and Animal Names

The following is a list of almost all the plants and animals mentioned in this book. The common name as used in text is followed by the scientific name: genus and species in most cases. Where only a general identification is made in the text, only the genus is given here, followed by "spp." In a very few cases only the family name is given.

FLORA

alpine lily (*Lilium parvum*)
Bald Mountain potentilla (*Horkelia tularensis*)
beavertail cactus (*Opuntia basilaris*)
bitter cherry (*Prunus emarginata*)
black cottonwood (*Populus balsamifera*)
blazing star (*Mentzelia* spp.)
blue flax (*Linum lewisii*)
blue monkshood (*Aconitum columbianum*)
bracken fern (*Pteridium aquilinum*)
brodiaea (*brodiaea* spp.)
buttercup (*Ranunculus californicus*)
California black oak (*Quercus kelloggii*)
California blackberry (*Rubis ursinis*)
California poppy (*Eschscholzia californica*)
cattails (*Typha* spp.)
Chinese houses (*Collinsia heterophylla*)
common horsetail (*Equisetum arvense*)
creosote bush (*Larrea tridentata*)
currant (*Ribes* spp.)
desert trumpet (*eriogonum inflatum*)
Douglas fir (*Pseudotsuga menziesii*)
elderberry (*Sambucus* spp.)
elephant heads (*Pedicularis groenlandica*)
fairy lanterns (*Calochortus amoenus*)
firecracker penstemon (*Penstemon eatonii*)
foxtail pine (*Pinus balfouriana*)
Fremont cottonwood (*Populus fremontii*)
giant sequoia (*Sequoiadendron giganteum*)
gooseberry (*Ribes spp.*)
hedgehog cactus (*Echinocereus engelmannii*)
huckleberry oak (*Quercus vacciniifolia*)
incense cedar (*Calocedrus*)
Indian paintbrush (*Castilleja pilosum*)
Jeffrey pine (*Pinus jeffreyi*)
Joshua tree (*Yucca brevifolia*)

larkspur (*Delphinium decorum*)
lupine (*lupinus* spp.)
madrone (*Arbutus menziesii*)
Mariposa lily (*Calochortus* spp.)
monkey flower (*Mimulus guttatus*)
Mormon tea (*ephedra nevadensis*)
mountain dogwood (*Cornus nuttallii*)
mountain hemlock (*Tsuga mertensiana*)
mountain pink currant (*Ribes nevadense*)
mule ears (*Wyethia mollis*)
paintbrush (*Castilleja miniata*)
pinyon pine (*Pinus monophylla*)
poison oak (*Toxicodendron diversilobum*)
ponderosa pine (*Pinus ponderosa*)
prickly poppies (*Argemone munita*)
quaking aspen (*Populus tremuloides*)
ranger's buttons (*Sphenosciadium capitellatum*)
red columbine (*Aquilegia formosa*)
red fir (*Abies magnifica*)
redbud (*Cercis occidentalis*)
rushes (*Juncus ensilifolius*)
sagebrush (*Artemisia* spp.)
sedge (family *Cyperaceae*)
Sierra iris (*Iris hartwegii*)
Sierra juniper (*Juniperus occidentalis*)
Sierra shooting stars (*Dodecatheon jeffreyi*)
sugar pine (*Pinus lambertiana*)
Tahoe yellow cress (*Rorippa subumbellata*)
thimbleberry (*Rubus parviflorus*)
toyon (*Heteromeles arbutifolia*)
water lily (*Nymphaea polysepala*)
Western bristlecone pine (*Pinus longaeva*)
white fir (*Abies concolor*)
whitebark pine (*Pinus albicaulis*)
wild mint (*Mentha arvenis*)
wild onion (*allium validum*)

wild rose (*Rosa* spp.)
willow (*Salix* spp.)
wolf lichen (*Letharia vulpina*)
yarrow (*Achillea millefolium*)

FAUNA

acorn woodpecker (*Melanerpes formicivorus*)
alkali fly (*Ephydra hyans)*
American goldfinch (*Carduelis tristis*)
American kestrel (*Falco sparverius*)
badger (*Taxidea taxus*)
bald eagle (*Haliaeetus leucocephalus*)
barn owl (*Tyto alba*)
beaver (*Castor canadensis*)
Belding's ground squirrel (*Spermophilus beldingi*)
bighorn sheep (*Ovis canadensis*)
black bear (*Ursus americanus*)
black-billed magpie (*Pica hudsonia*)
blue grouse (*Dendragapus obscurus)*
bobcat (*Lynx rufus*)
Brewer's blackbird (*Euphagus cyanocephalus*)
brine shrimp (*Artemia monica*)
brown trout (*Oncorhynchus trutta*)
Bullock's oriole (*Icterus bullockii*)
California gull (*Larus californicus)*
Canada goose (*Branta canadensis*)
chipmunk (*Tamias* spp.)
Clark's nutcracker (*Nucifraga columbiana*)
cliff swallow (*Petrochelidon pyrrhonota*)
common merganser (*Mergus merganser*)
common nighthawk (*Chordeiles minor*)
coyote (*Canis latrans*)
Douglas squirrel (*Tamiasciurus douglasii*)
eared grebe (*Podiceps nigricollis*)
golden eagle (*Aquila chrysaetos*)
golden trout (*Oncorhynchus mykiss aguabonita*)

great blue heron (*Ardea herodias*)
great horned owl (*Bubo virginianus*)
green-tailed towhee (*Pipilo chlorurus*)
hermit thrush (*Catharus guttatus*)
Kokanee salmon (*Oncorhynchus nerka kennerlyi*)
ladybug (family *Coccinellida*)
Lahontan cutthroat (*Oncorhynchus clarki*)
Mackinaw trout (*Salvelinus namaycush*)
mallard (*Anas platyrhynchos*)
marten (*Martes americana*)
Mojave rattlesnake (*Crotalus scutulatus*)
mountain bluebird (*Sialia currucoides*)
mountain lion (*Felis concolor*)
mule deer (*Odocoileus hemionus*)
northern goshawk (*Accipiter gentilis*)
osprey (*Pandion haliaetus*)
pika (*Ochotona princeps*)
plover (family *Charadriidae*)
porcupine (*Erethizon dorsatum*)
rainbow trout (*Oncorhynchus mykiss*)
rattlesnake (*Crotalus viridis*)
raven (*Corvus corax*)
red fox (*Vulpes vulpes*)
red-breasted nuthatch (*Sitta canadensis*)
rough-legged hawk (*Buteo lagopus*)
sandhill crane (*Grus canadensis*)
Savannah sparrow (*Passerculus sandwichensis*)
Steller's jay (*Cyanocitta stelleri*)
swallow (family *Hirundinidae*)
towhee (*Pipilo* spp.)
Townsend's long-eared bat (*Plecotus townsendii*)
tule elk (*Cervus elaphus nannodes*)
turkey vulture (*Cathartes aura*)
water ouzel (*Cinclus mexicanus*, a.k.a. American dipper)
weasel (*Mustela frenata*)
Western fence lizard (*Sceloporus occidentalis*)

Western tanager (*Piranga ludoviciana*)
white pelican (*Pelecanus erythrorhynchos*)
yellow bat (*Lasiurus xanthinus*)
yellow warbler (*Dendroica petechia*)
yellow-bellied marmot (*Marmota flaviventris*)
yellow-legged frog (*Rana muscosa*)
yellow-throated warbler (*Dendroica dominica*)

Appendix

Practical Resources—General

MAPS

American Automobile Association: AAA road maps (free to members) are an excellent source for road information, from major routes to minor unpaved access roads. The topography is not shown, but waterways, major peaks, and some major hiking trails are well identified. A few of the maps even have charts with detailed information on accommodations, campgrounds, recreation areas, golf courses, wineries, and boating facilities. For more extensive lodging and dining listings, pick up AAA's *Northern California & Nevada TourBook*, which is updated annually.

Benchmark Maps: This publisher makes an excellent, large-format map book called the *California Road & Recreation Atlas*. The Regional Maps section includes a U.S. Highways map, a map of the western U.S., and a map of California. Maps in the Recreation Guide section show locations of parks, forests, and wildernesses; campgrounds; ski areas; golf courses; boating, fishing, and rafting areas; a few hiking trails; natural wonders; notable towns; museums; and other attractions, all keyed to lists giving short descriptions and contact telephone numbers. Climate and weather charts are provided as well. The Landscape Maps section features 77 pages of 1:300,000 scale topography maps, which show and identify many features of the Sierra topography with notable accuracy (although contour lines for elevations are not shown.) Medford, Oregon, www.benchmarkmaps.com.

U.S. Forest Service Maps: These maps are sold at all the ranger stations and many visitors centers. They are useful for those who need to negotiate the fire roads on the way to remote campgrounds, lakes, and trailheads, but since the maps are not topographical, they can be disappointing to hikers. Forest Service information centers offer free pamphlets on many popular trails. These have basic maps and trail descriptions that can be sufficient for use on short-to-moderate-length day hikes.

Tom Harrison Maps: This publisher makes an excellent series of waterproofed topographical maps that show roads, trails, ranger stations, campgrounds, and pack stations. As of 2006, they had produced maps to cover at least 23 different Sierra regions, and it appears that the series is being updated and expanded on a regular basis. San Rafael, California, www.tomharrisonmaps.com.

United States Geological Survey (usgs) topographical maps: Once the only map resource available for backcountry travelers, the USGS 1:24,000 maps (also known as 7.5-minute quadrangles) cover every square inch of land in the United States, showing details of topography, established trails, roads, and locations of various permanent structures in the wilderness. In the computer age, maps on CD-ROM, commercially produced topographical maps, and equipment that prints maps to order increasingly are replacing the USGS maps at outdoor recreation supply stores.

CAMPING INFORMATION

Stienstra, Tom. *California: The Complete Guide to More than 1,500 Campgrounds.* San Francisco: Foghorn Press, 2003. A great resource for information on developed campgrounds.

U.S. Forest Service: See the end of each geographical chapter for Forest Service headquarters locations. The headquarters and ranger district stations can provide information on camping outside of developed campgrounds, along with local historical and recreation information.

RECREATION GUIDES — GENERAL
(see individual chapters for regional hiking guides)

Berger, Karen and Daniel R. Smith. *The Pacific Crest Trail: A Hiker's Companion.* Woodstock, Vermont: The Countryman Press, 2000.

Corless, Stacy, Kathy Morey, Michael White, and Thomas Winnett. *Sierra North: 100 Backcountry Trips in California's Sierra Nevada.* Berkeley, Calif.: Wilderness Press, 2005.

Libkind, Marcus. *Ski Tours in the Sierra Nevada.* Livermore, Calif.: Bittersweet Publishing Co. *Volume 1: Lake Tahoe; Volume 2: Carson Pass, Bear Valley, and Pinecrest; Volume 3: Yosemite, Huntington and Shaver Lakes, Kings Canyon/Sequoia.*

Morey, Kathy. *Hot Showers, Soft Beds and Dayhikes in the Sierra.* Berkeley, Calif.: Wilderness Press, 2002.

Parr, Barry. *Hiking the Sierra Nevada.* Helena, Mont.: Falcon Publishing, 1999.

Schaffer, Jeffrey P., et al. *The Pacific Crest Trail, Vol. I: California.* Berkeley, Calif.: Wilderness Press, 1996.

Semb, George and Patricia. *Day Hikes on the Pacific Crest Trail.* Berkeley, Calif.: Wilderness Press, 2000.

Winnett, Jason, Kathy Morey, Lyn Haber, and Thomas Winnett. *Sierra South: 100 Backcountry Trips in California's Sierra Nevada.* Berkeley, Calif.: Wilderness Press, 2001.

Recommended Reading

LITERATURE AND NONFICTION

Austin, Mary. *The Land of Little Rain.* New York: Penguin Books, 1997.

Clappe, Louise Amelia Knapp Smith. *The Shirley Letters: From the California Mines, 1851–52.* Berkeley, Calif.: Heyday Books, 1998.

Kerouac, Jack. *The Dharma Bums.* New York: Viking, 1958.

Muir, John. *The Mountains of California* (1894); *The Yosemite* (1912); *My First Summer in the Sierra* (1911). (Reprinted by many different publishers.)

Reid, Robert Leonard, ed. *A Treasury of the Sierra Nevada.* Berkeley, Calif.: Wilderness Press, 1992.

Reisner, Marc. *Cadillac Desert: The American West and Its Disappearing Water.* New York: Viking, 1986.

Snyder, Gary. *Mountains and Rivers Without End.* Washington, D.C.: Counterpoint, 1996.

Stone, Irving. *Men to Match My Mountains.* Garden City, New York: Doubleday, 1956.

Twain, Mark. *Roughing It.* 1872. (Reprinted by many different publishers.)

HISTORY

Berry, William B. *Lost Sierra — Gold, Ghosts & Skis.* Soda Springs, Calif.: Western SkiSport Museum, 1991.

Brewer, William H. *Up and Down California in 1860–1864, The Journal of William H. Brewer.* 4th ed. Berkeley and Los Angeles: University of California Press, 2003.

Browning, Peter. *Place Names of the Sierra Nevada.* Berkeley, Calif.: Wilderness Press, 1991.

Farquhar, Francis P. *History of the Sierra Nevada.* Berkeley and Los Angeles: University of California Press, 1989.

Holliday, J. S. *Rush for Riches — Gold Fever and the Making of California.* Berkeley, Calif.: Oakland Museum of California and the University of California Press, 1999.

Hoover, Mildred Brooke, and Douglas E. Kyle, eds. *Historic Spots in California.* 5th ed. Stanford, Calif.: Stanford University Press, 2002.

Howard, Thomas Frederick. *Sierra Crossing: First Roads to California.* Berkeley and Los Angeles: University of California Press, 2000.

Mallea-Olaetxe, J. *Speaking Through the Aspens: Basque Tree Carvings in California and Nevada.* Reno, Nev.: University of Nevada Press, 2000.

O'Connell, Jay. *Co-Operative Dreams: A History of the Kaweah Colony.* Van Nuys, Calif.: Raven River Press, 1999.

Weamer, Howard. *The Perfect Art: The Ostrander Hut & Ski Touring in Yosemite. Lafayette,* Calif.: Weamer Enterprises, 1995.

NATIVE AMERICANS

Heizer, Robert F., and Albert B. Elsasser. *The Natural World of the California Indians.* Berkeley and Los Angeles: University of California Press, 1980.

Heizer, Robert F., and M. A. Whipple. *The California Indians, a Source Book.* Berkeley and Los Angeles: University of California Press, 1971.

Kroeber, Alfred L. *Handbook of the California Indians.* Washington, D.C.: Bureau of American Ethnology of the Smithsonian Institution, 1976.

Ortiz, Beverly R. and Julia F Parker. *It Will Live Forever, Traditional Yosemite Indian Acorn Preparation.* Berkeley, Calif.: Heyday Books, 1991.

Powers, Stephen. (Heizer, Robert F., intro. and annot.) *Tribes of California* *(1877)*. Berkeley and Los Angeles: University of California Press, 1976.

Salcedo, Nancy. *A Hiker's Guide to California Native Places.* Berkeley, Calif.: Wilderness Press, 1999.

Index